S. E. Bowley.

COMMERCIALISATION OF THE REGIONAL PRESS

FOR MY PARENTS

Commercialisation of the Regional Press

The Development of Monopoly, Profit and Control

D. H. SIMPSON
University College, Cardiff

Gower

Published by
Gower Publishing Company Limited,
Gower House, Croft Road,
Aldershot, Hants. GU11 3HR, England.

British Library Cataloguing in Publication Data

Simpson, D.H.
Commercialisation of the regional press.
1. Newspapers - Great Britain
2. Advertising, Newspaper - Great Britain
1. Title
070.4'12'0941 PN5118

ISBN 0-566-00441-0

Printed and bound in Great Britain by
Biddles Ltd, Guildford and King's Lynn

Contents

Tables

Figures

Preface

An article based on this book has already produced fierce denunciation. The article 'How control has shifted on regional newspapers' carried the sub-heading 'Faceless men - commercial managers and not editors - now have the last word';[1] it spelt out Dr. Simpson's thesis that the Roy Thomson revolution in British provincial newspapers has led to a downgrading of journalists and editorial and to domination by a new breed of commercial managers - in advertising, circulation, accountancy, new production technology and computing, and in personnel. In particular advertising departments have expanded many times in size, while a roughly stable number of journalists are now forced to fill a larger space, with (consequently) more routine stories. Simpson also argues that financial controls and rules have been introduced and allow commercial management to dominate key areas of decision (deadlines, editorial budgets, pagination) which he claims were previously the prerogative of editorial. Accompanying his article were comments from six prominent provincial editors (mainly of morning papers) who dismissed it as exaggerated, biassed, needlessly pessimistic and untrue.

Most other people who read this book will find plenty to disagree with. I myself would point to a number of blemishes and some errors of fact and interpretation. In particular Dr. Simpson seems to be on unsafe ground in assuming that commercial goals were previously much less important than they became in the 1960s and 1970s. I believe he has in part, at least, swallowed a golden age myth of a time a generation or two back when editors, truth, and investigative journalism reigned supreme.

This book is, nevertheless, in my view a work of some originality and importance. Despite prompting (from myself, among others) the 1974-77 Royal Commission on the Press conducted no study about press managers. Consequently this case study is the first sophisticated study in existence of a range of British press managers spanning the commercial and editorial areas.

In other countries where such a literature exists - notably the United States, but also in Japan, France, Canada and Germany - there will be interest in seeing that the British provincial press is no exception to international trends.

Social science students of organisations, business management, and industrial relations will be interested in this book as a case-study of newspaper houses and a press chain - a type of organisation which encompasses creative and information outputs within a commercial/manufacturing setting.

Many journalists will, I suspect - while criticising the style and presentation - recognise much of what is said here. Editors - especially of the evening papers with which the study primarily deals - will probably resent the dismissive approach to their performance and their output. But my own experience of interviewing such editors (in both the mid 1960s and mid 1970s) suggests that they do indeed see a diminution of their authority and they do also resent their relatively low pay and low level of formal security.

Managers in the entire range of competing mass media - but especially regional television and local radio - may perhaps be cheered by the rather negative picture of the provincial press presented here. If so, I think, this would be unwise. The provincial press in Britain is more than just a magnet for attracting advertising revenue, and could be a lot more.

Regional press managers will, I suspect, have mixed reactions. Some will point to errors; some will be flattered by their portrayal as the new men of power; others will be annoyed by what they will regard as the author's prejudice and exaggeration.

Many social science studies are rejected by the subjects of the study as untrue and/or too obvious to need saying. But this study does, indeed, chart a massive build-up of commercial management in general - and advertising departments in particular - on British provincial newspapers. In my view what is now required is a more aggressive commercial-and-editorial policy. The highly profitable days of the early to mid 1970s (with which this book mainly deals) may or may not return to the British provincial press.

Dr. Simpson's book points to what he regards as an internal imbalance between advertising and editorial. Compared with Fleet Street, the British provincial press is much better endowed with advertising and profit than with circulation. I believe that the provincial press has a great future in Britain - but only if it can take the readers away from Fleet Street. Fleet Street may die of its own accord, but it may not. I believe that the provincial dailies must come out of their profitable local monopoly trenches and take the fight to the enemy. Otherwise the danger is that especially the larger provincial evenings will bore the readers - as they have done in the largest American metropolitan centres - and will lose them to more attractive competing media. The challenge is that the provincial dailies could - by providing a more comprehensive and interesting product than Fleet Street populars - make themselves into the dominant British press in sales terms. This is already the pattern in France, Germany, Italy, the United States, and also in Scotland.

The alienation expressed by some editorial executives - such as the news editors and features editors quoted in these pages - should not be ignored. Nor should the related alienation of many young and well-educated reporters. Dr. Simpson implies that the press managers see the 1980s as the era of profit earned (now that revenue has been expanded) by cutting costs. But his book implies a warning. Cutting costs could eventually kill the goose that lays the golden advertising eggs. While some costs - especially in production - may be cuttable, a lesson of this book is that management development and budgetory planning can be too one-sided. To the earlier boosting of advertising should now be added the expansion of circulation, promotion - and editorial.

(1) D. H. Simpson, 'How Control Has Shifted on Regional Newspapers' _Journalism Studies Review_ July 1980 pp 14-18

Jeremy Tunstall
City University
London EC1

April 1981

Acknowledgements

Firstly I wish to thank Professor G. F. Thomason for his direction and critical evaluation in supervising my doctoral thesis which provides the substance of this study. My thanks are also extended to Professor Jeremy Tunstall who read an early draft and whose comments helped considerably. I am also indebted to hard-working typists, not least my mother, Mrs. Joan Simpson,who changed barely legible manuscripts into readable drafts and actually typed my thesis. As regards this book I am most grateful to Mrs. Maureen Watts, Miss Megan Pugh and Mrs. Barbara Clargo for their typing assistance, and to Mrs. Mair Price for her care in drawing the diagrams. My thanks finally to those managers who freely gave their time, whose anonymity is preserved and without whom this book could never have been written.

However, I readily take responsibility for all that is presented here.

1 The publication of regional newspapers

I.I INTRODUCTION

The publication of newspapers in Western Democratic Societies is an important way of transmitting information, even truth, about events in, and affecting that society and its members. Because of this the press, as a whole, is viewed as something different in comparison to normal commercial operations, and its place in society is generally protected by various interest groups who see its healthy continuation as essential to the process of democracy. However in accordance with the ideologies of these liberal democracies the ownership of the press is in private hands, and presumably the deploying of capital in this way requires the usual commercial return. Any government infringement of this principle is either totally rebuffed, as in Britain, or placed within strict limits as elsewhere. Since the newspaper revolution by Northcliffe, proprietors in this country have utilised the medium of newspapers to disseminate personal points of view, even propaganda, although latterly the press has passed into the hands of commercial businessmen interested as much in a sufficient return on capital employed as in the information flow so required by the democrats. Whilst those proprietors interested in propaganda may have neglected the 'truth', those concerned with economic returns may find owning newspapers conflicts with this drive for profit. This provides a foundation for paradox, and it is the nature of this paradox, in particular the way it affects the organisation of newspapers which is the concern of this study.

Ensuring that the press not only fulfils its democratic function, but is also a viable commercial operation can be hypothesised to create its own tensions for those proprietors, publishers, controllers, editors or managers who are called upon to make the major decisions about the publication of a newspaper. The resolution of such tensions are affected by different constraints (of markets, technologies, personnel, etc.,) and by different dominant values (liberalism, commercialism, etc.,) as the situation of newspaper publication has altered over the present century. This is discernable in terms of the critical views which have recently been expressed about the nature and function of the Press in modern society. Thus Murphy has expressed very real doubts about the role of the 'free' press in a modern state, commenting that:

> 'at the local level, at least, where governments cover up, except on rare occasions, the press does not uncover, cannot uncover, and has no inclination to uncover.' (Murphy, 1976:p II)

His remarks refer to two weekly newspapers, but it is argued here that the organisational and management structure of regional daily newspapers ensure that they are also incapable of collecting such news that may allow them to fulfil any democratic freedoms normally demanded of the press. This incapacity may, in turn, be attributed to a conscious decision on the part of the controllers of the press, to pursue profit or money-making rather than the diligent search for, and presentation of, the truth. It is hypothesised here that, in the context of the regional press, the form and extent of this choice may be demonstrated.

Murphy has already shown, for example that reporters on weekly newspapers do not reveal enough to perform the silent watchdog role in which they are often portrayed. This study aims to show that commercial pressures on editorial are such that there is only time to collect the most routine of news, normally from institutional sources, (regular meetings of courts, councils, etc.,) in order that the advertisements can be interspersed with some news, to allow the final product to be called a newspaper. Commercial dominance of editorial departments by non-editorial staffs has been accomplished through a process of bureaucratisation of editorial work, which in turn has been achieved indirectly through control of any interaction the editorial department might have with others. The study is therefore not about news or its presentation and gathering, but rather about the way the processes by which pressure has been exerted on editorial to conform to the commercial demands of the organisation, have produced various constraints on decision making.

The study thus concerns the regional press, although the influence of the national press on its development cannot be minimised, in terms of organisation, ideology of publication and ownership. The history of the press has gone through several phases from the initial proprietor/editor/printer beginnings, through to the massive conglomerates which today own the press, as one interest amongst many. In the twentieth century there emerged a distinctive national London-based popular and quality press, initially owned by powerful individuals, in part for propaganda reasons. Latterly, however, this national press has been in the throes of a continuing process of change which may not, as yet, have finished. Ownership has changed, some titles have vanished and the press has become less political and more concerned to make a profit, or at least not a loss. These changes have occurred because of the demise of the original press barons and the competition of Independent Television for advertising revenue.

For a long time the national newspapers, deprived of their mentors, did not recognise the extent of the challenge and the need for response, and thus changes came later rather than sooner and were more fundamental than was once envisaged.

The provincial press has also gone through a change process which has been, for the most part, completed. In the nineteenth century the British press was regional but the provincial dailies and weeklies lost importance in relation to the national press after about I900. In the period when Fleet Street dominated the press new provincial newspapers were started as press barons extended their influence directly to the regions, and then were wound up through a process of rationalisation and amalgamation to produce a monopoly position for virtually every provincial newspaper. A more fundamental change occurred after I959 with the purchase of Kemsley newspapers by Roy Thomson and provincial newspapers, after that date, gradually became total commercial operations to make considerable profits. The ownership of the press was acquired for no other reason than to secure financial benefit, and editorial really did become the 'bit between the ads.' The particular change occurred most strikingly in Thomson Regional Newspapers but it was not long before the other major groups initiated similar policies to reach similar results. This study examines the process of this change to commercialism in three regional newspaper centres, publishing in total three evening, one morning, and twelve weekly newspapers. The rest of this introductory chapter describes the three centres and details the present organisational characteristics. Much of this information has been gathered by a lengthy interview schedule (see methodological appendix).

I.2 THE EVENING EXPRESS, THE EVENING TIMES, THE EVENING OBSERVER, THE MORNING MAIL AND TWELVE WEEKLY NEWSPAPERS

The newspapers that form the basis of the empirical work are published in three centres. In one, the Morning Mail and the Evening Observer serve a heavy industrial area, in another, the Evening Express and the Evening Times serve predominantly sleeping towns on the edge of a major conurbation, part industrial, part commuter, and part new town, and finally the twelve weeklies serve several communities in an industrial area.

The Morning Mail has a circulation of between 50,000 and I00,000, the Evening Observer between I00,000 and I50,000, and together are employed at this Centre (A) approximately I,000 people. The Evening Express and the Evening Times are both medium sized papers with circulations of between 50,000 and I00,000 and together provide employment for approximately 600 people Centre (B). The group of twelve weeklies has a combined circulation of approximately I50,000 and provides employment for approximately 250 people Centre (C). They are all members of the same regional newspaper group.

They were chosen for investigation because of their relative status within the total group, and thus would be likely to exhibit, if there were any, differing characteristics, of regional newspaper organisation. For instance, Centre (C) was examined because in status it must be at the bottom of any hierarchy and thus may provide a training centre for junior executives. It also had an added advantage in that it had recently installed a new technological process for the printing of the newspapers, it now being web-offset, instead of letterpress. Centre (B) was somewhat larger and had the more demanding routine of publishing two evening newspapers, and a move from a centre such as (C), to one such as (B), with the same job description, for instance, Personnel Manager or Production Manager would be a distinct promotion. Indeed even a move from a functional head of department to a deputy head would not be seen as derogatory to any career. It also had the new technological printing process, together with the newer composing technology, photo-composition instead of hot-metal setting. Centre (A) was one of the largest in the group and a move to here was almost considered a promotion, because of the prestigious morning newspaper and the evening newspaper which had a fairly high circulation.

During the investigation fifty-nine managers above supervisory level were interviewed, thirty-five from centre (A), twenty-six from centre (B) and the remainder from centre (C). For the purpose of the analysis, statistical as well as organisation, the interviewees are treated as a single population, although being employed in three different centres. However, being employed by the same regional newspaper group and because of career development patterns, they can perceive their jobs as part of that group as much as of part of the individual newspaper. Indeed the number of jobs that the sample had had in the last five years averaged 2.69, suggesting that most managers view their job as only a step on the career ladder. The figure indicates that these senior managers spend less than two years in any one job, within the regional group, and indeed for some functions the average number of jobs, in the last five years, was a high as 3.25 (advertising) suggesting a job occupancy of near one and a half years. Even within this sample of the total regional group newspapers there were interconnections of promotion and with the rest of the group many more.

From the interviews the following demographic information concerning career histories was obtained: the average time in present position (Table I.2); the average time with the present regional newspaper group (Table I.3); the average number of jobs held in the last five years (Table I.4); and the average time with present publishing centre (Table I.5). Other information on age structure, general education levels and professional qualifications of these managers can be found in the methodological appendix.

TABLE I.I

THE OCCUPATION OF THE INTERVIEWEES

	No.	%
Editorial	28	47.5
Advertising	I2	20.3
Production	6	IO.2
Accounts	6	IO.2
Circulation	I	I.7
Administration (and Personnel)	6	IO.2
Non-Editorial	3I	52.5

At the levels of figures for editorial and non-editorial statistical significance can be drawn, however for functions within the non-editorial anything that is determined statistically is done without any statistical significance, although it may reflect any indication or ideas gained qualitatively from the interviews.

TABLE I.2

THE AVERAGE TIME OF MANAGERS IN PRESENT POSITION

	Total	Editorial	Non-Editorial	Advertising
0 - 6 months	I6	9	8	2
6 months - I year	4	0	4	4
I - 2 years	I3	6	7	4
2 - 3 years	8	4	4	0
3 - 4 years	8	4	4	I
4 - 5 years	4	2	2	I
5 - 6 years	0	0	0	0
6 - 7 years	2	I	I	0
Over 7 years (specify)	3	2 (I3, 7)	I (IO)	0
Total	59	28	3I	I2
Average	2.30	2.56	2.I	I.46

Legend:- indicates less than

NOTE: The high number (9) of editorial staff in their present position less 6 months is due to a change in editor of one of the larger newspapers. He then proceeded to promote and appoint his own choice of subordinates. Without this influence the average occupancy for editorial would be much higher.

TABLE I.3

THE AVERAGE TIME OF MANAGERS IN THE REGIONAL NEWSPAPER GROUP

	Total	Editorial	Non-Editorial	Advertising
0 - 2 years	0	0	0	0
2 - 3 years	6	I	5	I
3 - 4 years	3	0	3	I
4 - 5 years	3	0	3	I
5 - 6 years	9	5	4	I
6 - 7 years	4	I	3	0
7 - 8 years	2	0	2	I
8 - 9 years	7	4	3	I
9 -I0 years	6	5	I	I
Over I0 years (specify)	I9	I2 a	7 b	5 c
Total	59	28	3I	I2
Average	I0.59	I2.75	8.65	8.54

Legend: - indicates less than

NOTE: a, Times are I0, I0, I2, I4, I9, 20, 2I, 30, 25, 25, 26, 27.
b, Times are I0, I0, II, I4, I4, I6, 44.
c, Times are I0, I0, II, I4, I6.

TABLE I.4

THE AVERAGE NUMBER OF JOB POSITIONS HELD BY MANAGERS IN THE LAST FIVE YEARS

No. of Positions	Total	Editorial	Non-Editorial	Advertising
I	8	7	I	0
2	I8	7	II	4
3	2I	I0	II	3
4	8	2	6	3
5	4	2	2	2
Total	59	28	3I	I2
Average	2.69	2.46	2.90	3.25

TABLE I.5

THE AVERAGE TIME MANAGERS HAVE BEEN WITH THEIR PRESENT PUBLISHING CENTRE

Time	Total	Editorial	Non-Editorial	Advertising
0 - 6 months	9	3	6	I
6 months - I year	I	0	I	I
I - 2 years	5	2	3	0
2 - 3 years	3	0	3	0
3 - 4 years	II	2	9	6
4 - 5 years	5	3	2	2
5 - 6 years	4	2	2	0
6 + years	2I	I6 a	5 b	2 c
Total	59	28	3I	I2
Average	7.24	9.22	5.4I	4.65

NOTE: a, Times are 7, 7, 8, 8, 9, 9, 9, IO, II, I2, I3, I9, 20, 2I, 24, 36.

b, Times are 7, 9, I6, 27, 44.

c, Times are 9, I6.

Tables I.2 and I.4 indicate a high degree of labour mobility among senior managers employed at the three newspaper centres. Overall, managers have had 2.69 positions during the last five years, have held their job for 2.30 years, and have been with their regional newspaper group for IO.59 years. At first glance there is a marked difference in stability between editorial and non-editorial functions, with the editorial managers staying longer in their employment and having fewer positions within the last five years. They have also been with their regional newspaper group for much longer. These findings may not be unusual as the tradition of regional journalism requires a localised knowledge, both at editor and reporter level. However, they are sufficiently close to the non-editorial figures to suggest that there may be similar motives or reasons for mobility in both areas.

The mobility of non-editorial staff by itself may also not be unusual, because the size of the individual centre does not allow for many promotion moves and ambitious managers would of necessity have to move. The critical factor here is the regional newspaper group which allows these promotional moves around regional newspapers of increasing size, with presumably a career pattern to the head office and beyond. (See Table 3.6 for the other interests of regional newspaper groups.) Because of such high mobility a conclusion must be drawn that managers, at least in the non-editorial functions, have a strong group loyalty, besides any perception of belonging to individual papers. The figures for editorial are sufficiently close to draw a similar, if not quite so strong, conclusion. If this is so then the commitment to the region within which, and presumably for which, the newspaper is published, must be low. This suggests one area of success for the ideology of regional commercialism, for such a low commitment to the region means that the region's news is not regarded in the highest possible way, thus allowing a relatively ordinary diet of news, which can be more easily gathered and presented, and thus managed.

For instance, an editor at Centre (C) was somewhat derogatory about the relationship of the paper to the community, insisting that the development of this was not his or the paper's prime function. 'The paper exists for profit; not for people. Therefore I am concerned with the profit for the paper and to this end I serve the wants and needs of the paper.' He later added that he did not see any 'dichotomy between profit and service,' as the two things went hand in hand. The editor showed no resentment to the intrusion of commercialism, indeed he actively supported it and because of his integration he legitimised the control over editorial by non-editorial functions.

What is also surprising is the rapidity of moves particularly among the advertising executives, who on average held 3.25 positions in the last five years, and had only been in their present position for approximately one and a half years. They had also only been with their regional newspaper group for 8.54 years, and as most of the interviews were conducted between I973 and I975 this suggests a date of entry in the mid-I960's when commercial attitudes were becoming to be held by the newspaper owners. This is supported by the relative staffing levels of Centre (A), which reveal that in I959 total advertising personnel was merely seven, by I972 this was II4, and at the end of I976, II9. The growth of advertising as a revenue maker obviously required increased staffs and management, however with such a lack of experience in the newspaper world of advertising, a period of stability to allow such experience to be accumulated would have been expected.

I.3 THE THREE NEWSPAPER CENTRES

The overwhelming impression gained from the three centres was of the commercial orientation of the operations. This is perhaps not unusual given the statement of the I977 Royal Commission on the Press that:

> 'the provincial newspaper industry is rather more profitable then manufacturing industry in general in terms of return on capital measured at historic or replacement costs' (paragraph 6.I7).

However, what was unusual was the extent of such commercialisation as in practically all matters editorial came second to the needs of non-editorial departments. This ranged from working conditions and pay through to the very make-up of the paper. Rather than the commercial or business side being in existence to allow news to be published, it was very much the reverse, a case of the business side using the medium of news, marketing it as though it were an industrial product, in order to gain the highest possible return on the capital invested.

There is, of course, a danger inherent in this policy in that it can produce a newspaper whose editorial is so dull and lifeless that readers and then advertisers disappear. By the mid-1960's this was unlikely, for if readers wanted local news, and if local business men wanted to advertise, then the local newspaper was practically the only choice open. The alternatives, local television, local radio and advertising free sheets were not seen as a threat. Indeed many commercial managers welcomed such developments as they promoted the ideas of advertising, and perhaps introduced new clients, who wished to advertise in all mediums. In both ways this meant an increase in revenue to the newspaper. (Royal Commission on the Press 1974-77a; paragraph 6.17)

At the time of the research, of the non-editorial departments, it was advertising which dominated, particularly at Centre (A). This situation displeased editorial staff, who on the whole felt constrained in their role. Journalists in particular disliked the strict control over their work, and editorial managers felt increasingly uncomfortable as they had to act more like managers and less like journalists. Although gaining control, advertising were also unhappy about the organisation of the newspaper enterprise. For them commercialisation had not gone far enough. Editorial staffs, to them, were still acting like 'prima donna's' instead of ordinary workers doing a routine job of work. For some commercial managers, the sooner journalists were paid by results, that is the amount they write, the easier will be the management of the newspaper. Thus the tension existing in the centres arose from a mutual resentment of the behaviour and attitudes of the two sections, advertising and editorial. Production, the other highly manned, and therefore costly department, was relatively insignificant in determining company policy at Centre (A), but where new technology had been introduced in Centres (B) and (C), they played a more important part. This is particularly true at Centre (B) where resentment and distrust occurred on a more complex three-way basis. The production manager, here a computer engineer rather than the normal time-served craftsman, became a controller of the excesses of editorial and advertising.

Although in each centre this tension existed between editorial and non-editorial, there were some differences, so that this mutual resentment was exhibited in various ways. For instance, as mentioned production technology was dissimilar, as was the size of the operation, and its proximity to urban areas. The size of the newspapers in pagination and circulation and their times of publication provided other differences. Thus before expanding on the main characteristics of this mutual resentment, it will be necessary to give pen-portraits of each centre.

I.3.I Centre (A)

This centre was considered to be one of the top four in the group, publishing a prestige morning and a large circulation evening. A move here was almost always viewed as a significant step in a career, and those executives who moved away, usually commanded more important posts within the group. The main office and printing works were situated in the centre of the city. The ground floor housed the printing machinery, the foyer and a few assorted offices including personnel, and on the first floor were the editorial, advertising and accounts departments, with the production manager's office. The studio was also located on this floor. The journalists working on the morning newspaper shared offices with those on the evening, and this was a source of resentment towards the non-editorial side, for once they had had separate offices, and had most of the first floor. The second floor contained the executive offices, including the editors, and the boardroom.

The centre was extremely profitable, even though the joint circulation had dropped approximately ten per cent over the previous decade. The evening paper, in particular, had saturation coverage in the main city, often exceeding forty pages, due to a high level of advertising, and it was rumoured that its profit kept alive the more influential morning newspaper. This, of course, was in competition with the London press, but had a distinctive regional character. It was much smaller than the evening counterpart because of fewer advertisements, reaching perhaps twenty four pages towards the end of the week, and very occasionally thirty two. Both newspapers had higher pagination levels than fifteen years previously, as a consequence of a large rise in classified advertising. The company operated advertising/editorial quotas, and thus the amount of space for editorial was greater than in earlier years. The general editorial view was positive towards this expansion of size and profit, but qualified on the static numbers of journalists who were now required to fill up to double the space.

The company had just undergone a change in management structure to provide greater commercial control of work operations. The previous organisation chart displayed seven executives reporting directly to the managing director, and any co-ordination of the commercial activities, or of editorial with production was left to him. However, he was not suited to this kind of organising role. His personal style of management owed more to the detached aristocrat than to the short-sleeved organiser. It is a style of management, that allows autonomy (a policy of the regional newspaper group) and also allows conflicts to be resolved without interference from above. As the policy of autonomy was only guaranteed by a sufficiently high level of profit, it was the revenue-making departments which assumed authority in any inter-departmental dispute, although in relation to production these comments need qualification.

There was a facility for monthly senior executive meetings, but they were only held at the request of the managing director. This was clearly part of his style, for problems brought to his attention could be solved either by a meeting or by individual action. Some senior managers thought the style had benefits. 'The timing of the management committee meeting is entirely at the discretion of the managing director. If I thought a meeting was necessary to discuss a problem I would contact the managing director, who alone would decide if the problem necessitated a meeting. We do not have regular meetings with a set agenda. This is not a good idea as making the agenda up occurs only because a meeting is due, not vice-versa. Sometimes we have such meetings three times a week, at other times once every two months. It all depends.' (General Advertisement Manager). The Display Advertising Manager thought the managing director inhibited discussion at meetings, whilst the Display Admin. Supervisor had been ignored at similar meetings. The Personnel Manager, amongst others, was more cynical, 'the organisation's managerial style depends on the function of the managing director. For instance, here we are given the mushroom treatment - kept in the dark and have shit shovelled on twice a day.' The editorial managers felt that most of their staff would be unable to name him, and the Sports News Editor (Evening Observer) said, 'I've seen him twice - on television! '

The change in the official organisation chart was to reduce to two, the number directly reporting to the managing director. These were two newly created Assistant Managing Directors, one responsible for the various advertising functions (now enlarged to four), and one for Production, Circulation and Personnel. This latter one also handled any problems arising from an interchange of editorial and production. The move to this more hierarchal management style was facilitated by the move of two senior executives, one retiring and one promoted. Thus internal jealousies were kept to a minimum. The new structure was working well during the period of the research the managing director able to become detached from the day to day running of the firm, and the two Assistant Managing Directors organising from the top, what was a very commercial operation. The editorial functions, from the organisation chart appear subordinate to one of the Assistant Managing Director's, much to his pleasure, but the editors when interviewed saw no such superior - subordinate relationship. They, after all, were responsible for the newspapers, but naturally had to have some direction in commercial aspects, this, though only from the managing director. The Editor of the Evening Observer saw the relationship of the editor and the managing director as one of 'Caesar and Jesus'. The Editors and the Assistant Managing Directors both thought each

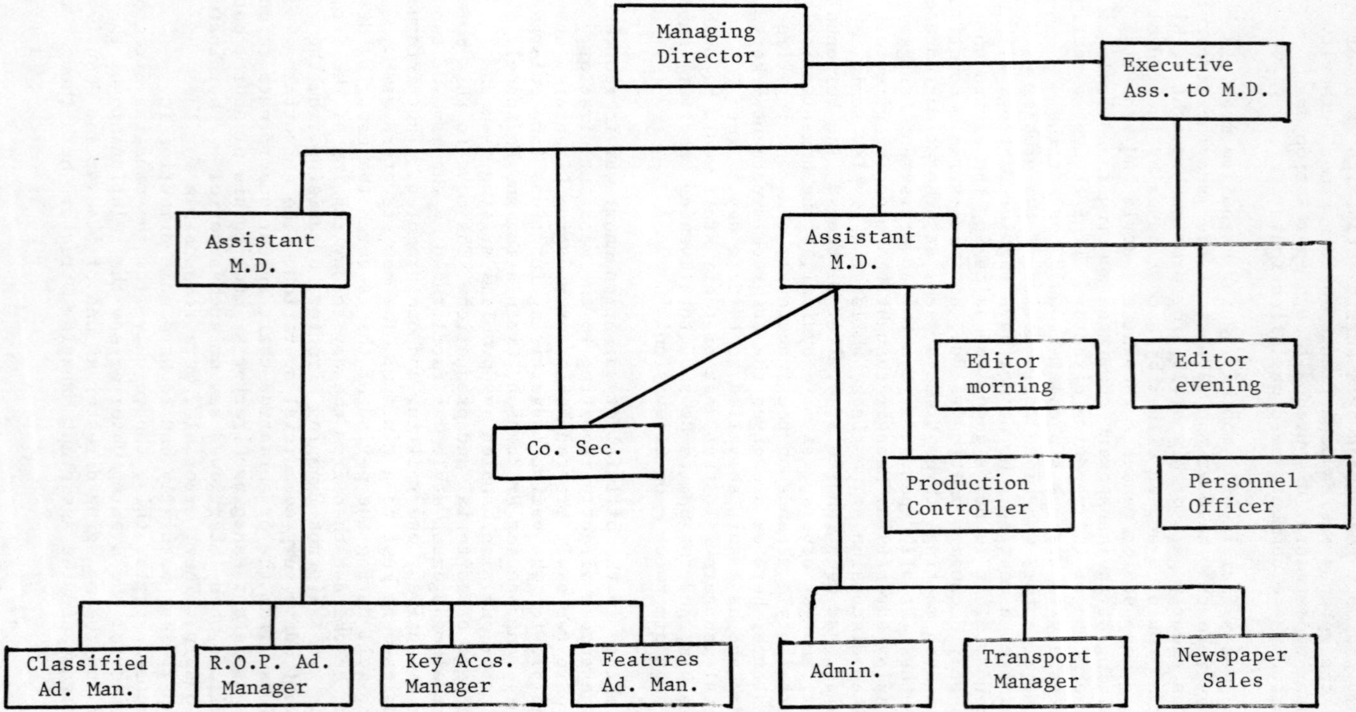

FIGURE I.I : THE FORMAL ORGANISATION CHART OF CENTRE A FROM 1973

to be superior to the other, however the balance was moving towards the Assistant Managing Directors. The Classified Advertising Manager summed up the situation, ' the trouble here is that editorial are used to thinking they are the number one department.' The editors were becoming more and more managers and less and less editors, and indeed career progression for some editorial managers would be into general and commercial administration. The proliferation of editorial managerial posts provided ample training ground. Of course, the different perspectives of the Assistant Managing Directors and the Editors is symptomatic of the non-editorial/editorial power struggle.

The re-organisation also affected advertising. Traditionally this was easily sub-divided into classified and display for each newspaper. Not only did this duplicate work, but it allowed little freedom on the part of the department to exploit and stabilise its markets. Advertising could be planned, giving more stability to pagination levels, and leading to the company becoming an advertising consultant, rather than an open market for the selling of goods and services. Thus four separate functional sections were created, classified, run-of-page, key accounts and features advertising. The Classified section had a fairly large and efficient 'tele-ad.' service, housed in a large office where numerous attractive young ladies would receive incoming telephone calls from prospective advertisers. This side of the work was important as classified advertisements would fill up to half of the newspaper. The end wall of the office noted the sales figures in relation to ever increasing targets. The operators were divided into groups headed by a supervisor, and competition between them developed, as their salaries had a sizeable payment-by-results element. The supervisor had responsibility for training the operators to use correct responses, to encourage the use of greater space and to ensure no mistakes occurred in advertising copy. A telephone call to advertise a car or house, would not be a simple process of insert, but the caller would be offered different forms of advertisement, of course at different costs, and alternative or rather more useful forms of wording. The classified department also had salesmen who would page firms rather than individuals to discover and fulfil their classified advertising needs. Car sellers, estate agents, local authorities for public notices and job vacancies fall into this category. For many of these, classified display was offered, whereby lengthy inserts were provided with some art work for background as this was thought to be more effective, though definitely more costly. It was all part of developing the company's consultative role.

In order to promote more and regular advertising the department would from time to time sponsor a section offering specific goods or services. For instance, household repair services, and general trade inquiries. Overall the classified department was efficient, and in the 'tele-ad.' room a feeling of high work pace, and the drive to sell permeated.

The other three departments were essentially, though not wholly concerned with display advertising. Over the recent years it had become apparent that a few large firms or shops were advertising in large quantities very regularly. The company thought they required special treatment by way of expert help in the design of advertisements, what form they should take, their position in the newspaper, and on what days they should appear. They were assigned to the Key Accounts Department. From such a development there is a possibility that advertisers, in such a prominent position could exert pressure on editorial content. when faced with such an assertion, without exception the managers said that they would not let that happen. Indeed any attempt to have a news story deleted would, many said, only double efforts to ensure that it was printed. A couple of managers made 'off-the-record' comments on the attitudes of some advertisers to the publication of damaging or unsympathetic stories. One large store reduced its advertising by fifty per cent, but as mentioned earlier, with nowhere else to advertise this was soon reversed. Another ignored the editor at the opera. Managers playing 'Caesar's wife' is an obvious response, for pressure if it existed would not need to be applied. Investigative reporting of what may be the local unacceptable face of capitalism did not take place either because the editor did not want to, or as evidence later shows, because there was just no time for such work.

The rest of display advertising was handled by the Run-of-Page (R.O.P.) Department, and included irregular or small advertisers. To promote display advertising the newspaper would promote certain specific events or utilise news items. Advertising here was organised by the features section, who would select topics for supplements only on the basis that it would generate at least a specified level of advertising. If not, no supplement. The opening of a new shop or factory was also a cue for the section to promote an advertising feature describing the event and persuading various other firms to advertise their acknowledgement or support of the venture. There were blatant 'puffs', and printed as such, but more subtle advertising-related material could appear. This was not so much that the editorial department would write an article for its advertising-pulling power, but rather there were various editorial features, which the advertising department could use as a basis to persuade clients to advertise. This involves some fore-warning of future features, but the lack of such communication was a source of frustration experienced by the features section of the advertising department.

The interviews with the managers in the advertising department left no doubt that advertising was the reason for the success of the company. To maintain and improve upon that success training and re-training had a high priority. For each news salesman there was a five week induction training programme, followed by a weekly training session for field salesmen, together with continual motivation by the field sales manager. In addition courses were held at regular intervals for specialised selling, industrial engineering, etc. The managers were all ambitious and many saw their pathway straight to the 'top'. This attitude was encouraged by the General Advertising Manager, later Assistant Managing Director, who had risen to this position from field work supervisor in three years. Even with promotion he felt under utilised, and would welcome further upward movement which might just stretch him. For the majority of the managers in this department the battle against editroial indiscretion and production's intransigence had not yet finished. The newspapers could yet make still more money.

Financial control was achieved by the Accounts Department, a situation unlikely to have been found fifteen years ago. Systems of budget allocations, of costing, of expense account controls, or bad debt repayments etc., had been gradually introduced producing a kind of financial stricture over the operation of various departments. Advertising, as a general rule had more flexibility with their spending, as it was likely to produce a concrete return, than Editorial, whose costing was often within the limits of a pound or two. For instance, expense accounts for advertising could be justified, even if it brought in late advertising, which could cost more to produce than the revenue it earned. Alternatively, editorial would have to reason at great length to have some freelance work paid for, or to have expenses paid, even if a worthwhile news story was the result.

Circulation, previously contracted out, was now thought important enough to be controlled internally, and it was subsumed under one of the Assistant Managing Directors. Marketing was relatively new, and based on the idea that the newspaper needs to be sold, it does not sell itself, as was once thought particularly by editorial. However, in the present day organisation, news gathering is less important, and thus regional newspapers may often have no local 'scoop' or important national news which enables the newspaper to sell itself. With saturation coverage by television, news stories can always be pictorially represented later in the evening. Therefore, the newspaper has to be sold by marketing it as a necessary good, for six days a week, promoting home sales (paper boy), rather than newsagent sales and introducing regular features, (citizen's guides, entertainment supplements, etc.,) which may appear to be a waste of money (as no new advertising is generated) but which maintains a steady, and high level of readership. The marketing aspect also extends to advertising, as the newspaper attempts to become an advertising advisor, even broker to local firms, suggesting various forms of advertising that are applicable to the firms' needs.

The Royal Commission on the Press 1977, in its research series No. 2, found regional newspapers not to have industrial relations problems of the nature experienced in the London-based press, and Centre (A) was no exception. For the most part production was there merely to print the newspaper, and had little direct influence. Everyone was wary of mistreating the department, the Key Accounts Manager, for instance, remarked, 'With the production department we have to have tact and diplomacy, persuasion to get that extra service. Usually they demand a bonus for this, which anywhere else would be accepted as part of the job.' Indeed it was generally agreed that the production workers were relatively good, that is compared to production workers elsewhere. They would do last minute work or change schedules, and bargain afterwards. Other workers often bargained before, which given the time element increased their negotiating power.

The method of printing was letterpress, with hot metal composition, and with many other offices this technology dated from the late nineteenth century, although with the arrival of a new production manager plans were in existence to move to photo-composition. Printing, due to technical difficulties not yet overcome, would remain letterpress rather than change to web-offset. The previous production manager, as those before him, was the time-served craftsman who had, by a process of deadmen's shoes, reached his present position. Needless to say nothing changed as this managerial policy was maintained.

The personnel department was both geographically and organisationally isolated. Tucked away at the back of the foyer, the department appeared to bother no one, and it was bothered by no one. When asked of its role, most managers were at ends to describe one, although nearly all felt it could perform a more useful function, even if they did not know what that was to be. The Display Admin. Supervisor, who had left and rejoined was more forthright on its role. 'They should promote a regular news-sheet for the employees. There's a breakdown with the personnel officer - he didn't even ask me why I was leaving. There's a new man now - don't even know who he is for instance (he had been in office for one month). The personnel office needs to be more geared up, not enough management development, need more involvement with the staff.'

The editorial department appeared very well organised, with the editor on the evening newspaper having reporting directly to him, the deputy editor and through him, the assistant editor. The four functional heads below this level normally dealt with the deputy or assistant editor, but access to the editor was always available. These heads were Features, News, Chief Sub, and Sports, although in addition there was a District News Editor and a Sports News Editor, whose position, status and authority were much the same. The work in the chief subs section was internal organisation of incoming news and features copy, the latter normally being prepared two days in advance. Sports news often came from regular or wire sources, but some reporters were allocated either the local football, rugby or cricket team, and there were specific correspondents for other sports. Sports news organisation followed, fairly closely, diary events, although reporters could easily manufacture a story by putting a proposition to, say, the manager of the local football team and his reply could easily be the basis of the lead sports story.

The collection of 'news' news was more complex. There were various sources: diary events usually from institutional sources; district reporters; and the wire or other newspapers in the group. The latter source was used when local people were involved in incidents outside the area. However, one headline blazoned across the front page 'Ex local man slightly hurt in bomb blast', suggested that more selection was required. The organisation of reporters was a problem, and the District News Editor felt more like a manager than a journalist as he was concerned with instilling discipline into his reporters to ensure a regular flow of copy. The Deputy Features Editor felt that news gathering had deteriorated over the past twenty years, because district reporters' jobs were no vocation for the ambitious journalist, who regarded such posts as mere training. The local correspondent known and revered by all was now a thing of the past. The morning newspaper had a similar pattern for work organisation, although in addition, there was a Night Editor and a Chief Assistant Editor. A major problem was the turnover of staff in the sub-editor's section, where journalists did not want to work nights.

Nearly all the editorial managers were aware of commercialisation and many of these had already come to view it as a necessary evil, for after all, to them the paper was bigger. This was an optimistic attitude covering up the growth of a situation they had little care for. Those managers most in contact with other departments had the clearest ideas of the pressures. There was more space, but fewer reporters and therefore the quality of editorial could suffer. The editors, many thought, had to fight battles to maintain the position of editorial as against advertising, or against any other pressures of costs, budgeting, number of reporters, deadlines, etc. There appeared to be a resigned attitude over commercialism in that a bigger paper meant more news, there was financial stability, and of more advertisements, many said that it would be wrong to turn away money. But there was also a feeling of isolation, as the editorial managers knew little of other departments and their problems, and felt that those departments did not want to understand editorial and its problems. It was a kind of impasse, resolved for editorial managers by sticking to their task of producing a newspaper they thought the people wanted to read.

I.3.2 Centre (B)

This relatively recent newspaper firm was housed in a modern building on a factory estate situated on the outskirts of a developing town. The circulation of the two evening newspapers was relatively modest, but expanding, and indeed to the north certain developments were to ensure the possibility of a vastly improved circulation in the years to come.

The opinion often expressed at this centre, was that it was a 'tight' operation, with costs being continually under review, particularly if there was a recession in advertising revenue. The newspapers had no tradition of readership or of advertising and many managers were aware that an image needed to be created, but editorial managers, due to the cost-conscious atmosphere, felt this image-building to be very difficult. The loss of regular news features and insufficient reporters caused consternation amongst nearly all below the level of editor, both of whom were of the managing editor type, and appreciated fully the commercial aspects of their work.

The printing technology was modern, with computerised photo-composition and web-offset. This was housed on half of the ground floor, with the other half being shared by the two sets of journalists who mostly kept a separate identity, although news stories were duplicated where appropriate. The first floor housed the studio, the advertising departments, personnel, production executives and administration. The second floor was much smaller and comprised of the boardroom and managing director together with the Assistant Managing Director, and the Executive Assistant to the Managing Director.

The organisational structure had not developed along precisely the same lines as at Centre (A), but did have one Assistant Managing Director, looking after the revenue gathering departments of classified advertising, display advertising, newspaper sales and marketing. Although not handling as much advertising as at Centre (A), the lack of specialisation in the advertising area was becoming a problem. The solution according to the Display Advertising Manager was to have managers for the different newspapers. Here, of course, the evening newspapers circulated in separate well-defined areas, whereas at Centre (A) about half the morning sales were in the evening's circulation area. Training was important and targets were constantly increased as the newspaper attempted to become the major selling mechanism for local trade and industry. There was greater managerial involvement at this centre than at Centre (A) as the operation was relatively new and still had some way to go before it would become firmly established, although the prospects were good. The Assistant Managing Director had a weekly meeting of his sales managers and kept in daily contact with them. The Managing Director had a regular monthly meeting of senior executives, and generally was fairly involved with the day-to-day operation. Reporting directly to him were the Assistant Managing Director, the Chief Accountant, the Personnel Manager, the two Editors and the Production Manager. For the most part these departments could function without direction from above, the only difficulty arising from the relationship between editorial and production.

The Production Manager at Centre (B) was an engineer, versed in the operation of computers. He was a professional manager and not a time-served craftsman, and his standing within the organisation was that much higher than at Centre (A). He was consulted over major decisions in the firm and his department was rigidly organised, with relationships with copy-sending departments, editorial and advertising, centring on the adherence to strict deadlines. The Editors and their departments operated in their relationship with production around the limits determined by the production department. The importance of production is perhaps the greatest difference between Centres (A) and (B), although the organisation of the editorial department was much the same as in Centre (A).

The production and editorial departments had in common relatively militant workers, and whilst managers of each department explained this in terms of a lack of tradition, in that their workers had not developed the loyalty normally associated with those who work on a newspaper, it was fairly obvious that two other factors were at least important, that of the 'tight' operation and relatively low pay. The working conditions resulting from the tight operation, particularly for journalists, were sub-standard and led to a neutral feeling over the newspaper. In particular the journalists had little pride in their company's output. Pay was low compared to the large city nearby, a situation not only producing a turnover of labour, but also leading those who stayed to rectify the position. This was often done by strike action, rather than lengthy negotiations which would 'break-down'. It was in this way the managers could talk of a lack of tradition.

The personnel function at this centre was more integrated with general management, and although not exercising as much influence as the personnel manager may wish, the general reaction was favourable. Personnel as a function is relatively new to newspapers, for traditionally the editor hired and fired his staff, and the trade union controlled recruitment in production. Elsewhere the staff were small in numbers negating the need for the recruitment aspect of personnel. At older plants the personnel manager took time to become integrated into the organisation, and, as at Centre (A) was isolated. At Centre (B) personnel had been important from the very beginning thus explaining its different role and status between centres. At Centre (B), the personnel manager talked of management development patterns of co-ordination training and recruitment policies rather than being a posting-box for other department's vacancies.

I.3.3 Centre (C)

The operation at Centre (C) was much smaller, involved weeklies rather than dailies, and had most of the editorial staffs in district offices. Its organisation structure was simple, and few difficulties arose apart from communication from the Editor-in-Chief to the majority of his staff. Most of the senior executives viewed their post as a stepping stone in their career, and for them employment was related to the group rather than the centre. They all reported to the Managing Director, who was happy with the span of control, presumably because it gave him the necessary experience for his next promotion. All the managers were aware, as they were in the other centres, of the rapid promotion available within the group, and appointments at Centre (C) would be crucial, in that perhaps only two years would be allocated for a manager to show his potential.

The centre was at the north end of the various areas in which its papers circulated. The present location and building were fairly new, having been chosen through a centralisation plan, and the activities of twelve weekly newspapers were co-ordinated from this centre. Printing was done by web-offset, and composition was gradually moving to photo-composition, but even given the number of newspapers there was still spare capacity and jobbing printing was being sought.

The pace of work and demands on managers were less than in other centres, although the need to extend advertising and control costs was evident. In particular the Editor-in-Chief was aware of constraints on the amount of space he could use. The centralisation had also meant that some news stories and features could be shared, whilst still retaining the community character necessary for a weekly newspaper.

If there was a problem at Centre (C) it was the dislike of the pace of a weekly, and although considered by many to be a training ground for executives, the operation did not and could not test them. For some it was boredom, for others they had to invoke their own sense of urgency in order that promotion would be sooner rather than later.

I.4 THE DEVELOPMENT OF NEWSPAPER ORGANISATION

Regional newspapers are essentially commercial, revenue maximising organisation, although they have not always been like this as the movement to overt commercialisation has only taken place in the I960's and I970's. This stage of their development, denoted as Regional Commercialism, has been described in the previous section and will be further analysed later. This stage however, must not be viewed in isolation, it had developed from an earlier one, and will in turn (some changes are now apparent) develop into a new one. The previous stage is characterised by an ideology of news or propaganda, a relatively strong managing director, owner or editor, and a sizeable and important editorial department. These were the characteristics of the most successful form of newspaper organisation in the first half of the twentieth century. They were most obvious in the London-based national newspapers of that period, and thus this stage is called Fleet Street. Its influence on the regional press must not be under-estimated, for by the exhibition of a successful form of newspaper organisation and of the interlinking of ownership, the characteristics of Fleet Street were exhibited by the regional press, albeit in a limited form, but nevertheless sufficient to say that the regional newspapers before I950 were organised differently from the I960's and I970's. There is therefore a process of change from the Fleet Street inferred model to the Regional Commercialism model.

The objective of these regionals was fast becoming that of revenue maximisation in preference to publishers' need to propagate their opinions. This trend towards commercial orientation was accentuated by the arrival in Britain in the I950's of Roy (later Lord) Thomson, and he quickly accumulated a small empire of regional and national papers, employing American and Canadian methods to bolster advertising. Papers had previously relied on display advertising (with a kind of persuasive sell) but the Thomson group of papers began to use the idea of regional papers being a market place for any goods small or large, and thus he exploited the potential for classified advertising:

> 'What he has done ... is to make not one or two pages into crude advertising vehicles, but to make whole newspapers 40, 50 or even 90 pages of them into sophisticated advertising vehicles.' (Southern I970, p.68)

Commercial managers were introduced and the advertising salesman reversed his previously subservient role.

This stage in development is characterised by an awareness by owners of the economic situation of regional papers, and obsession for more revenue and the subjugation of editorial departments in favour of commercial ones, notably advertising. Within this stage editorial and non-editorial are engaged in a kind of battle, editorial to ensure that the newspaper published is worthy of the name, and non-editorial to ensure a profitable return on capital. These aims if pursued with any amount of endeavour will be mutually exclusive. The collection and presentation of good editorial is costly and requires a flexible organisation. On the other hand the maintenance of a profitable return on capital will require a stringent control of costs and an organisation based on rational grounds. A tension develops between the two sides, resolved by that side having sufficient authority to pursue its aims, and ensuring all other departments in their activities provide the necessary support. A basis for the legitimacy of authority of editorial is based on traditional grounds whilst that for non-editorial is on rational grounds. During this stage this clash is resolved as the power of non-editorial is greater, based on the new wave of ownership and the concomitant ideology of newspaper publication.

A third stage can be isolated, that of Regional Technology, and indeed the regional press are embarking upon such a stage.

If stage two was about revenue maximisation, stage three is about profit maximisation. This is achieved by a reduction in the labour force and thus costs, by the introduction of greater mechanisation, providing greater managerial control inside the plant. Video-display terminals, and photo-composition are controlled by computers which also store and process information obtained by accounting, advertising and personnel departments. It has occurred first in the regions because of less union opposition, and because of some skilled labour shortages. However, as commercialism passed to Fleet Street so eventually will this new technology.

Therefore as a background to the commercial press, and the bureaucratisation of editorial work there is this development of regional newspapers form the Fleet Street type to Regional Commercialism to Regional Technology. This study examines the elements in the change procession that has occurred during this development.

The process of change, however, to be understood has to be placed in context of the economic and social history of the press, and the influence of Fleet Street domination of the press. Thus chapter two outlines briefly the history of the press, particularly in relation to the way the national and regional press have developed. To a large extent they have operated in different markets, and knowledge of this has helped newspapers survive. In other cases, acting in ignorance or defiance of economic markets, for whatever reasons has eventually produced crisis after crisis for much of the national press. The government has responded with three Royal Commissions in less than thirty years, but these and other interventions have done little to produce effective solutions. Again knowledge of the economic markets and social pressures are essential to the understanding of the relative failure of government intervention. The regional press has reacted in a very knowledgeable way, in most cases creating its own economic market and fulfilling the demands of it.

The influence of Fleet Street newspapers in the twentieth century on regional newspapers has been enormous. Not only have there been linkages of ownership, but of more importance here is the exhibition of what appeared to be a most successful form of organisation and management. This is strong central direction by one person, publisher or editor, or someone acting in both capacities. For the most part this person's authority was unquestioned, because of his charismatic method of control. A successful newspaper was never run by a committee, and this was demonstrated very aptly (although in differing degrees) by Beaverbrook, Northcliffe, Kemsley, Hartwell, etc. For some of these publishers a profit was not crucial, but propaganda through the promotion of their ideas to a wide audience dominated their newspapers, and was achieved by a relatively strong editor and editorial department.

To propagate opinions the 'correct' stories needed to be gathered and printed, and many journalists were required for this, and as competition between these press barons intensified the need for the latest news, from whatever geographical region, only reinforced the need for more editorial staff. This type of organisation in newspapers occurs when the ideology of publication is based on propaganda, and the publisher appears to have charismatic qualities. Chapter three focuses on the changes in the ideology of newspaper publication from the propaganda stage to that now based on profit, and in doing so analyses the particular Fleet Street style of management which had an influence over the regional press at least till the early I960's

The rest of the study, having examined contextual influences on the regional press, turns to consider the process of change in the three newspaper centres. The process centres on curbing editorial excesses, in particular when viewed from the commercialists, who after I959 became more numerous and more important. Advertising departments began to grow, particularly classified, and it became apparent that the newspaper could be marketed to certain age groups, in which advertisers are interested, and thus developed a marketing department. These commercialists wanted control of the newspaper to increase profit, and they had authority to do so because the owners were now not interested in propaganda or news (except at a minimal level) but rather money. Newspapers in monopoly positions should be able to saturate local markets in terms of newspaper sales, and advertising revenue, both classified and display. Indeed, they could go further and become an advertising adviser to the most important clients. More advertising is thus generated, which presumably, as in earlier years, would mean more space for editorial and more money for the exercise of their flair, but unfortunately for editorial it was just the reverse. Costs need to be reduced in non-revenue producing departments, and with production being tightly controlled by trade unions, inhibiting immediate change here it was editorial who were suspect to increasing control. There is no local competition and so therefore the latest and best news criteria do not apply. News is required, locally orientated, but its cost of collection, and presentation must be controlled, and in its activities editorial must fit in with the rest of the organisation, rather than, as many have observed the other way around.

The change process envelops editorial, until it succumbs to its new role, and this is often achieved by having managing editors, rather than 'journalist editors'. Alternatively editorial reacts, and the militancy of regional journalists is testimony to the nature of this reaction. Chapter four examines both the crucial elements in regional commercialism, (and the extent of its development) and the perception of both editorial and non-editorial to these changes. The underlying theme in the chapter is the way the new regional commercialism clashes with the organisation of regional newspapers before I959. One element of this clash, is the nature of editorial in a newspaper, and the outcome of such a clash determines the kind of organisational structure applicable to the management of this function. However the perception of editorial and non-editorial are also crucial to the kinds of activities in which they become involved. At one extreme the artistic nature of editorial work means informal rather than formal systems of organisation, whereas if editorial is merely a routine collection and presentation of news, then bureaucratic administration would appear to be wholly effective.

Chapter five examines the influence placed upon editorial through 'regional commercialism' by developing the notion of areas of interchange. Briefly an area of interchange occurs when members of one department have to contact members of another over an issue of mutual concern. Any decision made depends on the relative authority of the departments. In the Fleet Street model the authority of editorial was likely to exceed, in many cases, the authority of other departments. However with a change in ideology of publication, and a consequent re-orientation of objectives, the authority of non-editorial departments is increased sufficiently to determine decisions in the areas of interchange. The significance of such control is found in the internal operation of each department, because the control of interchange decisions means a re-organisation of work to meet the demands of such decisions. Of most concern is the editorial department for two reasons. First, because editorial's authority has been reduced by a change in ideology, and second, because the nature of interchange decisions are likely to be of a bureaucratic and rigid nature, which when interpreted within their department, will clash with their more flexible form of work operation. This chapter relies heavily on empirical material to develop this argument.

To ensure a continuation of control by non-editorial, particularly commercial departments, emphasis is placed on the adherence to rules, and indeed to introducing more control by stricter rules. (Chapter six). This is achieved by promoting managers relatively quickly, (Chapter five), which often means the introduction of new systems of operations, by new rules, at every promotion. Of course, ambitious managers realise the quick way to success, and fervently produce these new work operations, and ensure that their new rules are rigidly obeyed. These new rules are most likely to work within the new ideology, thus cutting costs and increasing revenue. Where they affect editorial it will be to control their activities within a bureaucratic framework, which is exacerbated by the mobility of managers, and again this is developed by empirical material.

The precise areas of control on the work of editorial, from the imposition of impersonal rules is detailed in chapter seven, whilst the next chapter examines the reaction of managers and particularly journalists to these changes. Finally, in the conclusion, the effects of this growth of commercialisation are assessed, in particular the internal organisational changes, in relation to the role of the press in western democratic society.

2 The recent social and economic evolution of newspapers

The social and economic evolution of newspapers in the twentieth century provides a necessary background to the analysis of study outlined in the previous section. The launching or revitalising of what came to be several mass-circulation newspapers in the first decade of the century, produced the Fleet Street stage, and indeed the intense competition which heralded the demise of that stage. The eventually ailing Fleet Street newspapers were supported by many regional newspapers in common ownership, and this resulted in the second, and third stages. The following sections report the recent developments in the newspaper industry and attempt to conceptualise these developments in terms of distinct economic market models.

Newspapers operate in markets and knowledge of the market, and how it works is essential to survival. A newspaper can control its own market either if it is in a monopoly position or if it has created its own market. The former applies to the regional press, while the latter increasingly describes the London based national press. For all newspapers, knowledge of the market is essential, for only then can the appropriate decisions be made, but as the I977 Royal Commission Report succintly remarked 'markets change', (Chapter 6, paragraph IO) and adaptation is necessary. The demise of Fleet Street is in part due to a changing market, but more so to a management and organisation structure which was unable to recognise the change and/or adapt to it. The opposite is true of the regional press.

2.I PERPETUAL CRISIS IN FLEET STREET

During the last fifteen years there have been numerous reports (I) published either describing the poor economic situation of the press, or prescribing solutions, for its continued existence in its present form. Most of these concerned themselves with the national press, for the regional press was highly profitable in some cases to the extent that they could offset the losses of some of the faltering national papers. A summary of this present state of crisis is necessary before analysing the historical and economic reasons for its occurrence.

The Economist Intelligence Unit remarked in 1966:

> 'No fewer than seven of the seventeen newspapers studied are in the unhealthy position of having a steady or increasing number of pages with a decreasing percentage of advertisements. This probably indicates that these papers are having to increase the percentage of editorial due to competition. In some newspapers this is undoubtedly carried beyond the point where the paper ceases to be profitable.' (Summary, p.29)

Another view from Harford Thomas on ownership trends:

> 'A relatively large number of independent newspapers of varied views is gradually being replaced by a remarkably small number of mass circulation national journals dominating the national newspaper field. At the same time the number of separate newspaper proprietors of importance has rapidly diminished owing to the growth of chains of newspapers and periodicals.' (1968 p.5)

But this increase in concentration of ownership, and lack of freedom of choice documented by the 1949 Royal Commission was to be far less of a danger than escalating costs. Once the peak in circulation (1957) had been passed, and restrictions in material supplies lifted, labour and newsprint costs began to rise disproportionately to any increase in productivity or increased revenue from sales and advertising.

The reluctance of proprietors to raise the price of their papers, in accordance with costs, especially during the circulation wars of the 1930's meant that newspapers were becoming heavily dependent upon advertising revenue to survive. The influence of commercial television, after its introduction in 1956 was both to enlarge the amount of advertising available to the media, and to take the largest, and to a certain extent disproportionate, share. The press was not geared to fend off such competition which intensified during the economic crises of the 1960's when a downfall in advertising (as it is liable to do) preceded a depression in the economy causing crises in the national press. These crises were heightened by the government's 'stop-go' economic policy, which did little to avert the death and near closure of many papers. Those papers with substantial profits (or financial support through large corporations) could weather these crises but the rest needed wholesale re-organisation or vast injections of capital to sustain them in these poor years. The near loss of half of the daily national newspapers (2) did not produce another commission, but led to the reports mentioned earlier. In fact the 1962 Royal Commission had all but by-passed the problem centring its reforms and proposals on the re-formation of a General Press Council to act as a guardian of Fleet Street, and on the disclosure of the ownership of papers. There was some discussion of increased concentration of ownership and of the reduction of the number of papers, with several proposals for manning reductions as a pathway to better industrial relations. Economic remedies, however crude, to make the government, or healthier papers, support the weaker ones, were rejected. The root of the trouble and the depths to which it has extended had been neglected by the commissions.

All the reports in the latter I960's concluded that inefficient management propagated by proprietorial rule had led to over-manning, low productivity, high costs, strong dictatorial unions all constrained by a technology dating from the latter part of the nineteenth century. They expressed fear over the near loss of several papers and over the lack of governmental and institutional concern with the reduction of the freedom of choice, especially as the threatened papers formed one side of the political spectrum.

The reports thought solutions requiring assistance external to the industry such as redistribution of advertising or use of government subsidies were inappropriate unless internal problems were initially solved. They suggested the security of publication could only be guaranteed by complete management re-organisation. Evidence for this came especially from the Economic Intelligence Unit Report which found that only the Sunday Times and the Daily Mirror had proved each in their own very different ways that efficient management is not inconsistent with successful journalism:

> 'Both these groups recognise the need for professional management with clearly defined areas of authority.'
> (Main Report, p.52)

Many of the papers still suffered from the old proprietorial influences of papers being used for the propagation of opinion. Instance the Daily Express:

> 'The newspapers in the Beaverbrook Group have traditionally been used as vehicles for the propagation of the later Lord Beaverbrook's personal philosophy and political ideals. It seems likely that the dissemination of political ideals was considered in the past to be more important than maximising profit.'
> (Main Report, p.29)

This type of management has been non-commercial, stemming from the dominance of the editorial staff in reporting news from as wide as possible and the publish-at-all-costs attitude of the proprietors. The E.I.U. in general saw this as a continuing inhibiting factor for the recruitment of experienced commercial managers.

By the mid-1970's, and in spite of all previous advice and help, the national press still had sufficient problems to warrant the third Royal Commission on the Press in less than three decades. The threatened closure of national newspapers was still a major area of concern for the subscribers to the 'freedom of the press in large numbers' argument but further worries were caused by the way the press itself had begun to solve its problems. Since 1962 concentration of the regional national press had increased, and the ownership had diversified out of the press, or alternatively outside interests had taken over. Monopoly trends threatened the freedom of the press, as did the diversification. The newspapers concerned would be reticent to criticise their other interests, and thus their impartiality would be called into question, and extension of the press into local and national broadcasting was also worrying. However, given the inadequacy of the two earlier Commissions it is ironic that when the press reforms itself this still brings criticism. The new managements were more commercial, and their papers had to be profitable, or they did not survive. Print trade unions were threatened that if stability of industrial relations was not achieved then the newspaper would close. The ideology of publication had certainly changed from the days of Beaverbrook.

2.1.1 The Era of Mass Readership and the Growing Dependence on Advertising

With the publication of the Daily Mail in 1898 there began the era of a Fleet Street dominated British press. A plethora of titles followed, many of them 'popular' in nature but

> 'From the beginning of the century to the first World War, Northcliffe's were the only daily papers to make satisfactory profits. Most others made losses. Several found it impossible to continue.' (F. Williams, 1957, p.28)

The competition continued with the circulation wars of the 1930's which were near disastrous for those papers which attempted to attain the magical two million circulation mark for their papers, necessary for increased advertising revenue. In part this competition arose from the introduction and development of display advertising, but such large and usually costly space in the newspaper was only profitable with large circulations. Classified advertisements on the other hand were usually more specialised and were thus aimed at fewer people. The Daily Herald and the Daily Mail were the forerunners in this battle for circulation and were soon joined by the Daily Express and the Daily Mirror, although these latter two both began to consolidate on their particular type of readership, and pull away from the circulation merry-go-round of the others, who were merely winning and losing circulation, one to another as readers built libraries, re-clothed themselves and re-furnished their homes, simply by subscribing to a different paper each month. (F. Williams, 1969, p.110). The Daily Express, with a bright editorial content built circulation on the stimulus of genuine readership demand and the Daily Mirror with its 'new sector' readership sold four, then over five million copies at its peak. The Daily Herald unfortunately though, with its two million readership did not have the impact Elias had predicted.

> 'Advertisers were less easily hypnotised by figures than he thought; they were less sceptical of the value of net sales certificates won by bribery.' (F. Williams, 1969, p.111)

But perhaps more important was the type of readership, for the small amount of money these people had to spend discouraged advertisers, more than their ephemeral nature. They were what the modern advertising consultant calls 'down market' working class and lower working class, C_2DE on the incomes grouping scale ABC_1C_2DE.

The ironical twist to this whole affair of circulation was that it was fought in a time of the greatest depression Britain has had, before or since. It was a time when companies had both little to spare for advertising and, when the benefit of advertising to a man existing on national insurance was questionable. Hard lessons were learnt about the nature of advertising, especially now that the press was dependent upon it to supplement revenue from sales. First, high circulation does not necessarily mean higher volumes of advertising at a higher price as it is the type of reader and how much money he has to spend which are all important. Second, during a depression advertising is regarded as superfluous by companies and will be the first item to be reduced in any re-appraisal of company costs. Third, even during a natural trading period an increase in price per column of advertising (based on increased circulation) may only have the effect of maintaining the company's advertising expenditure, while at the higher rate, reducing its volume. This, with the advertising/editorial ratios used on many papers, could reduce the total size of the paper. Lastly, in times of inflation, both labour and newsprint costs will increase more than the increase in sales revenue. If the increase in advertising revenue is not commensurate with the increase in costs, then this will impose heavy burdens on the financing of the newspaper, and may adversely, in the face of no external resources, affect the future of the paper.

One benefit that came from the circulation struggles was a permanent base for mass circulation newspapers.

> 'Between 1930 and 1939 the combined sales of popular morning papers rose by over one million and a half, and went on rising during and after the war. However distasteful the means, the habit of newspaper reading was permanently affected by the lavish promotion campaigns of the thirties.' (F. Williams, 1969, p.112)

The increase in circulation continued in the artificial circumstances of wartime and newsprint rationing after the war. Newspapers were cheap, and because of the rationing fairly small (some down to four pages) encouraging readers to buy two or more papers. Newspapers prospered during the post-war economic growth which continued into the I950's and provided an increased volume of advertising to supplement sales revenue in the face of increasing costs. Circulation reached its peak or 'saturation point' in I957, while the introduction of commercial television a year earlier seriously challenged the newspapers near monopolistic right to mass audience advertising.

2.I.2 Monopolistic Tendencies and the I947-9 Royal Commission on the Press

Concurrent with these developments were three Royal Commissions on the Press, the first two formed to analyse and recommend solutions to specific problems, the third having a much larger brief, including ownership, economics of the press, its reporting, editorial standards, its industrial relations and the functions of the Press Council. In contrast the I947-49 one investigated the monopolistic tendencies occurring in management and ownership, and the I96I-2 Commission focussed on the financial problems of costs and revenue, particularly newspapers increasing dependence upon advertising.

In their quest for greater circulation to attract advertising in the I930's, some of the proprietors of Fleet Street papers had branched out into the provinces, by either acquiring existing papers or starting new ones. Rothermere, Camrose, Kemsley and Cowdray, saw a 'potential goldmine in the provincial press'. (F. Williams, I957, p.I77). As a consequence of rising costs and intensified competition for advertising from the nationals, some provincial newspapers were forced out of business. But it was the extension of the methods of the press barons to the regions which left many newspapers here in a monopoly position:

> ' ... at the height of the struggle between the great trusts, independent papers that got in their way were forced out of existence without mercy. Others were bought and sold at fantastically inflated prices.' (F. Williams, I957, p.I78)

One such struggle in Bristol, Newcastle and Derby between the Berry brothers (later Lords Camrose and Kemsley) and Rothermere with his Northcliffe newspapers was eventually so expensive for both sides (Camrose was reputed to have spent more than one million pounds) that they had to compromise, with the Berry brothers withdrawing from Bristol and Derby, and Rothermere from Newcastle.

> 'In Bristol the effect was to leave a city which had formerly enjoyed the service of four independent morning and evening newspapers at the mercy of

one Rothermere invader ... ' (F. Williams, I957 p.I78-9)

Events such as this one produced complaints of increased monopolistic tendencies, and demands for some kind of investigation into the ownership of the press. Rising circulation did not mean more papers as 225 papers ceased publication between I9I8 and I956. The journalists in particular thought such trends to be harmful to the press, in that increased concentrations could adversely affect editorial content. They argued that the popular press, buy its very nature, over-emphasised entertainment and all its facets to the detriment of 'hard' news. The relationship between control and ownership and editorial content will be examined later, but on the subject of monopoly the journalists had somewhat exaggerated the position, which was contested by the proprietors, Lord Camrose being sufficiently motivated to document (Camrose, I948) his arguments nullifying the criticism of increasing group commercialism. (See Table 2.I)

Much of the critism was directed more at Lord Kemsley than anyone else, yet in reply he stated that newspaper groups had saved many unprofitable papers, and although this may be supported by the facts, it was true that monopoly as such did not exist.

TABLE 2.I

THE OWNERSHIP OF NEWSPAPERS BY THE MAJOR GROUPS

	London			Provincial		
	M	E	S	M	E	S
Daily Mail Group	I	I	I	-	I0	-
Kemsley Newspapers	I	-	2	7	9	4
Provincial Newspapers	-	-	-	-	4	-
Westminster Press	-	-	-	4	9	I

M = Morning: E = Evening: S = Sunday
(Source, Camrose, I948, p.I5)

'Out of a total estimated circulation of national Morning papers of I5,300,000, Kemsley's comanded 800,000; out of a total circulation of national Sunday's of 28,700,000, it claimed 4,900,000. In the provinces Kemsley morning papers sold I,400,000 out of a total circulation in that field of I8,500,000.' (Murray, I972, p.36)

However there was some concentration into fewer and fewer hands.

> 'By the end of 1929 the Berry brothers had twenty six daily and Sunday papers under their control, in addition to the Amalgamated Press. Lord Rothermere controlled fourteen and had a substantial interest in another three. The Westminster Press owned thirteen. The Invereste Paper Company nine. Between them these four groups with no fewer than sixty two daily and Sunday papers in their hands controlled close on half the entire newspaper press of the country.' (F. Williams, I957, p.I77)

Thus in economic terms the press, although having a different structure from that at the beginning of the century, was not in any danger of restrictive pricing policies or of suppression of general editorial freedoms. The Royal Commission summarised,

> 'We do not, ... therefore see cause for alarm in the decrease in the number of national morning newspapers from 2I in I92I to 9 in I949; but while the number is not alarmingly inadequate it is not so large that any further decrease could be contemplated without anxiety.' (I947, paragraph 3I3)

2.I.3 The I96I-2 Royal Commission: A Problem of Costs

By the time of the second Royal Commission on the Press the trend in monopolistic ownership had continued to the extent that the top three undertakings of all national Daily and Sunday papers had increased their share of total circulation Press, from 43% in I947 to 65% in I96I. (Royal Commission I96I-2, Report, p.I6). Concentration in the provincial daily field had only marginally increased and although in weekly newspapers the top five undertakings had doubled their holdings the extent of concentration was negligible. All this caused little alarm, except perhaps in the national press,although here attention was focussed on costs and revenue. It was the year of crisis I960-6I that provoked the second major investigation within I5 years. Three national Sundays, one national daily and one London evening all folded. Causality was thought not to lie with monopolistic ownership, but within the economics of newspaper production. Questions raised were how some papers boasting a circulation of nearly two million could not effectively compete in Fleet Street. The I96I Royal Commission on the Press had a different mandate from its predecessor in I947,

> 'to examine the economic and financial factors affecting the production and sale of newspapers, magazines, and other periodicals in the United Kingdom including
>
> (a) manufacturing, printing, distribution and other costs;

(b) efficiency of production; and

(c) advertising and other revenue ... ' (Report, p.3)

After a thorough analysis of the economics of newspaper production the Royal Commission revealed the existence of many inefficient practices concerning the use of labour. Of the other costs, newsprint and ink obviously varied with circulation and little cost reduction was possible here. The existing machinery was a fixed cost, although

'the development of new machinery and techniques has not been exploited to the best advantage.' (Report p.II4)

It was therefore decided that any progress in cost effectiveness was only in the short term at least, in the re-examination of the use of labour.

' ... it was estimated that a saving of 34% could be made in the manpower employed in production and distribution in the London newspaper offices.' (Report p.II4)

But perhaps such costs were a competitive element, if you could afford higher costs than your rival you survived and he didn't. It was a negative way of competing (though as with the News Chronicle a very effective one.) (3) Several criticisms concerned the multiplicity of unions at the workplace and called for moves towards one industrial union, a problem which when combined with a lack of unity, and pursuit of individual interests by the employers, had led to poor collective bargaining arrangements, in particular machinery for negotiation and circulation when

'the employees are too exigent in their demands on an industry in which profits must not be taken for granted.' (Report p.II4)

As a solution to these problems, apart from a closer look by management at their own methods, the Commission recommended that

'there should be a joint standing body of employers and unions charged with the oversight of planning and development and the whole field of newspaper production. Its general object would be to facilitate developments in machinery and techniques and plan for the long term manpower and training requirements.' (Report, paragraph I06)

The Commission also recommended that the Press Council be continued, but with further powers of investigation. The idea of such an investigatory body originated in the I947-9 Royal

Commission, but implementation was delayed until I953, and then only with an altered format, both tactics indicating the reluctance of the proprietors to have an outside body to investigate their own affairs. The newspaper proprietors found this proposal indigestible, if not nauseous. (Viner, I969) Eventually the membership of the council was not independent, or lay members as intended, but fifteen editors, and ten management who would then elect a Chairman from amongst themselves. Financially it only had an income of £2,500, increased to £4,I00 by I960, but this proved totally inadequate and precluded the council from pursuing many of its objectives of investigation of the Press.

This was realised in I960-I when there were calls from all quarters for it to examine the causes for the closure of the News Chronicle. The Council replied vehemently that the Secretary and assistant were too hard pressed,

> 'to act as a clearing house for the constantly fluctuating and infinitely varied economic fortunes of the British Press.' (The Press and the People, I96I, p.6)

The report of the Royal Commission, in the light of other closures - I7 in daily and Sunday papers since I949, I0 in provincial morning and 5 provincial evening from I937 - asked 'Did none of these deserve an inquiry except the largest?' Of more importance, detailed examination of the press was precluded by its very voluntary nature and the recalcitrant attitude of the proprietors.

> 'One attempt was, indeed, made to ascertain by questionnaire the costs and economic background of provincial newspaper production but this required the co-operation of the Newspaper Society which was not forthcoming, on the grounds, as we were told, that the economic factors underlying the deaths of newspapers were so clear that no inquest was necessary.' (Royal Commission, I962, Report paragraph 323)

By resurrecting the original ideals of the Press Council it would then be able,the Commission thought to pursue

> 'the general objects of encouraging the growth of the sense of public responsibility and public service among all engaged in the profession of journalism whether as directors, editors or other journalists; and of furthering the efficiency of the profession and the well-being of those who practised it.' (Royal Commission, I962, Report, paragraph 320)

Thus the Commission having found a major cause of inefficiency in exorbitant labour costs recommended both internal solutions (the joint-standing body mentioned earlier, and a reconstitution of the negotiating and consultation machinery) and external enquiry 'to study development in the Press which may tend towards a greater concentration or monopoly.' (5) Unfortunately neither came near to helping the Press in the matter of costs. As Murray reports

> 'its power and purpose remain exactly the same as they were. It wields no sanction beyond those of rebuke and persuasion. It has no authority to intervene when press mergers or take-overs are in the offing - nor can it claim that its records would be of any great value in making obvious a trend towards monopoly.'

Any information it acquires during investigation is kept secret, if not already public and

> 'in view of such restrictions it is hard to see how the public could ever be warned that another News Chronicle tragedy, large or small was impending.' (Murray, I972, p.I69)

Most of its work has centred around examining abuses of freedom of the Press in news reporting and content of editorial.

Certainly the Commission even with the new style Press Council moved no further towards controlling labour costs, although it provided some excuse

> 'that the ephemeral character of a newspaper means that the loss of one day's production can never be made good; that a stoppage of any length gives rise to a greater risk of losing the goodwill of advertisers and readers than attends other industries. This situation is said to result in pressure being exerted by employees at the eleventh hour of production.' (Royal Commission, I962, Report, paragraph IOI)

There is some truth in this statement but how and why should such a situation have been allowed to develop? 'More than one witness, when questioned about some wage rate or practice which seemed rooted in economic absurdity, said it originated perhaps fifty years before, no one knew quite how or why, and had become tradtiional.' (Murray, I972, p.II7-8)

Reference to the earlier years of proprietorial rule certainly provide reasons. First, at this time newspapers either made considerable profit, although there was little concern for how they did so, or had alternative sources of income. The circulation wars increased the pressures on proprietors for continuity of publication for readers were being urged by intensive campaigns to change papers and this gave the printing unions immense bargaining power, which could be readily used to increase earnings. Second, proprietors saw quality of editorial as important in securing permanent readers, and part of this was to provide "late news and exclusive news (as) key ingredients in the editorial contents of the newspapers" (Sisson, I975, p.89). This ultimately caused some disruption in the work flow of production processes, allowing the unions to bargain over increased work rates or changing patterns of work. Both enabled the printers to increase demands, which with the publish-at-all-costs attitude of the proprietors, together with sufficient profit, or alternative funds, were easily agreed to by management. The problem is now how to redress the balance of power, if at all possible, at the workplace. If the situation had arisen because of the economics of newspaper production, it may be somewhat difficult to reduce the union's exploitation of the situation.

In respect of Fleet Street, tacit agreements have been made that when one newspaper faces the loss of publication, the others do likewise. This prevents what the Webbs called the 'rolling strike' when the union forces each newspaper in turn to pay higher rates, by selective strikes. Joint action by management in this way merely enlarges the parties to any one conflict, although it may reduce the pressure on any one paper that could be in danger of closing. A lock-out of this nature must essentially be short term, for the loss of the reading habit of a daily newspaper by readers in any number would prove to be very serious. In many instances it will not be restored as quickly or as easily as it was cancelled. For instance, the E.I.U. reported 'that only about 70% of the News Chronicle readers transferred to other newspapers thus losing 400,000 readers from the total circulation.' (Financial Report, p.I3)

Thus the highly competitive Fleet Street prevents little unilateral action in relation to labour costs and it is no surprise that the Royal Commission was at pains to find any solution to this problem, although as shown later the monopolistic press has had a far greater impact in solving these.

2.I.4 The I974-77 Royal Commission: A full survey

The terms of reference of the I974-77 Royal Commission were so wide that the extent of investigation covered almost every conceivable aspect of the press. Their main concern was to ensure that the press could fulfil its role in a democratic society, which involved maintaining a freedom of the press, defined in paragraph 2.3, and a survival of the existing number of titles. Thus their analysis ranged from the traditional economic to discussion over the maintenance of editorial and to the reform of industrial relations. The Commission relied heavily on the economic analysis presented in I962, perhaps because the press had now arranged its own survival. Since I962, ownership had changed of the Times, Observer, Daily Express and the Sun, and financial stability had been achieved for the other national newspapers by diversification of interests. In addition by differentiation in the market each newspaper was trying to establish its own sector; thus achieving stability in type and number of readers. In view of this and the traditional objection to government subsidies, economic help was discussed but in the main rejected.

The Commission then turned to the effect on the press of this new type of ownership. It was worried that commercial interests elsewhere would lead newspaper owners to suppress criticism of these interests, and this led them to recommend extensions to the proposed charter on press freedom to safeguard the editor from undue internal and external pressures.

Editorial content was, for the first time, in a Royal Commission examined for its accuracy and possible bias, following accusations by many prominent politicians that the national press was biased against the Labour Party, the Trade Unions and left-wing political organisations and in particular of being sensational and incomplete over the reporting of industrial relations. The Commission found the press guilty on all of these counts and recommended that industrial relations coverage should be widened and improved. The concern over the lack of a left-wing 'serious' newspaper has, as the Commission said, a long history, (paragraph I.6) but they found no acceptable way of helping to launch and sustain one. Indeed they maintained this 'gap in the political spectrum'is partly filled by the periodical press. Other recommendations concerned the reform of industrial relations in Fleet Street, the re-organisation of training of journalists, and the restructuring of the Press Council.

However, monopolistic trends continued, labour relations were still unsatisfactory and management and owners were taking their own decisions to ensure survival of their newspapers. Thus the three Royal Commissions had examined some of the problems but had failed to suggest or get accepted any permanent, realistic or successful solution (5). As J. Curran noted of the last Royal Commission there was a 'widely held view in Fleet Street that its investigation was a waste of time - a view that its report did little to change' (I978, p.I).

2.2 THE MARKET MODELS

In order to evaluate the recent social and economic evolution of the press it is necessary to conceptualise the economic operation of these newspapers by means of several market models. By doing this the government policies can also be examined. The decision of the owners of newspapers will depend on their objectives and the means of their achievement in relation to the socio-economic market they are operating in. Indeed the perception of such markets is undoubtably crucial to the types of decision owners can make, and often such perceptions conflict with the actual workings of the model, which calls into question the continued survival of their newspapers. (Royal Commission, I977, paragraph 6.IO, 6.II)

The advertising-circulation downward spiral market occurs through intense competition where some newspapers find their share of advertising and thus revenue, declining, which often means a reliance on outside funds to maintain the position of the newspaper, or alternatively a reduction in quantity and probably quality of editorial. This leads to a drop in circulation, and advertisers respond by moving business to higher circulation newspapers. Revenue is reduced, editorial therefore suffers and the spiral only ends in closure. Competition in the form of which newspapers can afford the highest costs exacerbates the spiral, which can only be stopped by a dramatic occurrence such as new editorial line, new format, new size, etc., but this usually means a movement out of this spiral market into another.

Owners who by their decisions have created the spiral model, often move their newspaper into another market, the saturation market. Here a newspaper owner selects a particular circulation area and attempts to maximise his sales in this area. The market is partly created by the owner's decision made in reaction to the demands of advertisers who have increasingly become more selective about which goods and services can be sold to certain groups of the public. Thus if a newspaper owner can demonstrate to potential advertisers that he has a majority of readers of one or two categories he can be relatively certain of taking a substantial amount of advertising. This amount is also likely to be relatively stable, thus allowing the owner to more easily budget this expected revenue against costs.

The third typology, the regional-dependency market operates as an attempt to stall the consequences of the spiral market. The regional newspapers acquired in the 1930's by many of the national newspapers were, because of amongst other things the monopoly position, increasingly profitable, and provided a source of funds to sustain the national newspapers in avoiding the spiral. During the 1960's the 'regional commercialism organisational form' became operative and provided the major characteristic of this market model, that of profitable regional papers supporting the national papers. Of course the losses of the nationals could not be too great, and in due course many of these were changed to improve efficiency, cut losses and even make profits. For some it meant a move into the saturation market, and for others a realisation that costs could be cut, whilst still maintaining a reasonable standard of editorial. A variation of this market model occurs when funds from sources outside the newspaper industry are used, and increasingly this has found favour with many newspaper owners.

2.2.1 The Advertising-Circulation Downward Spiral Market Model

The solution of the labour cost problem is ultimately in the hands of the proprietor, which is not the case with the question of the downward spiral of circulation and advertising in which the proprietor is somewhat powerless compared with the market forces.

The problem has its roots in the dependence of newspapers on advertising revenue, and in its turn the dependencies of advertising, in volume, on the condition of the economy. Advertising is an efficient barometer of economic events, for it reduced fairly quickly in volume at the start of, and sometimes even before, a recession. Companies begin to question the desirability of advertising to a populace which will, with all probability,be constrained in its spending because of higher purchase (value added) tax, lack of loan funds, increased hire purchase requirements etc. During an economic boom period, advertising is likely finitely to procede an increasing in spending power.

It is at a time of recession when newspapers, which previously operated at the margin of profitability, are perilously close to closure, as revenue decreases while costs remain steady, or even increase. The 1962 Royal Commission noted the problem in relation to the News Chronicle, as to why it could not survive with a one and one quarter ($1\frac{1}{4}$) million circulation in a situation with competitors having four million plus readers. Of two policies such a paper could follow, the first is extremely costly in monetary terms in that losses are merely financed by loans or other means. This, apart from the presence of an extremely rich benefactor, is only a short term proposition, for even if the style and content of the paper are maintained during a recession, it is by no means certain that advertisers will return to that particular paper once economic conditions allow. This may lead to less circulation as advertising by itself may encourage readership, thus less advertising, less readership.

The alternative policy, and the one followed in recurrent crises is to reduce costs commensurate with revenue. This

> 'involves having a much lower level of editorial expenditure then the high circulation newspaper, and considerably fewer pages of text: only an exceptionally brilliant editor can hope to prevent a progressive loss of readers under such circumstances.' (Royal Commission 1962, paragraph 224)

A lower readership means that advertising rates are proportionately too high in relation to circulation to attract advertisers. This inevitably leads to less advertising, thus less editorial, thus fewer readers, thus less advertisers, thus less editorial ... A reduction in rates may not attract more advertisers, but merely further reduce revenue (same volume at a lower rate), which in its turn will require a reduction in costs, thus less editorial and a smaller paper, thus fewer readers, thus less attractive to advertisers who switch to other papers, thus less advertising ... The spiral leads to closure unless as the commissioners thought 'if sufficient customers can be persuaded that the quality of what they get makes up for the lack of quantity.' (paragraph 224)

Unfortunately those papers whose closure had led to the Royal Commission, were in direct competition with papers of larger circulation, broadly having readership from the same classes. A change of editorial policy may only alienate existing readers, yet persuade few or no others, at least in short term to buy the paper, thereby involving the papers in added costs over revenue, that would probably lead to an even earlier closure.

The Commission could find no solution of a legislative or fiscal manner to ensure the survival of newspapers. The report concluded

> 'The only hope of the weaker newspapers is to secure ... managers and editors of such enterprise and originality as will enable the publication to overcome the economic forces affecting them.' (paragraph 3I3)

The problem is not confined to National newspapers for many regional papers have closed once the advertising-circulation downward spiral is in operation. Little is heard of these papers, for prestige if involved at all, is usually confined locally, hence the development, because of so-called rationalisation, to a monopoly position and the acceptance of such a situation. A spate of closures I962-4 in Birmingham, Edinburgh, Leeds, Leicester, Manchester and Nottingham illustrate the trend. In particular the Manchester Evening Chronicle in competition with the larger circulation Manchester Evening News suffered from this spiral. Mr. L. Scott remarked,

> 'Local advertisers get better results from one paper and make more use of it: that newspaper becomes fatter and full of advertisements; those readers who are interested in advertising prefer it to the other paper, and so more advertisers get even better results from using it. This is a vicious circle that a second newspaper finds hard to break.' (Jackson, I97I, P.I8-I9)

The problem of the Evening Chronicle in Manchester has not been a failure to hold a substantial readership, but a failure through that readership to give advertisers a worthwhile return. They had tried to break down advertisers' resistance and to provide financial inducements for them to use the Evening Chronicle, but with depressingly little effect.

Advertising for the Chronicle

January to March	I96I	5,475 columns
" "	I962	4,693 "
" "	I963	4,029 "

The paper closed on June 26th I963. Thus the logic of Roy Thomson seems more than pertinent, 'The strong get stronger and the weak get weaker.' (Financial Times, 27.7.63.)

Eventually the weaker one is forced to cease publication but many owners pre-empt the developments in the spiral, and cut losses by merging or early closure.

The 1977 Royal Commission Report neglected this market and considered a now defunct one, that of competition with increasing circulation. Their conclusion was that small circulation papers would do best not to expand circulation because of doubts about increased advertising revenue. (Report, paragraph 6.5) Such advice to newspapers in a declining circulation market will do little to increase publishers respect of Royal Commissions. Of course some crises were more severe than others but this permanent struggle for survival of Fleet Street as a whole has several consequences. First, further closures or the constant threat of them. Second, an increase in concentration, both of ownership and circulation. Third, the diversifying of interests to support ailing papers, and fourth, the concentration of newspapers in one circulation area. The trend has been to magazines, or to an extension of control of regional papers. Fleet Street papers not having this support, have found that once proprietorial dominance has ended, they too have come closer to ceasing publication.

2.2.2 The Saturation Market Model

This model applies to both the regional newspaper and to some of the nationals. However, there is one distinct difference in that the regional newspapers enjoy a monopoly, whereas the nationals are in competition. The regional newspapers are sold in well-defined areas and to attract maximum advertising of all sorts, they attempt to saturate their circulation area. The national newspapers superficially are thought to be in competition with each other, although the popular/serious divide separates the market into two and thus reduces the competition. As previously argued this competition often results in the spiral market model becoming operative, and closure of some papers becoming inevitable. If this is the case then the competition is naturally reduced or even disappears. However, before closure occurs many papers attempt to reduce the extent of the competition and thus the effects of the spiral, by sub-dividing the market even further in what could be called a cartelisation of advertising revenue. This position is not reached by agreement but by the decisions of each individual newspaper owner.

For newspapers to operate this market model is a distinct change from previously, when objectives had been circulation maximisation from any readership group. The newspapers did not discriminate, indeed many revered the Daily Express, which in the 1950's and 1960's, out of the populars, had the highest readership amongst the AB groups. Newspapers have now changed to selecting certain readership markets and maximising sales within that market and that market alone, which is in effect a policy of saturation. Given the limited number of newspapers, this means that with each having its own circulation area, competition is vastly reduced or even eradicated, and the newspapers then only have to persuade the potential reader to buy and the advertiser to advertise, the process being absolute and not relative.

This market has developed but not for all newspapers. The initial division of newspapers into serious/popular still remains and within each category certain newspapers have tried to establish their own market and saturate it. Within the 'serious' division, The Financial Times has long had its own market because of its specialist nature, and has worked within this market for a long time. The other three 'serious' papers, The Times, The Telegraph and The Guardian are on the surface in competition, but have significantly different circulation areas. For instance, The Guardian has a Liberal tradition and has a great appeal in the education world. The Telegraph is bought by the commuting businessmen, and The Times by the senior civil servants. (Royal Commission, 1977, Report, paragraph 6.9; Interim Report, 3.15, 3.16). At the fringes of the circulation areas they do compete, but their editorial content is aimed at maintaining or increasing within their own areas, and given this structure to go against it may be suicidal. Events in 1967-8 concerning The Times illustrate this model.

> 'In January 1967 a five man "News Team" was set up which hired private planes with an abandon hitherto unheard of in Printing House Square. The new Business News Section and the Women's Page took on large expensive staffs. Extra outside columnists on Communications and Politics were retained. Altogether one million pounds was allocated to development of The Times in 1967.' (Seymore-Ure, 1970, p.106)

Such investment naturally allowed The Times to attract a wider audience, and this it did, circulation rising from 256,000 in 1965 to 432,000 in 1969. Thus the increased editorial (fixed) costs had had their desired result, but as The Times only received 34% of its revenue from newspaper sales, with variable costs accounting for 60% of total costs, a loss incurred if other revenue was not forthcoming. In prices per copy (1967 figures) a quality sixpenny newspaper cost nearly two shillings to produce, thereby resulting in a loss of one shilling and six pence per extra copy sold.

'Other revenue' could be obtained by either increasing the volume of advertising or increasing the cost of placing advertisements in the paper. The former was a possibility as The Times in 1965 had 35% of its paper in advertising compared to the Daily Telegraph's 53% but an increase here may well alienate existing readers. This latter is a policy which all papers follow, if possible, when circulation increases, but with market research, advertisers, selling a certain product can ascertain the people who want to buy their product, and the papers they read. Existing advertisers in The Times, would certainly pay higher rates if the increased circulation was of the type of the existing readership, but unfortunately, the new readers were not, they were under-graduates, young graduates, or young businessmen, teachers, etc., all with relatively expensive mortgages and young families, people who had little money to spare to interest the advertiser. The Management at The Times soon realised this and quickly reduced the extra editorial costs and circulation to its former levels, and it is now content to gain readership only as its present circulation groups grow.

The popular section of the national press has undergone similar experiences, particularly in relation to The Sun and The Daily Mail. The former has endured a change of editorial style by being released from TUC direction, a change of ownership from Odhams through International Publishing Corporation to Rupert Murdoch, and eventually through the latter's ownership a complete change of identity, enabling it to secure what has come to be known as a new sub-market below that of the Daily Mirror. Its move from the highly competitive 'middle ground' (F. Williams, I969, p.I56) has ensured its survival.

The Daily Mail had also experienced difficulties, losing nearly a million circulation from a peak of 2,648,000 in I96I. The paper also changed its shape - to a tabloid - and re-designed its internal pages in an effort to relinquish 'a highly vulnerable state under a proprietor who, to judge by the number of editors he was going through was rapidly losing his nerve'. (F. Williams, I969, p.I57) However, The Daily Mail has survived and has stabilised its circulation, sufficient for it to pre-determine, within margins, the advertising levels and revenue, and thus organise costs to this level.

The one newspaper that had not tried to select one circulation area and saturate, the Daily Express, has lost over half of its circulation ($4\frac{1}{2}$ million in the late I960's to $2\frac{1}{4}$ million in I977), and only averted closure by being sold to a commercially-proven business firm. Up until I977 it had still boasted of its wide-ranging readership, which had not attracted the necessary advertising revenue to justify the costs spent on publishing the paper. The new ownership had declared that younger readers are necessary for survival, an indication that even this newspaper is now attempting saturation of one section of the total market.

The I977 Royal Commission has certain sympathies with this analysis, and indeed as a recipe for continual survival it has a lot to recommend it.

> 'We reaffirm the conclusion of our Interim Report The ability of newspapers to specialise has helped them to resist the strong pressures towards concentration.' (Report, paragraph 6.I2)

2.2.3 The Regional Dependency Market Model

Certain national newspapers are part of a larger media organisation encompassing regional newspapers, who with their high profit support their unprofitable national counterparts. This model applies to The Times, The Sunday Times, The Daily Mail, The Financial Times, The Sun, The Guardian, The News of the World, The People and The Evening News (London).

A natural result of the increased control of the regional press by Fleet Street papers has been an extension of chain ownership. At the end of 1969, 55% of English and Welsh provincial evening newspapers were owned by five London based groups, and at the same time at least 200 weeklies were owned by the major groups, nearly 25% of the weekly total. Roy Thomson, once he had acquired the Kemsley group of newspapers in 1959, began to expand rapidly in the regions during the 1960's as did United Newspapers, and I.P.C. Beaverbrook Newspapers however maintained their Fleet Street and Scottish equivalent newspapers, without developing a regional newspaper support network. A further economic recession, combined with a falling circulation (from 4,321,000 in 1961 to 2,500,000 in 1976) of the Daily Express forced Beaverbrook Newspapers to print the Scottish edition of the Daily Express in Manchester, and to cease publication of the Evening Citizen in Glasgow. The advisability of investing in regional papers would now not be in question.

Of course the regional newspapers are operating in the saturation market because of their monopoly position, but their connection to many of the national newspapers makes the regional dependency market model a separate one.

The effect of the operation of this market, in popular or regional newspapers, whose increased profit levels were necessary to support Fleet Street newspapers, are the subject of the empirical work in the study, outlined in chapter one, and furthered in a later chapter.

2.3 ECONOMIC SOLUTIONS

The consequences of successive crises were instrumental in producing a plethora of enquiries, debates, investigations, commissions, reports, pamphlets and even books, most of which were held or published in 1966-7 and 1975-77 during the severest recessions of the 1960's and 1970's, periods when sterling was under threat and wage and price freezes commonplace. The effects on the press were nearly as traumatic as those in 1961-2, the plight of the Sun, Daily Mail, Daily Sketch, Guardian and Times having already been mentioned. It was now manifest that solutions proposed by the 1949 Royal Commission had been insufficiently successful, yet the second Royal Commission

> 'at the end of their labours in 1961-2 ... came up with little or nothing more than had been proposed by their

predecessors of fifteen years before. But many words had to be written and spoken, and many witnesses examined before the conclusion was reached.' (Murray, 1972, p.117-8)

Viner expresses sympathy with such comments

'The Commission took mountains of evidence and produced a molehill of a report mostly designed to pressure Trade Unions into accepting re-deployment or the dismantling of demarcation systems in the national press.' (Viner, 1969, p.8)

The lack of constructive suggestions by the first two Royal Commissions was due to a lack of realisation of the markets in which newspapers were operating. To be less critical would be to assume that they knew of such markets but were afraid of their consequences. Thus even if both Commissions were aware of the spiral market, they were hesitant to allow the natural movements to the saturation or the regional dependency markets, both of which involved a reduction in the numbers of newspapers, for in the saturation model there is only a limited number of definable circulation areas, a number insufficient to maintain the present number of national newspapers, and the regional dependency model involves monopoly in the regions and increased concentration in the industry. All such movements help to eradicate notions of the freedom of the press. This is, of course totally unacceptable for Royal Commissions, for implicit in their mandates is to find ways of maintaining or extending the present number of newspapers, and thus the regional dependency and saturation models are anathema to all members of Royal Commissions, even if they know of their existence. The outcome is that their analysis and therefore proposals tend to circumvent the realisation that the only practicable solutions have to involve the knowledge of the inevitability of the regional dependency and saturation markets.

The Third Royal Commission can be applauded for recognising the market conditions of the saturation model, and implicitly encouraging newspapers to continue to respond in this market. It turned its attention to the effects on newspapers of operating successfully in these markets, and it is perhaps ironic that during a period when the Royal Commission thought the press incapable of reforming itself and still maintaining the diversity of titles, the press had achieved some of that reform for the most part without the assistance and help of the Royal Commission and their recommendations. Perhaps the Royal Commission merely reminded those who had reformed, or were reforming where their social responsibility lay.

2.3.1 The Proposed Solutions

One solution centring around the reduction of 'first copy' or fixed costs was examined, though not solved by the 1962 and 1977 Royal Commissions (1962, Report, paragraph 54-73; 1977

Report, paragraph 6.I5) and by many of the recent reports (6). Their analysis exhibited a knowledgeable insight into the problems caused by a reliance on fluctuating advertising revenue to balance static or increasing fixed costs. Those newspapers with relatively more reliance on advertising as opposed to circulation revenue, in particular low circulation newspapers were the ones under threat in an economic recession, for changes necessary to reduce this dependance were too wholesale (for instance an increase in circulation by a change of editorial style) to chance the catastrophe of entering the advertising-circulation downward spiral. All of this, of course, benefits and increases the dominance of the strong over the weak newspapers, and the situation is exacerbated where costs overall are increasing.

> 'The potential influence of scale is tending to press out of existence the less powerful papers,' (N.B.P.I., I967, paragraph 2I)

in favour of the larger papers, which benefit both from large circulation and greater volumes of advertising. (Curran I978, p.263-5)

Thus the major problems of fixed costs and the necessary circulation to sustain them and the dependence on advertising to supplement circulation revenue, has questioned the survival of many papers, which inevitably threatens the widely held democratic principle of free speech. (See Chapter 3) Naturally those who see unprecedented consequences from such trends, have turned to that body which may have an interest in safeguarding democracy, the Government, suggesting ways in which the present numbers of newspapers would be maintained, together with the possibility of arrangements allowing newspapers to develop as the market situation allows.

The second set of solutions centre around a redistribution of advertising, by an administering body, perhaps a Government Ministry, or a Government financed independent Commission, or alternatively, the formation of a state publishing and printing corporation (7) to allow ailing newspapers to continue and fresh papers to start, yet this can only

> 'surely deliver the publication and their policies straight into the arms of the Government, or at least of those pressure groups who can exert pressure in Government circles Only in Utopia does the State benignly lease out expensive facilities to creative men and leave them to it.' (Winsbury I968, p. II)

Economic remedies, such as these or variations thereof were given some inspection by all the Royal Commissions. Detailed plans for levies on advertising revenue increasing percentage-wise as advertising increased, or merely taxes on revenue above a certain limit, were all rejected. The I962 Commission concluded 'that there is no acceptable legislative or fiscal way of regulating the competitive and economic forces so as to ensure a sufficient diversity of newspapers. The only hope of the weaker newspapers is to secure ... managers and editors of such enterprise and originality as will enable these publications to overcome the economic forces affecting them.' (Report, paragraph 3I3)

This scant advice, after a detailed enquiry into the costs of newspaper production, was reiterated in the inappropriate proposals made by the Commission. The industry now knew some of its problems, and had been presented with numerous figures detailing them, yet in terms of its management and organisation little was known, although the Economist Intelligence Unit (E.I.U.) in I966 commissioned by the national newspaper industry produced a wide-ranging report and it was included in the mandate of the I977 Royal Commission Report. The former was intended as a fact-finding investigation and thus 'you will not find in the report any advice about how the industry could best solve its problems.' (E.I.U. Introduction). Certainly the national press was deeply studied, and besides the already known disease of over-manning and thus high costs the report disclosed that 'the quality of management is uneven, and the industry is short of professionally trained managers,' and because of the close structure of the industry 'one poor management can create trouble for all.' (E.I.U. Management Survey, p.56). The problems of the press were therefore much greater than the Commissions had found and more serious than the proposals had anticipated.

The I97I Royal Commission, even with its wide mandate failed to consider management and organisation of the press, although some mention was made in Working Paper No.3 on Editors by Jeremy Tunstall. Other studies had remarked on the inadequacy of the Commission's analyses in respect of advertising, technology or of alternative funding (8), with one even suggesting that it had been the decline of the journalists as a force within newspaper organisations that had heralded an era of incompetent management.

It is amongst the accountants, the lawyers and the printers at the highest levels of newspaper management 'that there is the grossest incompetence, and it is here that the power, the prestige and money lie.' In providing for the future he asserts that 'the Press should be run on business lines, subject to market and commercial forces, and have as its prime aim the making of money by selling more copies and getting more advertisements. But this entails relaxing the ideology of "the Fourth Estate" and the defence of democracy' (Boston, I970, p.9).

There is thus still a wide area of unresearched material in the internal processes of newspapers, in respect of their management methods, the managerial influences on editors and how far the profit-motivated commercial managers have a say in the organisation of editorial matters. These questions remain unanswered and until they are notions of a charter of the freedom of the press to safeguard the editor, remain somewhat antiseptic, for only when the management of a newspaper is understood can such a charter be meaningfully interpreted for newspapers.

Moreover and perhaps more fundamentally a free press can only exist if the press itself can survive by either economic or social means. On the first it has been shown that knowledge of particular markets as depicted by the models earlier is essential for survival. Alternatively, the second social survival may involve the government, and although successive Royal Commissions have vetoed such ideas nevertheless the government has some economic and social say by virtue of its policies and indeed it is the contradictions of these which has lead newspapers to seek their own solutions by operating in either the saturation or the regional dependency markets, both of which, by the influence of commercialism internal to the organisation may bring doubt on the viability of any externally-decided charter of the freedom of the press. The contradictions became complete when it is seen that public policy has done little to stop the newspapers moving into these markets.

2.3.2 The Contradictions of Public Policy and the movement to Saturation and Regional Dependency.

In accepting that Royal Commissions had been unable to influence the continuing demise of the press it might have been thought that public policy through government action would have acted to help the press solve its problems, rather than to inhibit change necessary for its survival.

In attempting to redress the balance between revenue gained from advertising and that from circulation a favoured proposal was to raise the selling price of the paper, to 'a price nearer their cost of production.' (Royal Commission, 1962, Report, paragraph 284). A price at the full cost of production of course, will eliminate a newspaper's dependence on advertising, but such a price would deter many present readers from buying the paper, and quicken the move to fewer national papers. This happens as circulation falls so fixed costs are distributed on fewer papers, thus increasing their price. Even raising the price substantially above its present levels may only make those profitable newspapers, more profitable, ultimately at the expense of the weaker and poorer ones. However, the argument for raising prices, when both inflation has cheapened papers, and the market can support such a rise without a reduction in circulation, is a solid one. The policy of cheap papers 'is a matter of history' (Royal Commission, 1962, Report, paragraph 271), yet when an opportunity to rectify this imbalance is proffered, government policy strait-jackets the idea. Public policy in recessions is necessarily deflationary and is usually too rigid to allow exceptions, so when the Daily Mirror in mid-1967 applied for a price increase, paragraph 10 of the White Paper was administered such that increases are allowed only 'if after every effort has been made to reduce costs.'

On this basis the N.B.P.I. Report No.43 referred swiftly to the E.I.U. report, and the cost structure of editorial departments of popular papers in general, stressing that they spent more money on average to produce less editorial material than the qualities. This philistinic approach to newspaper costs structure was the basis of the spurious, yet governmentally correct, decision to refuse the increase. Further evidence confirmed their approach, specifically

> 'The I.P.C.'s (owner of the Daily Mirror) own estimate of the extent of over-manning ... is put at about £0.5 million, this being equivalent to another 25-30 percent.' (paragraph 33)

and more generally

> 'and we consider that the practical possibility of reducing dependence on advertising revenue can be, and is, exaggerated ... the prior emphasis is time should be placed on a reduction in costs, and that cost reduction should precede any attempt through higher prices to readjust the balance between the revenue from sales and that from advertising.' (paragraph 47)

The grandiose conclusion on government intervention that newspaper managements should put their house in order first, was the complete antithesis of all previous attempts to aid the press in the solution of its problems. The decision was all the more mysterious in context of the price increase for newsprint (50% of production costs, and 30% of total costs) allowed in April of that year. Scathing criticism followed, that the N.B.P.I. 'ought to have been clear that the financial plight of the newspaper industry was far worse than simple manning reduction on the printing machines could cure.' (Winsbury, 1968, p.14). However, 'an increase from 5d to 6d for a paper drawing 70% of its revenue from advertising would provide an increase of only 6% in total revenue.' (Thomas, 1968, p.64). Thus, although the proportion of income, arising from circulation would change little, papers operating at the margin would have had a base for future survival.

The Government, for the only apparent reason of a change in economic climate as reflected in public policy (White Paper on Productivity, Prices and Incomes Policy after 1969), reversed its previous policy of not allowing price increases for newspapers. The existence of unavoidable increases in costs was still paramount in allowing price increases, although the N.B.P.I., investigated the proposed claim in the light of 'as on the occasion of our Report No.43, the scope of achieving cost reduction and the general financial position of the owning company.' (N.B.P.I. 1970). Evidence from elsewhere has suggested that as the severity of the economic recession had now waned, several newspapers, which previously had been near to closure, were less in need of assistance. But in this instance the

N.B.P.I. allowed the increase, and although there had been and there was to be some increases in the price of newsprint, the basis for such a decision concerned the Board's assessment of the nature of costs and the ability of the newspapers to reduce them.

> ' ... most of the possibilities for savings are essentially related to long-term projects from which benefits can be expected to accrue only over a number of years ... it would be unrealistic to think that sufficient savings can be generated in the short term to obviate the need for some price increase.' (N.B.P.I., 1970, paragraph 76)

Public policy now acknowledged that most savings were in long-term projects having stated two years earlier something quite different, but it was difficult to imagine how the state of the press had changed so significantly in such a short period, for developments since 1966-7 have shown little implementation of any of the solutions mentioned although there had been 'considerable efforts to bring newspaper costs under control and to increase (newspaper) efficiency,' (N.B.P.I., 1970, paragraph 39) yet the report still suggested areas where newsprint and manpower efficiences would be introduced, and where the distribution system could be rationalised, all to save costs. Management was also criticised, in that 'with one or two exceptions it is not clear that newspaper managements have succeeded in working out a co-ordinated editorial and advertising strategy designed to maximise profits.' (paragraph 14) The only apparent tendency towards any solution is thus a movement out of the advertising-circulation downward spiral into the saturation and regional dependency markets.

Following recommendations by the1962 Royal Commission the monopoly legislation of 1948 was extended in 1965 by the Monopolies and Mergers Act, to cover newspapers. In particular, section 8 empowered the Secretary to the Board of Trade (later the Department of Trade and Industry) to refer for investigation to the Monopolies Commission any proposed merger of newspapers or companies owning newspapers having combined circulation of over 200,000. Seven reports have been made, one concerning two national newspapers, and six concerning the acquisition of regional papers by companies owning national newspapers. Common to all was the required guarantee of editorial independence (see Chapter 4) and that they were all deemed not to act against the public interest. Common to the last two, were misgivings by the Commission over the trend towards 'a press which consisted predominantly of a few large groups, each running one or more national newspapers and a considerable number of local newspapers.' (Monopolies Commission 1972, paragraph 76, 1973 paragraph 79).

Presumably, as a solution to the problems of the press, such a process could act against the public interest, but the Commission preferred to disregard it, 'it is not our function to pronounce upon the condition of the press generally (I968, paragraph III) and merely suggest 'if present trends continued, the Government should consider whether it would be appropriate to arrange for a special inquiry into this problem.' (I972, paragraph 76, I973, paragraph 79). This was included in the terms of reference of the I974 Royal Commission.

Concentration of the Press, had previously been viewed with a certain suspicion although the takeover of ailing papers, whose survival could be guaranteed by new ownership, was construed as a necessary evil. What was alarming about these mergers was that highly commercially-orientated companies were taking over profitable newspapers, with the blessing of the Monopolies Commission. This is another irony of the situation, that as Royal Commissions pronounce against concentration, public policy in the intervening years accelerates the trend!

The first such report was in December I966, over the proposed transfer of the Times to the Sunday Times which is owned by the Thomson Organisation. The Commission mentioned the financial difficulties of the Times yet pronounced ' we find it surprising that the company found it urgently necessary to look for rescue by a change of ownership ... the company's financial prospects do not appear desperate.' (Monopolies Commission, I968, paragraph I50)

They also thought that Times independence could be guaranteed and

> 'could have avoided its present difficulties if the problem of increasing (its) circulation had been tackled energetically some years ago.' (paragraph I50)

(Hindsight proved this to be somewhat unfortunate advice - see earlier) Even with this evidence, the Commission supported the merger, yet it noted that

> 'It would be a continuation of the movement towards concentration in the ownership of the press, which must ultimately tend to stifle the expression of variety of opinion.' (paragraph I6I)

In this case the Commission saw no danger to democracy as the combined circulation of all regional and national dailies owned by Thomson would rise to only 7%, but into different categories the percentages rise (for instance, 44% of the quality Sundays) and put into regions the real meaning of monopoly is exhibited. This was dismissed by the Commission 'as its provinvial newspapers, although numerous can scarcely be regarded as influential by comparison with national newspapers.' (paragraph I62)

Such reasoning allowed Thomson to acquire in January I968 the three newspapers of Crusha and on Limited, in North London, a small company which was in no danger of collapse (profit

1962-66 was between 44% and 57% of capital employed), but sought refuge with a larger company to enable it to provide expertise in re-equipping and expansion. Even so, 'it had ample reserves for replacement and development' (Monopolies Commission 1968, paragraph 88) and there was seemingly no financial necessity for the merger. Although the Thomson organisation only increased its circulation share of the weekly press from 2.9% to 3.3%, the Commission was concerned over the monopolistic tendencies in the locality of the Crusha Newspapers, but as the latter "already enjoys a monopoly ... the merger would not create a new monopoly" and thus this could not act against the public interest.

Another proposed transfer was investigated by the Commission in April 1972, that of the County Express Group of newspapers to Berrow's Organisation Limited, a subsidiary wholly owned by News International Limited, publishers of the News of the World and the Sun. The merger would allow Berrows to have a monopoly of weekly papers (except Dudley Herald) in Worcestershire, but the Commission found this of little concern after assurances of editorial independence had been given. Again the papers in question were not financially threatened, but as the owner had no heirs, he wanted his papers to be kept within a newspaper publishing company. Again the Commission questioned the desirability of national-based groups acquiring further newspapers, but allowed the merger, naively accepting assurances that News International 'has no policy of actively seeking out local newspapers for acquisition.' This contradicts earlier evidence, when Berrows 'had made overtures on previous occasions' for the transfer of the paper.

The Commission (para. 48) was also misguided in approving assurances on the independence of other local papers, when the County Express group papers are expanded. 'But this does not necessarily mean that any increase in circulation would be at the expense of neighbouring independent newspapers.' (paragraph 66). Experience from elsewhere had proved the contrary. (9)

In October 1973, the Commission reported on a similar type of merger between Westminster Press (owned by Pearson Longmans, publishers of the Financial Times) and 18 weeklies in Kent and Sussex owned by Morgan Grampian. None of the latter were in monetary difficulties, although finance would be required in due course, for re-equipping. In this case Westminster Press would increase its share of the weekly circulation from 8.2% to 10.2% but the Commission decided that

> 'Westminster Press ... does not fit very exactly into the pattern of a group running one or more national newspapers and a considerable number of local newspapers.' (Monopolies Commission, 1973a, paragraph 80)

Surely the Financial Times, as with the Times, has an influence of a greater proportion than is commensurate with its circulation, and thus Westminster Press should have been considered as other national groups had been previously.

2.4 CONCLUSION

The social and economic evolution of newspapers has centred around three organisational types, operating within certain economic markets. The Fleet Street type operating in the advertising-circulation downward spiral has had to re-orientate its policies, as that market could not contain so many newspapers at least with the excesses of management so prevalent. The regional press was very profitable and was beginning to support the Fleet Street press, a combination of the regional commercialism organisational type operating in the regional dependency market. At the same time many newspapers were beginning to see the advantage of creating and thus controlling their markets. Utilising this saturation model the overall market can be split into discernable sections, allowing a reduction of competition amongst national newspapers which have become more commercially aware as the regional newspapers had done. Most of these changes have occurred in spite of three Royal Commissions on the press and in defiance of other government assistance.

This study recognises that Fleet Street Newspapers are in the process of change, but that regional newspapers have for the most part completed one phase of change. This chapter has concentrated mainly on the national press and less on the regional in reflection of the existing literature, for the history of the development of the regional press up to 1960 in Britain still has to be written. However, it has been at the national press which the arguments over the freedom of the press have been made, and it is here contended that the movement of much of the Fleet Street press into the saturation and regional dependancy markets will have important implications on the management and organisation of these newspapers. In particular operation in both markets rests on a commercial awareness, which is exhibited in the regional press, which has saturated its market and is providing the back-up to many national newspapers. It is the extent of the influence organisationally of that commercial awareness which provides the area of study. These effects are studied later, but first attention needs to be drawn to the ideology of newspaper publication, the existence of which is necessary before any newspaper is published.

NOTES

(I) See in particular H. Thomas, I968; R. Williams, I957; R. Winsbury, I968; F. Williams: I96I; C. Wintour, I972; R. Boston, I970; E. Moonman, I969; Economist Intelligence Report, I966; D. Murphy, I976; C. Cleverly, I976; F. Hirsch and D. Gordon, I975.

In addition the proceeding, and minutes and reports of three Royal Commissions, I949, I962, I977; The Reports of the Monopolies Commission into press takeovers; The National Board for Prices and Incomes (relevant reports); The Cameron Inquiry I967, and the annual reports of the Press Council.

(2) The Daily Mail, The Times, The Guardian, The Daily Sketch, The News Chronicle, The Star and the Daily Herald. In fact of the latter three, the News Chronicle and The Star folded in I96I and I962 respectively, and the Daily Herald changed its name to The Sun in I964, eventually to be bought by Rupert Murdoch and revamped considerably. The Daily Sketch also suffered and was merged with The Daily Mail in I968.

(3) See Royal Commission on the Press, I96I-2, Report, paragraph 2I of conclusion.

(4) Article 8 of the Constitution of the Press Council.

(5) The concern of this study is with changes in the regional press prior to the third Royal Commission and it is for this reason that attention had been mainly directed on the analysis of the two earlier Royal Commissions and why the following analysis relates more to the situation before the third Commission than that after it.

(6) See in particular Seymore-Ure, I970, Chapter 3; E.I.U. Report, I966; N.B.P.I. Report No. 43; Cleverly I976.

(7) See Curran I978b, pp.266-7 for an example.

(8) See Winsbury, I968; Curran, I978.

(9) C. Morris, I963; and the early circulation battles for the new Thomson newspapers published at Hemel Hempstead.

3 The changing ideology of newspaper publication

3.I IDEOLOGY AND THEORY

Mass circulation of newspapers has existed in Great Britain since 1896. They provide information and entertainment to nearly the whole of the population, which superficially, seems a reason why newspapers are published, at least from the viewpoint of the reader. Thus their importance cannot be minimised. However the owner, though admitting the entertaining and information side of his paper, may have different ideas about publication. Indeed it could be said that there are ideologies of newspaper publication, and such ideologies are important in determining and legitimising the objectives of newspaper firms, or the activities of constituent departments. It will be shown later that in certain cases ideologies allow departments or individuals to pursue certain policies to achieve defined objectives. Briefly, in an example, this could be that if ownership of newspapers for power and influence was the ideology, then propaganda through news gathering of a certain type would be the objective achieved by a policy of having large editorial departments, whilst other departments would be more supportive and of less significance. Alternatively if money and profit are central to the ideology then maximisation of advertising revenue may be the objective achieved by well-paid and well-trained commercial managers, with a somewhat subservient editorial department.

Ideologies are therefore here determined as highly personalised. They are the ideas of individual publishers and these are fairly accurately interpreted by those people working for them. Knowing the ideology will thus say much for the management and organisational style and structure. It is not suggested that such ideologies once found can be tested, scientifically or otherwise, rather the ideology is a body of ideas, of beliefs, which in themselves are absolute to the individual and cannot be tested. What can be investigated is how there ideologies through translation structure organisation and effect policies and if the members of organisations live up to the demands of these ideas and beliefs. A difficulty may arise here, for the perception by any employees of that ideology and how it is related to practice, may differ from the proprietor's stated or demonstrated viewpoint. A solution to this difficulty, often used in the short term was a dismissal, and in the long term, the selection of personnel only on the criterion that they agree with the proprietor, (I) or in some cases agree to agree with the proprietor (2). However, it is suggested that the proprietor goes to great lengths to ensure that his, and only his, ideology is the one to guide the activities of his employees. Thus great weight can be placed on the pronouncements of senior executives as well as those of the proprietor, as to the nature of the ideology. Thus

> 'the whole range of communication activity which the individual's particular institution engages in, can in most cases be related back to the guiding dogmas.' (Brown, I969, p.I56)

It is postulated that the ideologies are centred on the following: one, that newspapers should promote news for information and discussion; two, that they exist merely for power and influence achieved by propaganda of a particular kind; and three, that they are business enterprises marketing a specific product to achieve relatively high returns on capital.

There is also a body of ideas which exists to explain the role of the press in society. These may be normative, that is concerned with what the press should be or do, or analytically descriptive attempting to explain the observed behaviour of the press. This body of ideas attempts a global view, and is (substantially) different from an ideology which is highly personalised. This body of ideas is labelled theory. In respect of the British press, which is the concern of this study theories of how the press acts or should act in a political democracy become of significance, not for the theory itself, but rather its influence on how ideologies may be formed or changed. Indeed in many cases the nature of the theories lends legitimacy to the ideologies of publication (3). There is not always a direct relationship, but rather a partial justification for newspapers pursuing particular policies, and again a brief example helps. Nearly all theories of the press preach the need for independence of government interference which in part legitimises the ideology based on money and profit, even though policies pursued within the framework of this ideology may denigrate news to a totally subservient position.

These theories are not intended to be axiomatic, nor in th strict sense theoretical, in that they can be proved or disproved by empirical observation. They are often propounded by writers as a doctrine abstracted from what the press has done or based on notions of what it should do (the latter are the majority). It is thus belief in the doctrine which is central making rigorous testing redundant as perceptions themselves will differ even of the same social phenomenon.

For this very reason of the important relationship between theory and ideology (4) the theories of the press are summarized below before analysing in detail the changing ideology of newspaper publication.

3.2 THE THEORIES OF THE PRESS

> "In Germany the invention of some mysterious process by which all the copies of a book were seen to be exactly alike was brought into England in I47I by Caxton.'
> (Collett, I933, p.I)

This together with the introduction of the roman type of Calvin and Knox in the Reformation, was not used for regular press publication until the beginning of the eighteenth century, (5) as until this time the printing of books and pamphlets had occurred, normally at the discretion of the taxing authorities. Another factor affecting distribution was, of course, the ability of the populace to read any material printed, although by the second half of the eighteenth century almost every large town had a weekly newspaper.

The role of the press in forming or reflecting society has been open to continuous debate, as has the freedom of the press in terms of not only on the granting of such a freedom, but what that freedom practically means. The press has been described as 'The Fourth Estate of the realm, ranking only just, if at all, behind the Lords Spiritual, The Lords Temporal, and the Commons.' (F. Williams, I957, p.6) and indeed to protect it in this role the United States Constitution has its first amendment called the First Freedom. (6)

The press is an integral part of a communication process, and indeed it could be said this is a primary reason for any newspaper. Further, 'it has been clear that the extention of communication has been part of the extension of democracy.' (R. Williams, I962, p.I9). But if communication is neglected in favour of propaganda and profit, then democracy itself may come under attack. Moreover such an attack may be against the public interest, as monopoly advertising and the drive to sell lead to a culture intent on restricting rather than extending the communication process, and if this argument holds any credibility the press may be failing in its responsibility to the community, local or national. What is now under investigation is whether the influences of theory have been important in the formation of the ideologies of press publication.

3.2.I. The Authoritatian Theory of the Press

The taxes on the press in I7I2, I725 and I757 had been preceded by numerous attempts to regulate and control the activities of printers, made by the authorities to stop the monarch's subjects actually knowing anything about the working of government. For instance in I637 a decree of the Star Chamber limited the number of printers and master type founders upon punishment of whipping, the pillory or imprisonment. Indeed the Tudors granted these 'exclusive patents of monopoly to selected, well-disposed individuals, who were permitted to profit from these monopolies so long as they refrained from rocking the ship of state.'

(Siebart, I963, p.I9). In I643, after the abolition of the Star Chamber, the House of Commons authorised a Committee of Examination to appoint persons to search for scandalous pamphlets and to seize lying pamphlets, presses or printers. (Collett, I933, p.2)

After I700 when some regional and London based weeklies began to grow in circulation the authorities turned to press taxes as well. In I7I2 to meet these taxes, half sheets cost 2d, and in I725 the tax element was Id per sheet. Street sellers were also hounded, as anybody might take into custody a hawker of unstamped newspapers upon reward of twenty shillings. Further acts, and larger penalties were introduced at intervals throughout the eighteenth century, with stricter controls during the period of the French Revolution. Stamp duty was re-imposed under George III after I8I5 as per table (Collett, I933, p.9)

TABLE 3.I

STAMP DUTY ON PUBLICATIONS I8I5

	Great Britain	Ireland
Advertisements - each	3. 6.	2. 6.
Almanacs for one year - each	I. 3.	9.
Almanacs for several years (each year)	I. 3.	9.
Perpetual Almanacs - each	IO. 0.	7. 6.
Pamphlets - per sheet of I copy	3. 0.	2. 0.
Newspapers	4.	2.

Some discounts were allowed, but not sufficient to stop the editor of the Examiner to write on his newspapers - "Paper and Print 3½d, Taxes on Knowledge 3½d, Price 7d."

In this way only material supporting the monarchy and government could be printed and distributed. 'When the earliest form of newspaper appeared it too was assigned to individuals who in return for the exclusive monopoly of purveying news were all too ready to agree to publish only that which forwarded the policies of the state.' (Siebart, I963, p.20). Censorship, laws of seditious libel, and treason and the accompanying courts, together with taxes, controlled the press. Indeed

> 'During Walpole's long reign (end I742) as first Minister in England, political writers were secretly put on the payroll, newspapers were tied

to the government through funds from the secret service account and opposition editors were alternately threatened with prosecution and seduced with bribes.' (Siebart, I963, p.25)

Political comment was avoided in an attempt to obtain higher circulation and these early provincial papers confined much of their editorial to mere description, usually of international and national events. The cornerstone of the authoritarian theory of the press was based on the 'authoritarian philosophy of the nature and function of state' under which 'all instrumentalities operating within the state should advance the objectives and policies of the state.' (Siebart, I963, p.26). It was not so much that current issues could not be debated but rather there should be no attempt to discredit or unseat the authorities themselves.

During the early nineteenth century this government control was defeated in two main ways. First, the growth of middle class reform newspapers, (7) particularly in the North emphasised the social problems of the growing industrial society, and they proposed reforms, not only of these, but to encourage the development of a profitable industry, which for the most part was in their hands. Some of this material was undoubtedly seen as seditious by the authorities and led to another controlling Act in I836. Secondly, as the legal press expanded (8) so did the monopolists who recruited more and more apprentices, who when qualified as journeymen in increasing numbers found little work available and they were forced into illegal printing. Taken together with the growth of political parties, who needed some printing outlet different from a government controlled one, the authoritarian principle began to crumble. No longer could the authorities achieve total dominance of communications by control of the state-registered monopolies. 'The number of stamped newspapers in I835 was 35,823,859; the number in I85I was 95,I63,395.' (Collett, I933, p.22I).

This particular theory describes one historical stage of the press. However it shows how the press, as one form of communication, can transmit the instructions, ideas and attitudes of the ruling group (and) 'as a matter of policy (exclude) alternative instruction, ideas and attitudes.' (9). In a democratic nation it is somewhat inconceivable that such a press could exist, although any state moving towards totalitarianism, of the left, or right will begin to need an authoritarian press to use communication to protect, maintain or advance their social order based on one particular minority.

3.2.2 The Libertarian Theory of the Press

The middle-class reform newspapers began to detail programmes of solutions to outstanding social problems, determined according to the newspaper and its political slant. The latter came as a result of the growth of political parties, these in turn emerging from the supremacy of Parliament over the Crown, and with the phasing out of a single authority, multiple opinions became expressed via the press, the only means to do this.

The connection with government had to be severed

> 'When a definition is called for that states the ideal relationship between the press and the government in a democracy, the one most often used is that of John Milton, elaborated in Areopagitica, where he argued not only for unlicensed printing but for a public policy favouring free and unlimited discussion as the surest way of arriving at truth' (Gerald, 1956, p.5)

'One only has to look at the classical liberal model of society to understand how central to it press freedom is.' (Lee, 1976, p.22). The search for knowledge and truth could not exist without the freedom of the press, and as A.J. Lee continues it is not so much that knowledge and truth are important, but rather the search for them.

> 'In the liberal pursuit of certainty it was as much the pursuit as the certainty that counted, reflecting not an indifference to ends, but a psychological attachment to a faith in the ultimate harmony of ends. Liberals generally embraced freedom on the understanding that it entailed truth, and with the assumption that neither freedom nor truth could harm either the individual or his universe.' (1976, p.23)

Thus the Press assumed the role of informing the populace (increasingly the electorate) of the decisions of the elected government. However, 'it was diverse enough to give political representation to major parties.' (Gerald, 1956, p.6) or even to factions within each party.

> 'Libertarian theorists assumed that out of a multiplicity of voices of the press, some information reaching the public would be false and some would be unsound. Nevertheless the public did not have the right to restrict that which it considered false and unsound. If it did, it would inevitably tend to suppress that which was critical of the state or was contrary to the opinion of government officials. The alternative procedure, as exposed by the libertarians, was to let the public at large be subjected to a barrage of information and opinion, some of it possibly true, some of it possible false, and some of it containing an element of both. Ultimately the public could be trusted to digest the whole, to discard that not in the public interest, and to accept that which served the needs of the individual and of the society of which he is a part. This is the "well-known self-righting process." '(Siebart, 1963, p.51)

In the British context, political parties did use party funds to support newspapers. The Conservative and Unionist Party subsidised what they thought were Unionist papers, and Unionist Party funds subscribed £10,000 for Express ordinary shares in I9II. The Liberal Party had the support of the Daily Chronicle, which in I9I8 was being sold by its owner Frank Lloyd. Lloyd George wished to keep the paper behind his coalition policies and in October I9I8 it was bought for £I,650,000. 'Most of the money came from the political fund which Lloyd George's wealthy admirers had contributed for his support - and no doubt for their peerages.' (Taylor, I972, p.I58) The latter were normally given when party funds were low, and obviously by the government or impending government (or Prime Minister). The pledge of press support in I9I8 was organised by Lord Beaverbrook.

> 'He pledged the support of the Daily Express and set out to canvass others ... Beaverbrook brought Rothermere (proprietor of the Daily Mirror) and Edward Hulton (Daily sketch, Evening Standard, The Illustrated Sunday Herald, etc.) to dinner with Lloyd George in Downing Street ... Lloyd George promised to make Rothermere a Viscount, and Hulton a Baron. Beaverbrook declared that he wanted nothing for himself except to be dis-peered. All three press lords were thus won over and duly supported Lloyd George at the general election.
> In the summer of I9I9 Guest reported to Lloyd George that Beaverbrook was demanding more K.B.G.'s for his old associates in return for continued press support.'
> (Taylor, I972, p.I60)

Latterly another opinion in questioning the libertarian theory expresses the disdain of so many popular papers, 'I would argue that the News of the World, or the Daily Sketch or Sunday Mirror are about as necessary to democracy as an outbreak of typhoid.' (Boston, I970, p.4)

A slightly different version of this theory has been given elsewhere. Under the heading 'Commercial', Raymond Williams has suggested that communications system can exist on a commercial basis, 'it is argued that men have the right to offer for sale any kind of work, and that all men have the right to buy any kind that is offered.' (Williams, I962, p.II8). Subsidies are not needed, as commercial viability is the sole determinant of the structure of the press. However, the breakdown of perfect competition can lead to authoritarian tendencies, thus 'Anything can be said, provided that you can afford to say it and that you can say it profitably.' (R. Williams, I962, p.II9)

A degenerate form of this libertarian theory eventually produces either, two political sides of the press, or strong individuals who determine what people ought to know. The press thus protects and guides society as though it were a duty. However, the way in which that society should act is determined not by the society itself, but by the prominent political parties or individuals.

This theory could only be substantiated in practice if there were many newspapers of differing outlook or as Gerald remarks 'the Miltonic theory of competition in ideas' (I956, p.6) Its reliance on Adam Smith and the classical economists is all too apparent and indeed frightening, although equally worrying was the way the ideas permeated into an era when the Smithonian idea of competition hardly applied. Gerald writes of the British press in I956 in respect of this theory which

> 'Assumes that a private press will give expression to a multiplicity of tongues and that out of the many-faceted points of view expressed a working society will emerge that will be liberal, tolerant, sympathetic, progressive and self-energising.' (p.I86)

A. J. Lee commenting on the press nearly a century earlier is critical of the maintenance of such a theory.

> 'The prospect of a golden age, both for Liberalism and for the press, was not then an illusion. The illusion was that it could be perpetuated indefinitely.' (I976, pp.25-6)

There are numerous reasons why this theory eventually became suspect, not least the problem of obtaining and maintaining perfect competition. In respect of the newspaper industry speed and efficiency increased to produce bigger papers competing not only for readership but advertising, and from this situation the circulation-advertising downward spiral began to operate producing the monopoly position described by Ian Jackson. Also the assumption of enlightenment began to be questioned. The freedom of expression was merely a freedom for a privileged few, who by the breakdown of this theory had the right to jeopardise the welfare of the majority. The economics of publication in a declining market could not afford the luxuries of allowing every man a freedom to speak regardless of what he had to say. This was anarchy not the democratic policing of government as the libertarians wished.

3.2.3. The Social Responsibility Theory of the Press

The concentration of the Press, together with the cost of entry into the market destroyed the freedom of entry. This was further enhanced by the declining markets in which the newspapers operated. The regions experienced a decline of 46% in their morning newspapers between I92I and I969, after I974 no regional evening newspaper was in competition with another, and from I9I8 to I957, at least 225 provincial weekly newspapers had ceased publication. The Fleet Street newspapers have declined in numbers by I976 to four populars, three serious and one specialist. Further the political opinion expressed by all are less extreme than they once were, as papers attract circulation not to extend the communication process, but for the advertiser.

The newspapers that are thus left are in a position of power. They control one of the major means of communication of information and governmental decisions. This power can be and has been abused, and according to one source, in many ways.

I) 'The owners have propagated their own opinions, especially in matters of politics and economics, at the expense of opposing views.

2) The press has been subservient to big business and has at times let advertisers control editorial content.

3) The press has resisted social change.

4) The press has often paid more attention to the superficial and sensational than to the significant in its coverage of current happenings and its entertainment has often been lacking in substance.

5) The press has endangered public morals.

6) The press has invaded the privacy of individuals without just cause.

7) The press is controlled by one socio-economic class, the business class.' (Peterson, I963, pp.78-9)

These criticisms of the press if correct, suggest that the influence of the libertarians has vanished, and the press once again can become authoritarian, only this time in the direction of the owners rather than the Crown. Another commentator puts it differently 'So the position is that newspapers do not survive or fail according to how many people want them, but according to their suitability as media for advertising. This is a distinctive feature of this large part of communication in twentieth century Britain.' (R. Williams, I962, p.28)

To avoid the interference or even control by government of a monopolistic press, abusing its position, the social responsibility theorists of the press advocate that the press has the following requirements.

I) 'To provide a truthful, comprehensive, and intelligent account of the days events in a context which gives them meaning.

2) Be a forum for the exchange of comment and criticism.

3) To project a representative picture of the constituent groups in society.

4) To present and clarify the goals and values of the society.

5) To have full access to the day's intelligence.' (Peterson, I963, p.85)

These may seem high ideals, perhaps to the extent of being dreams of utopia rather than aims for reality. However, to strive for such ideals is incorporated in the social responsibility theory, and to monitor such efforts, independent institutions should be formed. 'In a system that emphasizes private ownership it is of utmost importance for the public to maintain constant contact with and evaluation of the press system so as to note the degree to which it is performing its assigned social function.' (Gerald, I956, p.I86) In the British context three Royal Commissions on the Press within 20 years show some public concern over the conduct of the press and a Press Council encourages 'a sense of public responsibility and public service in the press.' (Peterson, I963, p.78)

This body was criticised for its ineffectiveness up to I962, and so after the second Royal Commission its powers and finances were bolstered. In general it adjudicates on any complaint against the press brought by any member of the public, although recently taken with great seriousness, its powers are moral rather than legal, and its effectiveness transitory rather than permanent.

3.2.4 A Democratic Theory of the Press

This has been suggested as an ideal for how the press should perform, and is primarily the idea of Raymond Williams. 'There are two related considerations; the right to transmit and the right to receive.' (I962, p.I20) These rights are incontrovertible, to be used by the majority. Their protection will be guaranteed by public service of some kind, allowing active contributors the control of their means of expression, in this case the press. The basis for such a system of communication is the sharing of all human experience, but the practical difficulties make it unreal in its pure form, however some of the component ideas have been introduced (IO) as part of an ideology of press publication. Indeed the very idea of communication, in its pure form, being the sharing of human experience has had some form of moral influence over some of those proprietors who might have thought to ignore the concept completely.

3.3 THE IDEOLOGY OF NEWSPAPER PUBLICATION

Ideology in this context is a body of ideas which form the basis for publication of a newspaper, and it can thus explain why owners publish newspapers. The ideological themes based on news, propaganda and profit are probably implicit in some degree in all ideologies, however whichever is most important in any ideology will determine the objectives and policy of that newspaper and thus be an important influence on the style of management and organisation.

3.3.I News

There have been owners of newspapers who have viewed their own newspapers as part of a news communication process, and their ideology of publication is centred around the theme of news, which it is more important than other themes. It could be said that all newspapers publish some news, however small, but news may not be the basic idea about publication of such newspapers.

Nearly all the theories of the press lend social legitimacy to this ideology, least of all is the authoritarian theory as news coverage is highly selective and political, although most legitimacy comes from the theories propounded by Raymond Williams 'Communication is the sharing of all human experience.' (1962, p.22) The libertarian theory which implies reproducing as much news as possible in the 'search for truth and knowledge', is a liberal theory involving a freedom of the press, both in a negative way, from government restriction, and a positive way to allow 'the sufficiently enlightened' and 'the greatest number of qualified persons to engage in open discussion and competition.' (Mill, pp.21-8) The social responsibility theory, recognising the economics of the newspaper market also suggests that news is of paramount importance. The most obvious example of a type of newspaper based on this ideology is the 'national institution', and in Great Britain, The Times has undertaken this role.

The abolition of the newspaper stamp tax in 1853 heralded the surge of many radical and popular papers. The Times in the mid-nineteenth century had succeeded in becoming politically independent, and thus its news reporting and opinion became to be considered as independent, setting some form of standard, by which the other, politically orientated papers could judge their own news reporting. Delane of the Times in 1852 outlined the duties of the press, which if not followed elsewhere, provided a certain ideology for the Times.

> 'The first duty of the press is to obtain the earliest and most correct intelligence of the events of the time, and instantly, by discussing them, to make them the common property of the nation ... The press lives by disclosure: whatever passes into keeping becomes a part of the knowledge and history of our times; it is daily and forever appealing to the enlightened force of public opinion - anticipating, if possible, the march of events - standing upon the breath between the present and the future, and extending its survey to the horizon of the world.' (F. Williams, 1957, p.8)

The independence of the Times from overt political influence has led to a label for its news of a paper of record, which was reinforced, more recently, when a transfer of ownership was contemplated. One witness to the equiry held by the Monopolies Commission wrote

> 'The Times holds a unique postion in the world of newspapers. It is the quality newspaper of London and the rest of England. It is read by the most responsible people in the country. It has great potentiality for influencing informed public opinion both at home and abroad and this cannot be measured merely in terms of its circulation. Control of the

Times will give very considerable power to any individual or group of individuals.' (Monopolies Commission, I966, paragraph I02)

The takeover took place after assurances from Lord Thomson on three counts; that editorial independence be maintained; that the paper maintains its traditon as a paper of record; both leading to the importance of its editorial opinions as a cutting edge. (Monopolies Commission, I966, paragraph I03)

This ideology does not extend to other British newspapers, in spite of their claims, but rather to other countries, where the following newspapers could be said to be published on the basis of part or all of this ideology; *Le Monde*, *Washington Post*, *La Stampa*, *De Welt*, etc.

The ideology of publication of the first newspapers to be published on a regular weekly, then daily basis, was also centred on news. In the early eighteenth century there were the 'one-man-band' operations, followed somewhat later by regional papers campaigning for social reform. Both types of newspaper were also published for profit and propaganda and thus had mixed ideologies.

Of the former it has been said

> 'The typical form of ownership in the nineteenth century had been a printer, a printing family or a small company. It was rare for more than one paper to be owned by the same person or company.' (R. Williams, I962, p.27)

> 'Newspaper proprietors had customarily been recruited from the ranks of printers and publishers, and the tradition of publisher-editor was deeply-rooted and long-lived. It was surely a major factor in the success of the family business, where experience of both the regular work of journalism and of the business management of a firm were found in the one man.' (Lee, I976, p.84)

Although the same historian has asserted that such proprietors did not have an ideology of news. 'There can be little doubt that the proprietors of early Victorian newspapers ran them in the vast majority of cases in order to make a profit.' (I976, p.49) This is axiomatic, for such newspapers were a business, and profit was needed to survive, but why should such 'businessmen' invest in newspapers? The same historian provides his own answer. Losses were common and often led to closures, ' ... between I860 and I803, £250,000 was lost in newspaper bankruptcies ... Such risks as these losses point to, however did not seriously deter new capital investment. ... The political, economic and social attractions were too great ...' (Lee, I976, p.90)

These businessmen ran newspapers on the basis of profit and the public good in which the dissemination of news and opinion was central. As C.P. Scott said

'A newspaper has two sides to it. It is a business like any other ... But it is more than a business. It has a moral as well as a material existence and its characters and influence are determined by the balance of these two forces.' (quoted in F. Williams, I957, p.I93)

GOT BOOK

This ambivalence or 'symbiosis of business and philanthropy' (Lee, I976, p.77) stood newspaper proprietors apart from the hard-headed capitalist. Proprietorship was seen in part as contributing to the ideal of public duty, but it was combined with an imperative of commercial success, producing in the end a kind of capitaliste oblige. (Lee, I976, p.95) Many of the nineteenth century newspapers boasted of Gentlemen as directors or investors, some of whom began to use the local press, 'as an indispensible means of promoting local, cultural and social activity.' (Jackson, I97I, p.5) If the proprietor has as his sole objective, profit then circulation, to bring sales and advertising revenue could only begenerated by an attractive, saleable paper. This by and large was achieved by news presentation which gave the editor some prominence, and as newspapers became more established the positionof the editor became more important. (Royal Commission on the Press, I977e, p.272) In contrast nineteenth century newspapers had standards of management which were

'universally poor. The few pictures that we have of the day-to-day running of these business indicate that even in the case of the largest concern management was, if it existed at all, very basic.' (Lee, I976, pp84-5)

For instance, such newspapers 'were not quick to exploit advertising after the I850's.' (II)

Within the one-man-band category several papers aimed at the working classes, were published by those public minded men who were anxious to educate the people and permit them to educate themselves were Cobbett with his 'Political Register', William Carpenter with the 'Political Letters' and Henry Hetherington with his 'Poor Man's Guardian'. This latter proprietor, self-educated in newspaper publication had the following philosophy

'Of almost imperturbable temper, of unbounded energy, filled with indignation against every abuse, he conducted his newspaper with a constant regard to the rights of others; he never degraded it for the sake of profit. He was always ready to admit the reply of anyone who thought himself misrepresented by him ...' (Collett, I933, p.I4)

Another example of newspaper proprietors having the ideology of news are the regional newspapers in the second half of the nineteenth century. Primarily within this category are the group of Northern middle-class reform papers in Manchester, Leeds, Sheffield, Salford, etc. In many cities two or more papers were published, following the libertarian theory, with each proprietor following a distinct political line,

'The editors of the larger urban newspapers of the North saw themselves as intermediaries between political, economic and social theorists and particular local readerships.' (Jackson, 1971, p.11)

This ideology spread to the new mornings introduced later in the nineteenth century.

'With the end of the newspaper stamp tax (in 1853) Manchester, Liverpool, Bradford, Birmingham, Leeds, Newcastle, Nottingham, Edinburgh, Aberdeen, Sheffield, Darlington, Plymouth and Belfast, all became possessed of vigorous organs of local opinion, many of which were to make great names for themselves in the history of British Journalism.' (F. Williams, 1969, p.36)

The propaganda element in the 'one-man-band' and 'regional campaigner' type of newspaper was against social evils rather than for direct personal gain. Indeed the tradition of the pursuit of news in a campaigning way has been continued to the present day, however, as the empirical evidence later shows, this is very much diminished. In a basic way it is the difference between investigative and descriptive reporting. It will be shown later that the latter has become more popular with regional (and some national newspapers), and that the former has to all intents and purposes disappeared, as the editorial function has become subservient to the commercial success of what is now an enterprise, which happens to have a newspaper as its product. Studies in the 1960's by Beith and Hill come to largely the same conclusions. However, they see fault with the inexperienced journalist, but Murphy in 'The Silent Watchdog' feels there are other influences

'if the young journalists are trained to work in a particular way in the context of an economically motivated organisation, one must ask why.'

In particular the role and power of the non-editorial staffs.

'how are relationships between editorial staff and administrators in newspaper firms actually negotiated.' (Murphy, 1976, p.36)

One purpose of this study is to examine these intra-organisational relationships and processes to provide answers to this question.

Ideologies based on total news are now rare. News is still reported, perhaps only as an offering from the conscience, but not for its own sake, it is subservient to profit and propaganda, two themes which form the modern ideologies of newspaper publication.

3.3.2 Propaganda

The libertarian theory of the press suggests that there should be many outlets of news, biased or unbiased, and that people therefore have a wide choice. A proprietor owning a newspaper for merely propaganda, finds, according to this theory, that he is doing nothing wrong, particularly if there are others like him. The Fleet Street newspapers of the first half of the twentieth century fit neatly into this category.

Propaganda as a theme in ideologies of publication chronologically follows news (except for the government controlled media of the sixteenth and seventeenth centuries.) Many of the early newspapers did propagandise - the regional campaigners for instance did in a political way. It could even be said that the national institution is involved in propaganda by being neutral over all issues, in that it involves a tacit acceptance of maintaining the prevailing order. However their prime concern was, and is, news, which cannot be said of those newspapers within the category of proprietorial dominance, where personal propaganda was of great importance. Northcliffe and Beaverbrook were closest to holding this ideology in a pure form.

Northcliffe, primarily a journalist who became a businessman, ran his papers at a profit instead of subsidising them, apart from the Times which he regarded as a 'national monument'. He was immune from political influence which besides annoying the politicians, allowed him to pursue any news story from any desired angle. This he did but only on stories he regarded to be in the public interest. He did not embark upon any vilifying campaigns, as Beaverbrook did, rather his influence could be seen in an 'emotional sympathy for all the unprivileged and the underdogs', or in assailing bureaucratic authority. 'His campaigns against "Hide the Truth" officialdom brought him calumny, not only from officials but also from countless diehards in whom persisted the English innate dislike of publicity.' (Clarke, 1950, p.13)

When Lord Beaverbrook was asked, by the Chairman of the Royal Commission on the Press 1947-9 what his main purpose in conducting newspapers was he replied, 'I ran the paper purely for the purpose of making propaganda and for no other object.' (Royal Commission, 1949, Q. 8656) However, he quickly qualified this in terms of his financial independence of political parties,

> 'I do not think a paper is any good for propaganda unless you run it as a commercial success. That is essential if you are to have a good propaganda instrument. My purpose originally was to set up a propaganda paper, and I have never departed from that purpose all through the years. But in order to make the propaganda effective the paper has to be successful. No paper is any good at all for propaganda unless it has a thoroughly good financial position. So that we worked very hard to build up a commercial position on that account, but never sacrificing propaganda; always making, but never in the news.' (Q. 8660)

When Beaverbrook was asked what kind of propaganda he said 'Particular issues; my own issue, the issue I have advocated all these years.' (Q. 8660) Beaverbrook was referring to Empire Free Trade, but as he implies there were other issues which dominated his papers, entirely at his direction. A.J.P. Taylor (1972,p XII ff) lists fourteen items which Beaverbrook supported or initiated, including isolation, increased spending and no entry to the E.E.C.

This ideology was dominant and several others have endorsed this opinion, 'Beaverbrook used newspapers to further his own beliefs.' (Christensen, 1961, p.48) Indeed he reversed the trend of political parties having influence in the press. 'He hoped that newspaper ownership would win him political power by enabling him to impose his views on political leaders.' (Driberg, 1956, pp. 140-1)

The proprietorial dominance of a paper in ideology and organisation initiated by Northcliffe and Beaverbrook was not confined to their papers. Thus Rothermere, Astor, Kemsley, Camrose, Cadburys etc, each dominated the character and organisation of their paper, the two aspects becoming indistinguishable. When Harold Hobson was appointed editor of the Sunday Times in April 1950, Lord Kemsley said 'It is, of course, to be understood that I will retain my active control of the paper as editor-in-chief and that final authority in all matters of policy will reside in me. In my absence the deputy chairman (Lionel Berry) will exercise my authority, and furthermore it is my intention that a member of my family should always occupy this position.' (Russell, 1972, p.278) Thus Kemsley 'acted the part of the omniscient autocrat,' (Braddon, 1965, p.267) and 'Lord Camrose was a bluff, dominating and dynamic figure who bought the Daily Telegraph from the Lawson family in 1928 (when circulation was 84,000) and built it up to more than a million ...' (New Statesman, 1974b)

The ideology of propaganda applies most directly to the original barons of Fleet Street. However the newspapers that they owned were still involved in propaganda even after their death. The ideology of publication had been continued by a group of nepotistic successors; at the Daily Mail and London Evening News by Vere Harmsworth, the grandson of Lord Rothermere; at the Daily Telegraph and Sunday Telegraph by Lord Hartwell, the second son of Lord Camrose; at the Daily Express, Sunday Express and Evening Standard by Sir Max Aitken, the son of Lord Beaverbrook; the Observer by David Astor (editor) appointed in 1948, the son of the proprietor; at the Guardian Lawrence Scott, grandson of C.P. Scott; and the Times was controlled by the Astor family until 1967.

It is not certain, though, that these nepotistic successors have been active in any propaganda campaigns, rather the newspapers have drifted attempting to continue in the manner of a previous era, whilst attempting to offset any financial losses. The result, for the most part, has been newspapers without a well-defined ideology which has led to closure or near closure for many of them. The nepotistic successors do not have the charisma of press barons to dominate their newspapers or organisations, nor do they seem to realise fully the need for commercialisation. For instance, according to one authority Lord Hartwell is

> 'a painfully shy and reticent personality. He speaks in a low, almost inaudible mumble, is prone to stuttering, and even his handwriting is so difficult to read that his messages to editors and writers take teamwork to interpret.' (New Statesman, I974b)

and the Economist Intelligence Unit found at the Daily Telegraph

> 'During our investigation it was difficult to discover any clear cut commercial policy ... but in our opinion the organisation is not planned and directed as a normal commercial business. Top management is dominated by the proprietor whose interest may not necessarily be those of the conventional entrepreuner.' (Report, I966, p.25)

> 'Lord Hartwell is the complete antithesis of the original press baron.' (Wintour I972, p.I85)

Also Sir Max Aitken

> 'For Max, one suspects has never been greatly interested in newspapers for their own sake. His work was at the Express, his life elsewhere. So it remains today. His male friends are all yachtsmen or businessmen or both.' (New Statesman, I974a)

However the E.I.U. report that

> 'It seems likely that the dissemination of political ideals was considered in the past to be more important than maximising profits. Therefore there may have been a tendency to neglect the foundation for efficient and continuing management ... the present management structure methods and control system are in our opinion unsuitable for long-term business needs and will almost certainly need to be reorganised when the present executive Chairman retires.' (Report, pp.29 and 3I)

This ideology of propaganda corresponds closely with the Fleet Street charismatic type of management and organisation (discussed in the next section). The nepotistic successors are not strong enough to withstand an attack on the traditional values that dictate publication. Indeed many newspapers, as mentioned in the first chapter, re-assess their market position and attempt by 'saturation' to become more commercial. Such a policy, however, was not initiated in Fleet Street, but rather in the regional press.

3.3.3 Profit

This ideology centres on money and profit. Newspapers are treated as as though they were a product of a manufacturing firm, and ideologies that conjure up newspapers fulfilling a democratic function are absent. Newspapers have to make money to survive, or they, like other unprofitable enterprises, are closed down. One consequence of the publication of newspapers by this ideology, as shown later, is the sharing of services between newspapers enabling unit costs to be reduced. This intertwining results in increased concentration in the newspaper industry, something despised by the libertarians, yet perhaps welcomed by those supporting the social responsibility theory of the press. If a newspaper is profitable, it can afford to be more critical in its approach, and take an independent line. Indeed, this has been the policy of the newspapers owned by Thomson, who, whilstaccepting a reasonable return on capital utilised, allows editorial freedom. He was the initiator of the type of newspapers which corresponds with the regional commercial category outlined in chapter one.

Lord Thomson, a Canadian, arrived in Britain in the I950's, primarily to buy and run British newspapers at a profit. He bought the 'Scotsman' in I952 and by a reverse take-over bid (I2) he acquired the Kemsley Newspaper empire in I959, which at that time included the Sunday Times and numerous regional newspapers. Thomson openly declared his intentions to the Kemsley's who equally openly disapproved, by commenting (in I952) 'that when he bought newspapers he left their politics and their policy entirely alone.' (Braddon, I965, p.I83) He had, however, given previous notice by his approach to Canadian newspapers, whose owners could not 'find any affinity with a man who not only owned radio stations but also claimed that he ran his one miserable newspaper as a business and only for its profits. In Canada in those days, one bought newspapers for political or prestige reasons, not for their profits, which were negligible; anyone who claimed that he published for profit alone was immediately suspect.' (Braddon, I965, p.I83)

This suspicion was not confined to Canada. The commercial orientation and the search for profit at the expense of opinion was of course anathema to the existing press lords. Raymond Williams had noted with fright this trend as early as I962.

> 'There is a widespread dependence on advertising money, which leads to a policy of getting a larger audience as quickly as possible, to attract and hold advertisers. From this it becomes one of the major purposes of communication to sell a particular paper or programme. All the basic purposes of communication - the sharing of human experience can become subordinated to this drive to sell.' (p.32)

Thomson is the archetype proprietor having this ideology, although some roots can be traced to J.S. Elias, later Lord Southwood, Chairman of Odhams, publishing the People and the Daily Herald. He was uninterested in newspapers except for their profits, and he was very eager to push circulation upwards to attract the greater prizes in advertising. However, the Daily Herald was not editorially independent for it voiced the opinion of the Trades Union Congress. Thomson has extended this ideology further,

> 'This is in fact Thomson's great contribution to British journalism, that he has thrown the whole apparently inevitable philosophy of publishing into the melting pot. By successfully assuming a proprietorial attitude, the opposite to that of all other great proprietors, he had shattered the feudal concept that editors owe unquestioning allegiance to the policies of their barons. By asserting that newspapers exist to serve the community in which they exist he has denied the Press baron's right to use newspapers as an instrument of propaganda. He has reiterated a thousand times that he personally operates newspapers only to make a profit ... ' (Braddon, 1965), p.364)

Certainly in the regional press Thomson has gone to the other extreme, profit not opinion, though to the distaste of some observers. 'What was once a means to some larger policy has become in many cases the policy itself. The organisation of communication is there not for use, but for profit ... ' (R. Williams, 1962, p.33)

Thomson has preached editorial freedom, so long as the paper is profitable. However, this is only one kind of editorial freedom (12).

The changing ideology of newspaper publication has been one of the major reasons for the trend towards commercialism, in the regional press and latterly elsewhere. Central to this book is the examination of such trends in the regional press. However, whilst asserting that such changes have been taking place, this assumes a pre-commercialism state of existence, knowledge of which is necessary before such changes can be examined. After all, a process of change implies a process linking two separate states. To understand the process of change not only must that process itself be studied, but concomitantly the beginning and end states. The analysis now turns to examine the major characteristics of the beginning state (pre-commercialism) by an investigation into the management and organisation of Fleet Street newspapers.

3.4 FLEET STREET MANAGEMENT AND ORGANISATION

The concern here is to examine the organisation and management structures which were associated with the 'hey-day' of Fleet Street. This will lead to the discernment of an organisational type, the Fleet Street type, around which were modelled almost all newspapers. In brief this would be characterised by domination by one person, a search for the most exclusive and latest news, an accent on editorial rather than advertising, and a newspaper enterprise that existed to publish news and opinion whilst making an economic return, rather than using news to make a profit. Regional newspapers were organised in much the same way, not only because such an organisational type was the most successful, but also because many of the regional newspapers were owned by Fleet Street enterprises. For instance by I930 the Berry brothers owned at least 26 provincial morning and evening newspapers and Rothermere at least I4. The lack of a press baron may be a major difference for some, however they were often dominated by a strong proprietor or editor, usually prominent local figures. These newspapers were more concerned with news and opinion, and had organisations to achieve this end. In pursuing this analysis it will be possible to show how the regional press was organised before the onset of commercialism, and further, help in understanding how the changes in the I960's and I970's occurred.

The evidence presented here necessarily comes from secondary sources, many of which are biographies and autobiographies of the dominating people in Fleet Street. For the most part they are romantic remembrances from proprietors, editors, and journalists, of succession of scoops, but provide some insight into how newspapers were actually published. For instance, by the very fact that all this literature concentrates on editorial to the detriment of any other function, is itself significant.

All of this does provide information, often by implication, as to how editorial departments were organised. What is most startling is the near total domination of a newspaper by its proprietor, who in turn was often the subject of adulation and hero-worship by the staff. Information on the regional press is sparse, (I3) even though much of it was owned by the Fleet Street 'barons'. From what evidence is available it appears they were modelled on the Fleet Street type.

3.4.I The Organisation of the Fleet Street Press

In general in this Fleet Street category what is being suggested is that the demands of the proprietor receive unswerving loyalty from employees, and thus their reaction to the means to achieve the proprietorial goals will be of agreement, and legitimacy of his authority, his purposes, and his organisational structure and achieved. In a conceptual way the legitimation of the 'barons' legitimacy resembles the work of Weber on charisma (Weber, I947, pp. 328)

In terms of newspapers one activity will be the gathering of news, which in itself may invoke a sufficient degree of loyalty from journalists to allow orders to be obeyed without question. When this is combined with a proprietor who has established a new form of newspaper, extended the communication process and is highly successful in producing such newspapers, then the loyalty and respect are reinforced. Other newspapers in competition will try to copy such characteristics along the lines of proprietorial dominance to hopefully achieve a similar success, and although they may not have initiated some new trend they may be seen to be developing (or exploiting) it. Northcliffe and Beaverbrook would seem to fit clearly in the former category whilst in the latter would be Kemsley, Camrose and Rothermere.

Dependent on the source of legitimacy is the structure of the organisation and the managerial style, and in the case of Fleet Street newspapers the claim to legitimacy arises because of the personality and character of the proprietor, for instance, Beaverbrook. 'His personality is the one constant power that shapes its (the Daily Express) doings wherever he may be in the world.' Similarly, 'the Daily Mail and the Daily Express were created by their proprietors, Northcliffe and Beaverbrook, - men not at all ordinary.' (Edelman, 1966, p.142) Other proprietors dominated their newspapers, to the extent that it became accepted

> 'that all outstanding papers have in effect been one-man bands in the sense that they were largely the product of one man's inspiration and conviction ... it is equally demonstrable that no paper of any distinction was ever masterminded by a board.' (Bairstow, 1970, p. 50)

This notion has acceptance by modern editors, in particular the editor of the Evening Standard has remarked,

> 'A newspaper must have more than a formula for its contents if it is to be a success. There must be a sense of identity and purpose and of usefulness. And that can only be provided by the editor, or the publisher, or both.' (Wintour, 1972, p. 22)

Although this characteristic is self-evident it provides some understanding into the long period of dominance of the Fleet Street type of organisation as the major one for newspapers. The one-man domination and propaganda as the ideology of publication interact and reinforce each other and as successful newspapers are created and run by one man, so therefore must that man be allowed to determine what news should be published. The staff of the newspaper, realising the position, actually support the proprietor in doing whatever he thinks is correct. These notions appear to be widely held and it reinforces the belief in the authority of, and thus loyalty to the proprietor.

A characteristic of an organisation dominated by one man is that all decisions are made by him, and are usually not subject to any control or sanction. Such decisions will often appear irrational in that they hold no respect for any normal ways of working or uneconomic to outsiders, but because of the nature of the particular proprietor, even these decisions are accepted as normal, and most often proved correct. Decisions over appointments, particularly of senior personnel appear in this category. Take for instance Beverley Baxter's first week at the Daily Express. Later he was to become the editor, but on his first Sunday he was a leader-writer, on Monday he was transferred to the reporting staff, and on Friday the editor called him and said Beaverbrook 'says that beginning next Monday you are to be the Literary Editor and take on the whole page except the leader column.' (Wood, 1962, p. 138; see also p. 212)

Similarly the idea of a scoop fits into this pattern. Here the 'bedding' of the paper would be held up until the last possible minute to allow for the latest news, in order to beat rivals. Journalists were employed in great numbers to obtain such scoops, (I4) which increased expense by holding up production schedules, increased labour costs through overtime, and perpetuated over-manning to facilitate constant changes of the main news pages. Thus the will of the proprietor, or more often subordinates acting so that they attempt to satisfy their perception of what was the proprietors will, held sway over any rational motives to promote commercialisation. Indeed there was something akin to devotion for most of the staff as shown by Christiansen, the editor of the Daily Express, when talking about control of the paper, 'I did not have control of policy except that I controlled every word that went into newspapers ... The policy was laid down by the proprietor, Lord Beaverbrook, and I was the man who made the policy attractive to the people by presentation ... I was perfectly prepared to follow his political policy and at the same time project it.' (Christiansen, I96I, p. I48) And by the rest of the staff 'Beaverbrook recruited young men with ideas who could write and his papers paid the highest salaries in Fleet Street. Hence he was never troubled by a labour dispute. It was more than money which held the papers together. Beaverbrook secured a personal devotion from all who served him.' (Taylor, I972, p. I72)

In cases of doubt of loyalty amongst his staff, Beaverbrook would use persuasion to maintain control, and if anyone disagreed with his policies, they often could not disagree with his persuasive arguments merely because they emanated from him. He remarked to the I949 Royal Commission on the Press, that in any difference of opinion with his editors, 'I talked them out of it.' (Taylor, I972, p. I72)

In any decision that Beaverbrook made there was hardly any indication that agreed or normal rules were followed. He acted as he wished, governed only by his principles which were liable to constant change. In part this aspect of his undoubted ability, although appearing at times anarchist, increased the devotion of his employees or followers. He transferred this style into the Ministry of Aircraft Production in I940-I ignoring completely the bureaucracy and its accompanying rules found in Whitehall. His short stay was characterised by threats of resignation from related Ministers and counter-threats from himself. However he achieved magnificent results, but had to be removed before the threatened mass resignations became a reality. (I5)

The Fleet Street proprietors were successful in the way they ran their newspapers. A single authority, and apparently irrational decisions and appointments were combined with propaganda campaigns determined by the proprietors. For them a successful newspaper needed good journalists, and to provide the support for the campaigns, many of them, and, as a force within the organisation, were more numerous and more powerful than other groups. This power, of course, deriving from the proprietor himself. Most of the foregoing has concentrated on Beaverbrook, but other proprietors governed their newspapers in much the same way, in particular Kemsley, Camrose and Northcliffe. (I6)

3.4.2 The Fleet Street Organisational Type

It is possible from the sources of foregoing evidence to outline the main characteristics of the Fleet Street type or organisation. The most successful newspapers were either created by and/or dominated by one man, and such proprietors for the most part held an ideology of publication based on propaganda. The newspapers were often vehicles for the dissemination of their own ideas, normally concerning issues of the day. For them, money, though not unimportant, was secondary to news, especially the latest and most exclusive. Those proprietors more concerned with money were less successful, and indeed the one man who openly worshpped the 'money god', Rothermere, ('His ambition which he just failed to fulfil, was to be the richest man in Britain' F. Williams, I957, p. 226) was a near disaster for any newspaper he attempted to direct. In I93I his financial ventures into regional newspapers were so inept, that he had to sell shares of the Daily Mirror on the open market in order to raise some necessary liquid resources.

The hierarchy of these organisations, naturally, was topped by the owner, who either became or gave substantial power to, the editor. Often the title differed, editor-in-chief, editorial director, chief editor ... etc. but the implications were the same, the dominance of the editorial department, both economically and politically (status) above all others. This meant that there was always a surplus of journalists ready to report any story at any time. Syndicated or 'wire' news in this era did not assume their present importance, for there was a constant drive to be first with a new story, or to uncover some new facet of an existing one, or failing that to invent a new campaign. All these would produce a paper, different in content and style from the rest. The proprietors, in general, were not satisfied with a difference in emphasis or treatment of similar news stories, only new stories, or at worst, new angles would suffice. A News Editor of the Daily Mail working under Northcliffe in I9I9 sums up these constant news pressures.

> '(Northcliffe) would ring me up before breakfast to call my attention to things in our own paper, and in the rival papers ... He would continue his telephone bombardment through the day. I would go home late, limp of body and weary of mind. I would wake early with a vague dread of the day in front on me, and would take no breakfast until I had seen the other papers and learned whether I had won or lost the previous day in the incessant quest for 'scoops'.' (Clarke, I93I, p. I26)

To the proprietor it was the editorial department which was most important. After all it was the department which made the newspaper possible, and further, probably the only one that could make it successful. There were sufficient journalists for defined career structures to emerge, with the local reporter, lower in the hierarchy, being able to rise to be one of the many special correspondents working in Fleet Street. Besides their normal career progression, there were also the glittering prizes that could be bestowed upon any one of them, merely at the will of the proprietor.

To formalise their position senior journalists founded the Institute of Journalists which lists in its charter the obtaining 'for journalists as such, formal and definite professional standing.' This is very much the elite of journalists, allowing entrance to newspaper proprietors, managers and directors, (provided they can qualify as journalists) for whom membership of the National Union of Journalists was ineligible. The later association, formed in I907, began as a wage-fighting machine, particularly on behalf of many northern provincial journalists who pay was low and working conditions poor. However, the N.U.J. was (and still is) divided between those who perceive it as a trade union, and those wishing it to be a vehicle for the advancement and recognition of the status of the journalist. (I7)

Any survey of the literature on the press until recently will reveal little information on the business side. (I8) This apparent neglect derives most probably because of the attractiveness of writing memoirs of journalistic experiences. The neglect is apparent because implicit in this literature is the notion that the non-editorial section of the enterprise exists merely to serve the editorial department. This is not exactly correct, for although the business side created less interest than the editorial its existence was crucial to any newspaper. However in most newspapers the proprietors' interest in propaganda and relevant editorial lead to the subjugation of the business side. One publication, for the training of journalists attempts to explain the position. It is sponsored and edited by one of the Fleet Street proprietors, and does give some insight into the relative importance of various functions within newspapers. William Mabane, a director of Kemsley newspapers, writes in this publication of the importance of the editor and his department. The editor 'endows the newspaper with its saleable quality' and 'it is on the editorial foundation that the whole structure of management must be built ... All other problems depend upon the editorial purpose of the newspaper - the readership at which it is aimed.' (I950, p.358) He further deliberates on costs 'Certainly there are, particularly on the editorial side, extremely heavy and exceptional costs which it is deemed wise from time to time to incur ... The competition for special articles, for series of articles, and for writers or cartoonists deemed to have box office appeal is intense, and prices paid are very high.' (I950, p. 36I) Even given the importance of editorial, there presumably was some control of these costs, if only to enable costs to be equalled by revenue, even if editorial have a large say in determining management policy.

However the implementation of Mabane's dual function in practice is very difficult, 'merely because of the implicit nature of the editorial function. The editor as an artist is a far more frequent phenomenon than the editor as a businessman, and Micawberish consideration of halfpennies more or halfpennies less are not agreeable to the artistic soul.' (I950, p. 358)

The reasoning becomes tautological. Editorial costs must be controlled, but to achieve a better paper, higher ciruclation, greater influence and perhaps change, superior news coverage and news presentation (with the necessary scoops) are needed. To achieve these, costs in editorial will rise rather than fall, and if management policy of success is pursued, then editorial costs are bound to be high. Control can only be exercised by the editorial dpeartment itself, and as it views itself as pre-eminent this is highly unlikely. Thus Mabane himself has an implicit acceptance that the survival of the newspaper is in the hands of the editorial department. The economics of this then produces 'an unusually high reward for success, and an unusally heavy penalty for failure, (they make) large profits or large losses. There is no normal, and little chance for mediocrity to survive.' (I950, p. 358)

Figures provided by the I949 and I977 Royal Commission Reports indicate that in I947 average editorial costs were 27.7% of the total costs, but by I975 had dropped to I5%. Such a high percentage in I947 is a result of efforts to ensure the newspaper was successful. However efficient was the rest of the organisation, if it was built upon a bad editorial then failure, it was thought, was the only result. In I965 the Economist Intelligence Unit reaffirmed this, 'There does not appear to be any consistent relationship between profitability and the quality of management.' (Report, I966, p. 2I) Further they conclude by giving some credence to the Fleet Street method, 'Possible brilliant editorial can carry poor management, whereas brilliant management cannot carry poor editorial.' (Report, I966, p.57)

The business side was not wholly neglected by the Fleet Street proprietors, in that they either took major financial or economic decisions themselves, or paid one person a large salary to do the same. What they did neglect, as the evidence from the Economic Intelligence Unit Report of I965 indicates, was to build an effective business organisation. The whole organisation was built around the proprietor, by the proprietor and for the proprietor, and when the proprietor relinquished control, for whatever reason, the newspaper enterprise, as the E.I.U. suggests, struggled to survive.

3.5 CONCLUSION

There was some commercialisation of the press after I930 when circulation began to rise and investment was at greater risk because of intense competition, but the changes were gradual and did not diminish by any significant proportion the position of editorial and the control of organisations by these Fleet Street proprietors. The E.I.U. Report in I965, although undertaken to help improve the fortunes of the Fleet Street newspapers, provides a useful insight of the types of organisations that had developed during the period when Fleet Street was dominated by the press barons. The following comments from the E.I.U. are a summary of their general findings, (I9) although they did make comments on individual newspapers (pp. 2I-49)

> 'In some organisations the essential drive and interest from the top is directed solely towards the editorial functions ...'
>
> 'When all allowances have been made for variations within the industry, its most striking feature, and possibly its greatest problem, is its dominance by a small number of highly individualistic proprietors with their own personal interests and philosophy of managements.'
>
> 'Some proprietors appear to have little interest in modern management methods and techniques yet retain almost absolute authority over the organisation. This tends to stifle the initiative of the other members of the management team and indirectly has an effect on the calibre of managements.' (Report, I966, p. 52)

Some editorial departments

> 'have almost unlimited freedom of action. On some of these newspapers the Editor does not work within a cost framework or budgets (on other the cost framework is largely set by the Editor himself) ... In this type of organisation it is heresy to suggest that there should be any control over editorial expenditure by commercial management, or the function should be subjected to any form of management discipline. The traditional view appears to be that the editorial staffs should not bother with the financial and commercial problems of their company, and the commercial management should not interfere with the editorial function.' (Report, I966, p. 6I-2)

Fleet Street newspapers, owned by men having an ideology of publication centred on propaganda, had an over-heavy reliance on news gathering and presentation as the key to success. This was not always determined by the amount of profit or revenue acquired, but rather by the level of circulation required by the proprietor to disseminate his views. Most of the owners of the Fleet Street press in this period saw a direct relationship between the size of editorial departments, their 'flair and artistry' in acquiring the latest and most exclusive news and the level of circulation. In pursuit of such policies some papers rarely made a profit, and because of this some ceased to be published, but others continued with funds from other sources. The way the Fleet Street press was organised had significant influences on the regional press, both through ties of ownership, and by the demonstration of what appeared to be the most successful way of organising a newspaper enterprise. The rest of the book is now concerned with the way regional newspapers as organisations coped with the change from editorial to commercial domination.

NOTES

(I) Michael Foot, a declared socialist, was editor, and wrote leaders for the Conservative Evening Standard. Taylor, I972, pp.550-I for details.

(2) F. Hirsch and D. Gordon I975, found political views of journalists differed with those of the paper but the journalists still stayed. See also Royal Commission on the Press I977, Working Paper No.3, p. 320)

(3) See A.J. Lee, I976, on how 'liberalism' influenced the development of the press in the second half of the nineteenth century.

(4) See Brown p. I56. There appears to be some confusion in Brown's article over the application of the word ideology. In a later passage, p. I57-8, Brown refers to Peterson's social responsibility theory of the press, and he asserts that this is really an ideology. However, if ideology is a personal set of beliefs and ideas of publishers then the social responsibility theory is not an ideology, except insofar as any publisher holds such a view. A more informative paradigm exists if a normative framework is interposed. The socially responsible theory is undoubtably normative, - that is the press, to put it bluntly should be socially responsible. In this sense it is more theory than ideology.

A. J. Lee also uses both terms, particularly in relation to liberalism. He says 'It is commonplace that the theory of the press which prevails in most Western democracies, including Britain is a 'liberal' theory.' Later he refers to liberalism being an ideology. It is not both ideology and theory, although there is some connection. Liberalism did include a theory of the press based on many competing papers of differing news and opinions. However the proprietors of such papers would not publish merely to fulfil the requirements of a theory, but rather to propagate opinion and/or to make money. If there were many such proprietors, the liberal theory of the press gives legitimacy to their ideologies.

The debate can become more semantically orientated and perhaps obfuscate the main argument. To avoid this one can assert that ideology applies to individual beliefs and ideas which form a basis for a system of action. Theory however applies to those sets of ideas attempting to explain certain phenomena - in this case often the relation of the media to other social institutions. They are often normative, portraying a desirous utopia, yet sometimes attempting to analyse and then explain the function of the media.

To illustrate, on p. I63, Brown refers to 'older components of press ideology - the press as 'watchdog' or ' the fourth branch of government', ' both of which are component elements of theories expounded in later pages of this work.

(6) See B.W. Rucker, I968, and D. Carter.

(7) See D. Read: Press and People, and L. Madden: How to find out about the Victorian Period, Ch. 3.

(8) See G. Unwin: Industrial Development in the Sixteenth and Seventeenth Centuries in England, for an account of how craftsmen moved out of the physical jurisdiction of such regulations.

(9) R. Williams, Communications, p. II7. The author uses the word system rather than theory but in the same way attempts to explain the role of the press in society.

(IO) See R. Boston: The Press We Deserve, pp. 8-IO, on the Le Monde where journalists have 40% ownership.

(II) Lee, I976, p. 87 see also Royal Commission on the Press I977, Working Paper No. 3 p. 279.

(I2) For details see F. Williams: The Right to Know, pp. I72-4.

(I3) An omission noted by Royal Commision on the Press I977, Working Paper No. 3, p. 286.

(I4) See E.I.U. report. In particular the Daily Express used to keep two photographers at London Airport, but often used agency photographs.

(I5) For an entertaining account of his rule at the Ministry of Aircraft Production, see Taylor, I972, Chap. I7.

(I6) For Kemsley see Hobson, Knightley and Russell, I972; Murray, I972; Kemsley I950; F. Williams I969: For Camrose see F. Williams I957 and I969; New Statesman I974b: For Northcliffe see Clarke I93I and I950; Andrews I964; The Times I952; King I969.

(I7) Any sample survey of the N.U.J.'s house journal. 'The Journalist' between I907 and I930 will demonstrate the division of militants and professionals.

(I8) One exception, apart from the E.I.U. report mentioned, is John Goulden, Newspaper Management, but this is a rather simple and straightforeard account of newspaper management, sponsored by the National Council for the training of journalists. A glance at two annotated bibliographies, both American, will confirm the paucity of books in this field. Even those that exist are American. The bibliographies are;

W.C. Price: The Literature of Journalism: An annotated bibliography.

W.C. Price and C.M. Pickett: An Annotated Journalism

Bibliography I958-68.

(I9) These comments do not generally apply to the Thomson Organisation in respect of the Sunday Times, nor to I.P.C. in respect of the Daily Mirror.

4 Regional commercialism

'Among the most powerful forces in national life today are the centripetal forces making for centralisation and uniformity in government, in education, in amusement and in standards of taste. The National Press is one such force, but the Provincial Dailies exert an influence in the opposite direction ... They can stimulate an interest in local affairs and in the work of local authorities and regional bodies; provide a forum for local discussion for both local and national affairs, and formulate and express a distinctively local opinion. By fostering and reflecting diversity of character, of custom and viewpoint, they contribute to the richness of the nation's life and the toughness and stability of its institution.' (Royal Commission, 1947a, para. 314)

'The ownership of the means of communication old and new, has passed, or is passing, in large part to a kind of financial organisation unknown in earlier periods, and with important resemblances to the major forms of ownership in general industrial production. The methods and attitudes of capitalist business have established themselves near the centre of communication.' (R. Williams, 1962, p. 31)

The changes in the regional press have been immense. On the surface the type of paper produced in the earlier part of the century is totally different from that in the present era; there is no competition, and ownership has changed. The rest of this work is concerned with a study of these changes, the nature of them, and of more importance, how they were achieved, particularly in the 1960's and 1970's when commercialism became much more overt. In part this becomes the guiding ideology as opposed to political propaganda through news. To achieve commercialism there is a requirement of a more rational, even bureaucratic form of organisation, certainly more formally determined than the informal set of relationships evident in the Fleet Street model. The demands of a commercialised bureaucracy will conflict with the demands of the editorial philosophy with its accent on artistry and flair. The outcome of that conflict will shape the organisation of the newspaper, although of more concern is the process by which that outcome occurs. To a large extent this process is a power struggle with one function, non-editorial, trying to inflict its will on another function, editorial. Editorial by way of the Fleet Street model, with traditional undertones, finds some legitimacy in its authority to dominate the pre-commercialist regional newspapers. Whilst post-commercialism non-editorial, by virtue of the profit motive find some legitimacy in their authority to control the non-commercial activities of editorial. Non-editorial have a belief that the commercial bureaucracy set up by them is there to work within, and for, yet to control the necessary artistic and creative editorial input. What changes is the level of necessity for artistic input as news gathering, interpretation and presentation is increasingly considered by non-editorial to be capable of being bureaucratically organised. Of course the perceptions of editorial staff are considerably different.

4.I The Regional Newspaper Industry in Monopoly

The importance of regional newspapers must not be under-estimated, as is shown in the following tables on their proportionate share of circulation, advertising and employment in the industry. (I)

TABLE 4.I

THE NUMBERS OF REGIONAL NEWSPAPERS

	I948	I96I	I969	I974	I976
Regional Morning	28	2I	22	I9	I9
Regional Evening	77	75	79	79	82
Regional Sunday	6	5	7	7	6
Regional Weekly	I307	I2I9	II63	II28	IIOI

Source: Annual Reports of the Press Council.
(All figures relate to 30th June of the respective year)

In I973 when Beaverbrook Newspapers Limited, because of financial difficulties closed the Evening Citizen in Glasgow, there was no provincial town in Great Britain with more than one evening newspaper; the monopoly situation had arrived. It was not abrogated by competing morning newspapers, for although in I974, nineteen were in existence, seventeen had sister evening papers having the same ownership, one was published where no evening existed, and only had a circulation of I0,000, and only one was in competition with newspapers belonging to other groups.

TABLE 4.2

THE CIRCULATION OF REGIONAL NEWSPAPERS

(Compared to National Papers) ('000)

	National Morning	London Evening	Provincial Morning	Provincial Evening	National & Provincial Sunday	Weekly & Bi-Weekly
I937	9,980	I,806	I,600	4,400	I5,259	8,56I
I947	I5,634	3,500	2,700	4,800	28,256	II,908
I957	I6,76I	2,858	2,000	7,000	30,I80	I2,372
I959	I6,I57	2,483	2,000	6,700	27,892	I2,267
I96I	I5,835	2,203	I,800	6,700	25,6I2	I2,702
I974	I4,882	I,275	2,088	6,560	24,383	I2,594
I976	I3,976	947	2,087	6,420	20,838	I3,36I
Change Since I937	+ 40%	- 48%	+ 30%	+ 46%	+ 37%	+ 56%

Source: Annual Reports of the Press Council.
(All figures relate to 30th June of the respective year)

TABLE 4.3

THE DISTRIBUTION OF ADVERTISING REVENUE (%)

	I960	I964	I970	I974	I975
National Newspapers	I9.8	20.7	I9.5	I7.9	I6.8
Regional Newspapers	23.8	23.6	25.8	30.3	29.2
All Press	70.9	69.3	72.2	72.I	70.I
All Media	I00.0	I00.0	I00.0	I00.0	I00.0

Source: Annual Reports of the Press Council.
(All figures relate to 30th June of the respective year)

TABLE 4.4.

THE NUMBER OF WEEKLY NEWSPAPERS OWNED BY THE MAJOR GROUPS

	All	Total of Top 6 No.	Total of Top 6 %	Thomson	Daily Mail	Westminster	United	News Int.	Iliffe
I948	I,307	58 [a]	4.4	0	6	32	I6	0	4
I96I	I,2I9	I37	II.2	29	I9	49	20	0	20
I967	I,I64	20I	I7.3	37	35	62	28	22	I7
I968	I,I60	200	I7.2	35	36	66	25	2I	I7
I969	I,I66	220	I8.9	3I	38	78	35	2I	I5
I970	I,I70	236	20.2	33	38	83	48	2I	I3
I97I	I,I50	2II	I8.3	26	38	82	32	20	I3
I972	I,I34	226	I9.9	33	30	85	3I	32	I5
I973	I,I37	230	20.2	33	32	83	33	32	I7
I974	I,I28	247	2I.9	38	36	97	3I	28	I7
I976	I,I0I	252 [b]	22.9	38	35	97	32	28	22
I976 Circ. [c]	I3,36I	2,89I	2I.6	393	469	I,258	277	288	206

NOTES:

I. In I948, in addition to the groups mentioned, Consolidated Press Ltd., owned 20, and Kemsley Newspapers Ltd., 9 weeklies. With these added, the total % of the top 6 major groups was 6.7%

2. In I976, in addition to the groups mentioned, other major groups controlling 20 or more weeklies were:-

F. Johnston & Co.Ltd., Falkirk	24	(253,000)
Scottish and Universal Investments	20	(275,000)
Surrey Advertiser and County Times Ltd.	24	(II7,000)

This brings the total % of major groups owning more than 20 weeklies, to 29.I%.

3. Figures for circulation in thousands. If the three groups in footnote 2 are added, the percentage figure rises to 26.5%.

Source:

Annual Reports of the Press Council.

(All figures relate to 30th June of the respective year).

TABLE 4.5

THE NUMBER OF REGIONAL NEWSPAPERS OWNED BY NATIONALLY BASED GROUPS

Company:	Thomson			Daily Mail			Westminster			Beaverbrook			News Int.			Reed		
Newspapers:	Times S. Times			Daily Mail E. News			F. Times			D. Express S. Express E. Standard			Sun News of World			Daily Mirror Sunday Mirror Sunday People		
Date	M.	E.	W.	M.	E.	W.	M.	E.	W.	M.	E.	W.	M.	E.	W.	M.	E.	W.
I948	-	-	-	-	8	6	4	9	32	-	I	-	-	-	-	-	-	-
I96I	5	8	29	I	I3	I9	I	8	49	-	I	-	-	-	-	I	-	-
I966	4	9	37	I	I2	26	I	9	62	-	I	-	-	2	25	I	-	6
I967	4	9	37	I	I3	35	I	9	62	-	I	-	-	I	22	I	-	6
I968	4	II	35	I	I3	36	I	9	66	-	I	-	-	I	2I	I	-	6
I969	4	I2	3I	I	I3	38	I	9	78	-	I	I	-	I	2I	I	-	6
I970	4	I2	33	I	I2	38	I	I0	83	-	I	4	-	I	2I	I	-	6
I97I	4	I2	26	I	I2	38	I	I0	82	-	I	6	-	I	20	I	-	6
I972	4	I2	33	I	I3	30	I	I0	85	-	I	6	-	I	32	I	-	8
I973	4	I2	33	I	I3	32	I	I0	83	-	-	6	-	I	32	I	-	8
I974	4	I2	38	I	I3	36	I	I0	97	-	-	7	-	I	28	I	-	8
I976	4	II	38	I	I3	35	I	I0	97	-	-	3	-	2	28	I	-	9

NOTE: Daily Telegraph Ltd., and The Observer Ltd., do not own any regional newspapers. The Manchester Guardian and Evening News Ltd., own one regional evening (the Manchester Evening News, which supports the Guardian) and one regional weekly newspaper.

Source: Annual Reports of the Press Council. (All figures relate to 30th June of the respective year).

TABLE 4.6

OTHER INTERESTS OF NATIONALLY-BASED NEWSPAPER GROUPS 1974

I The Thomson Organisation

a) 25.0% V, 24.2% NV, Scottish TV

b) II.0% V, Metropolitan Broadcasting

c) Substantial interests in Holiday Travel Firms, Advertising in Telephone Directories, Magazine Publications, Books, Exhibitions and Oil.

2 Westminster Press

a) 2.0% V, 2.5% NV, Birmingham Broadcasting

b) 7.5% V, Metropolitan Broadcasting

c) Substantial interests in book publishing

3 News International

a) 9.0% V, 38.2% NV, London Weekend TV

b) Substantial interests in magazine publication

4 Daily Mail

a) 22.I6% Ordinary and Preferred Shares
24.6% Unsecured in London Broadcasting Company

b) 2.5% V, 2.5% Redeemable Preference Shares in Greater Manchester Independent Radio

c) Substantial interests in Wharfing, Transport and Trade

5 Reed International

a) 29.6% V, 2I.2% NV in Associated TV

b) 6.5% V, 6.5% NV in Radio Clyde

c) Substantial interests in various manufacturing industries

Legend: V - Voting Shares, NV - Non-voting Shares

Source: Annual Reports of the Press Council

TABLE 4.7

THE CIRCULATION OF REGIONAL EVENING NEESPAPERS OWNED BY THE MAJOR GROUPS (%)

	Thomson	Daily Mail	Westminster	United	Iliffe	Total
I96I	I4.0	I3.0	5.4	6.6	8.7	47.7
I966	I6.I	I3.7	7.2	7.I	9.2	53.3
I967	I6.5	I3.7	7.3	7.2	8.4	53.I
I968	I6.3	I4.I	7.3	7.I	8.5	53.3
I969	I5.9	I3.8	8.7	6.8	8.3	53.5
I970	I8.0	I4.0	8.0	I0.9	8.0	58.9
I97I	I7.8	I4.0	8.0	I0.5	8.3	58.6
I972	I7.8	I3.9	8.3	I0.4	8.3	58.7
I973	I7.4	I4.2	8.4	I0.0	8.I	58.I
I974	I7.4	I4.3	8.5	9.9	8.4	58.5
I976	I6.4	I4.0	8.2	9.5	7.9	56.I

Source: Annual Reports of the Press Council.
(All figures relate to 30th June of the respective year)

One consequence of such a position is the stifling of the press in its free expression. Kemsley Newspapers in their evidence of the I947 Royal Commission advocated that 'Just as Parliament is made alive by the cut and thrust of debate, so in the country at large, the Press provides a great forum of opinion out of which, if expression be free, the truth will emerge.' (Royal Commission, I949b, p.I03) For the vast majority of people where evening papers circulate there can be no such cut and thrust of debate as only one opinion can be broadcast. There are national newspapers but they are more devoted to national rather than regional issues, or as one commentator has observed that 'We haven't got a national press, what we have got is local newspapers that are distributed nationally. Fleet Street is a London Press that gives London news and Londoners views of the rest of the country. It is London events, London gossip, London Exhibitions, plays and films that get discussed.' (Boston, I970, p.5)

If the majority of such newspapers are all of the same political shade, it may invoke a restraint on the exercise of the freedom of the press and the nature of democracy that this entails. Another study (Jackson, I97I) has produced figures giving evening newspapers as 40% Conservative leaning and 40% as politically neutral, and although showing some bias these figures presumably do not give immediate cause for alarm. However, the study suggested that the neutrality persuades newspapers to drop contentious issues, and later it will be argued there are overriding commercial reasons for the maintenance of such a policy.

The monopoly situation becomes more apparent when weekly newspapers are included. Table 4.4 shows an increasing concentration, combined with dropping numbers, whilst Table 4.5 also shows that many of these weeklies are part of a group, itself owning several evening newspapers. Indeed Table 4.7 shows that the concentration of the latter is such that five groups control nearly 60% of the total circulation of evening newspapers. The interdependence is completed by the relationship of the national press to these groups, as shown in Table 4.5

Government policy as espoused in monopoly commission reports shows little sign of halting or reversing the trend or in ameliorating the consequences of it. In April I972, the Monopolies Commission expressed concern on the tendency towards concentration of ownership of weekly newspapers, and in October I973, they reiterated their fears adding that although one transfer by itself may not be objectionable, the total of such transfers may well be so. In May I974, in another report on the proposed transfer of weeklies to a nationally-based group, the Commission whilst agreeing to the transfer, again expressed concern on what could be an undesirable concentration of ownership. The Commission have at times, produced somewhat extraneous arguments allowing the trend towards increased concentration to continue, citing the maintenance of employment, the maintenance of publication, the rationalisation of the regional press etc., but the Commission has rarely delved with any great insight into the freedom of the press, and thus its conclusions begin to lack the authority that has been expected of such enquiries. Indeed freedom of the press combined with 'in the public interest' are sufficiently vague and open to numerous interpretations, that short of overtly evident corruption, censorship or bias, most situations are permissible and thus legitimised. However, the Press Council with an accent on impartial objectivity, when called to give evidence on the Courier Printing and Publishing takeover found it did not have sufficient information on which to cast a judgement. Indeed the Press Council, being so inextricably tied to the press and its present ownership, was glad to see such questions passed to other bodies. In its I974 Report, it stated

> 'It is not surprising ... to find that among the terms of reference of the Royal Commission into the Press are ... the distribution and concentration of ownership of newspapers ... ' (The Press and the People, I974,p.88)

Whilst this discussion could become isolated in the semantics of the freedom of the press in relation to increasing concentration, the purpose here is to recognise that concentration of the press is occurring and little is being done to stop it and furthermore this concentration means that regional newspapers are increasingly tied to other regionals, weeklies or a national newspaper in some form of group ownership. In essence the object is to work at the internal effects of such trends which may shift the freedom of the press debateaway from traditional grounds. As can be gathered from Table 5.7 there are five major groups administering national, regional evening and morning, and weekly newspapers, which are the Thomson Organisation, Associated Newspapers, News International, Westminster Press Group and United Newspapers. Some of them have relatively long histories for instance, Allied Newspapers,the Westminster Group and United Newspapers started accumulating regional newspapers in the 1930's although the Thomson Organisation controlling Thomson Regional Newspapers only acquired the fairly massive Kemsley Newspapers Limited in 1959. What is now different, apart from the increased concentration of ownership amongst these groups, is the different ideology of publication which produces a different utilisation of resources within the group. For instance it was once thought that a journalist would obtain his training in the provinces before promoting his career to the national newspapers, although it is now certainly true that journalists are more likely to make a career in the regions by the management of editorial or alternatively switch to commercial management of a newspaper. More important however is the career pattern of the commercial managers who can obtain experience in weekly, regional and maybe national newspapers of differing sizes, all within the same company. In some groups other interests (see Table 4.6) are increasingly important such that managerial development can continue (or start) in oil, property, holidays, advertising, book publishing, local radio, television, etc.

Another change is in the gathering of news. It is now realised that with group ownership news can be more easily shared and the individual gathering of certain news is replaced by a collective gathering. This results in a reduced need for news gathering by each regional paper, an in increase in news management or presentation, which relatively increases the management of editorial departments by number and importance. The management of news is similar everywhere and thus career patterns can be developed here as with the commercial side. News gathering on the other hand requires some local knowledge, and a list of contacts in order that the news can be obtained easily. However, as news gathering becomes less important, fewer contacts are required, thus journalists as a whole become more mobile, increasing the trend towards mobile career patterns.

These are just two changes, which have arisen from this new ideology and group control, however, there is a need to examine from what position did these changes occur. The prime motivator of the changes was Roy Thomson, when he took over Kemsley Newspapers in 1959 and it could be said that the ideology of regional commercialism started here. Other groups reacted to the Thomson changes by imitation although somewhat more slowly, as Thomson himself later realised 'And it was not by chance that other newspapers in seeking advertising assistant, frequently included the words "Must be Thomson trained".' (Thomson, 1975,p.161)

As the Thomson takeover is the point of departure for the following analysis, it will be necessary to outline the regional newspaper position found by Roy Thomson in 1959.

4.2 THE REGIONAL PRESS BEFORE REGIONAL COMMERCIALISM

With the now infamous reverse bid Roy Thomson acquired Kemsley Newspapers Limited in 1959, and his empire thus started with, amongst others,eight provincial evenings and five provincial mornings. Immediately Thomson attempted to make them more commercial, money not news became the primary objective. To a large extent the position, structure and organisation of regional newspapers can be gathered negatively by reference to what Thomson actually did. For instance the introduction of organised classified advertising by Thomson infers that there was little or no emphasis on this before he took over. Information can also be obtained from secondary sources, autobiographies and biographies of those working in the regional press, but these are very few in number. Lastly, and within the empirical work, several of the interviewees had had sufficient experience to have worked in pre-commercialist days particularly those on the editorial side. With these three sources it ahs been possible to construct some detail on the regional press before the onset of commercialism.

The regional newspaper before 1960 in certain areas had more competition locally, either by an evening or morning newspaper, competing primarily in news, rather than advertisements, although these were necessary for survival. In general, circulations were much higher, as papers strived for larger circulations to promote opinion. This type of ideology of publication is obviously derived from the then current Fleet Street type, however its importance may not have been so overriding as in the nationals, because of the lack of ability of regional newspapers to dominate opinion, and although this could be done locally by its very nature is secondary to national influence. Many papers were controlled by nationally-based groups, such as those in the Kemsley or Rothermere organisations, and their ideology and thus method of management was influenced by the Fleet Street ideology of publication.

The evidence given to the 1947 Royal Commission on the Press emphasises the role of regional newspapers in providing as wide a range of local news as possible and influencing local opinion, although for many it was the choice of the former which inherently provided for the latter. Much evidence expressed the thought that the regional press were ignored in any discussion concerning the media, but Hirst, Kidd and Rennie Limited, attempted to redress this by suggesting that the 'regional and local newspapers are the backbone of the country's Press.' (Royal Commission, 1949b, p.92) Indeed they may be more important because their emphasis is on news rather than opinion, on honesty rather than popularity. This is echoed by the report of the 1949 Commission which stated

> 'There are ... papers whose purpose ... is merely to be a newspaper. These are the papers produced by

professional journalists whose interest is first and foremost in the creative exercise of their craft ... Pride in the production of a good paper and pleasure in the prestige which its ownership confers, are not negligible motives ... They are especially potent in small community where a local daily or weekly has a more intimate relationship to its readers than is possible for the national and the larger provincial papers.' (Royal Commission, I949a, p.26)

Further it was argued the local press ought to be able to stimulate and even educate local interest.

' ... I believe newspapers have some responsibility in encouraging public interest in worthwhile matters- such as the development of citizenship and its responsibilities. In this connection we have given many articles which were designed to encourage interest in local government, and on the importance of exercising the franchise (though of course, not in any particular direction). I also feel that newspapers can do much in improving public taste, and we also devote a considerable proportion of space to cultural movements and to sincere critism of art, music and drama.' (Royal Commission I949b, p.II)

Evidence such as this suggests that this emphasis on the collection of local news will result in a pre-ponderance of journalists, many with local knowledge. Indeed the collection and presentation of local news will dominate the newspaper organisation, with the editor assuming a position of high authority within the managerial structure. This is reflected in the declared organisation chart of one of the regional newspapers covered in the empirical research.

For many editorial managers these were the good times, when standards were high, the editorial function was dominant, the editor was pre-eminent, and the newspaper was a vehicle of news and opinion. Many of those interviewed expressed alarm at current trends, and yearned for days when editorial was dominant. The Assistant Editor (Special Features) of the evening at Centre A said 'In the I950's the standard of journalism was far better. The reporters, sub-editors were better qualified as people to do the job.' He thought that editorial standards had dropped, that commercialisation had reduced the editorial role, and that advertising had now taken over as the leading light. He continued 'Editorial now has a minor role - this paper has become a vehicle for making cash. The editorial is the space between the advertisements. The editor was the big man, but not now - often the editor was the M.D. but they now come from the commercial side.' The Deputy Editor of the morning at Centre A largely agreed 'Twenty years ago the company leaned fairly heavily to editorial. Twenty years ago the journalists were good - they got hard news stories, but today they don't want to know ... In the last twenty years there has been a decline in the standard of news.'

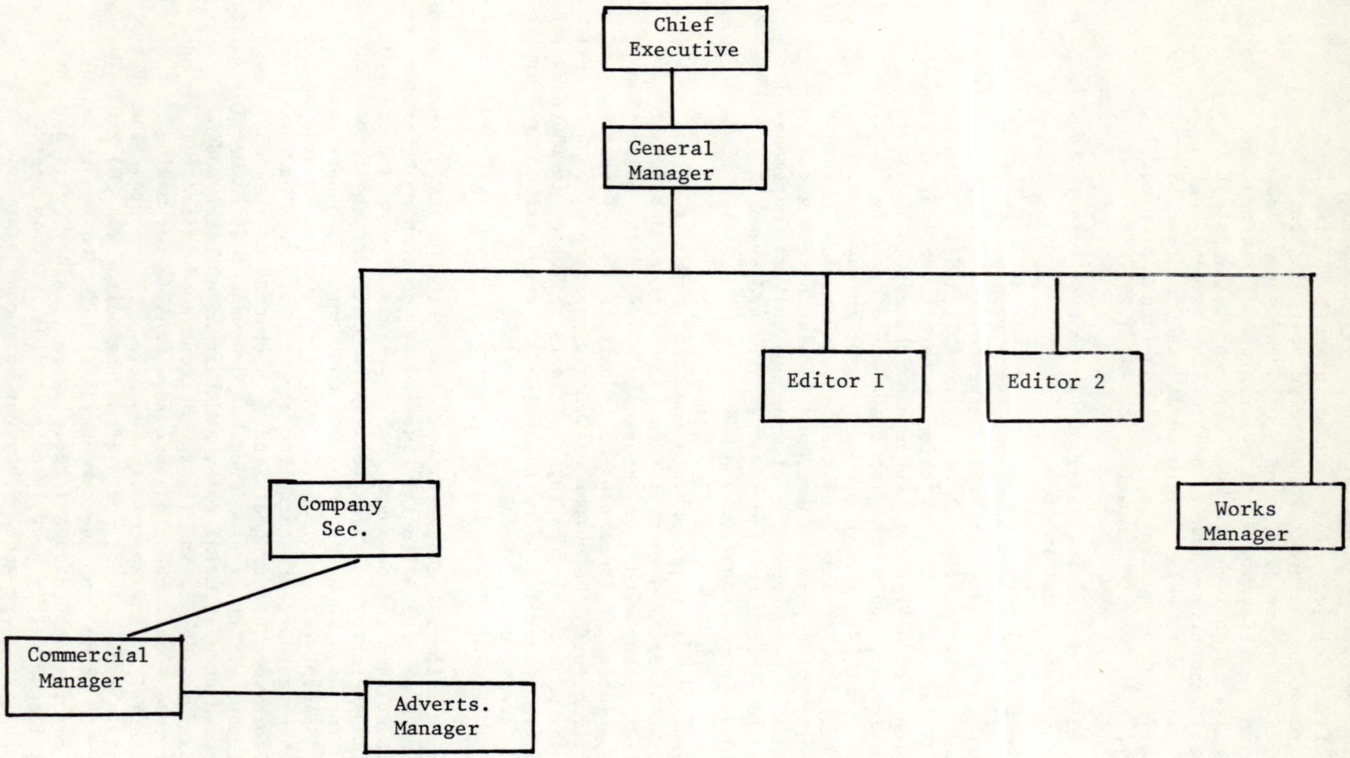

FIGURE 4.I : THE FORMAL ORGANISATION CHART OF CENTRE A PRE-I964.

Other editorial managers referred directly to the position of the editor. 'The editor is not the lone important figure nowadays.' (Night Editor, Centre A, evening) The Chief Sub-Editor (morning Centre A) remarked 'The editor was once a despot.' The News Editor (Centre A, morning) said 'The Editor's position has declined over the years because of the rise of the business side of things' and he felt it was reflected in the whole editorial department. 'The number of reporters has declined over the past ten years as the editorial department has declined in importance.' Even commercial managers realised the dominance of editorial in pre-commercial days. The Night Production Manager at Centre A remarked 'Well twenty years ago Editorial were all powerful very important.' The Deputy Production Manager (Centre B) commented that 'Editorial are not quite so important, the Editor is not what he was fifteen years ago. The company is now run from a balance sheet.'

Other managers expressed views that they were more content in the pre-commercial days than at present. They felt that the organisation was 'a much more homely place to be in.' (Features Editor, Centre A, morning), and that, 'there was more of a personal touch - now not the same closeness' (Sports News Editor, Centre A, evening). Some managers had worked for one of the newspapers owned by a Fleet Street proprietor, and some in those where a relative was the Managing Director. The Assistant Company Secretary (Centre A) said of this earlier era,

> 'Well then there was a very personal touch. The owner had his son as managing director and this personal way gave much to personal contact. The owner kept things very much alert with direct instructions to his son and from there direct ones to the head of departments.'

The Personnel Manager (Centre B) saw the early days as 'More of a proprietorial thing.' The Sports Editor (Centre B) 'With the old M.D. there was more of a personal touch - now its the era of financial wizardry - its very much a business.' Many bemoaned the growth of commercialisation, because the cash nexus often ignored the flavour of the local community, which they thought was necessary. The Display Advertisement Supervisor even said 'it was probably not as good a newspaper as before with the homely, master-servant relationships.'

One notable editor of a regional newspaper, Sir Linton Andrews, has outlined by way of his function, the importance of an editor. He compares the editor and his team of journalists in both a military way, and by relation of schoolmaster to his staff. In Chapter six of his book he develops the ideas of editorial training in news gathering, presentation, up-to-the-minute news, etc. but singularly fails to place such activities within the total publication of newspaper. There is no mention of advertising, accounting, production, circulation, and perhaps most important of all, the management of the editorial department. All of these are not conceived as of problems, unless they stem from poor journalism, all of which leads him to conclude, 'I am not wholly persuaded that there has been so sad a decline in editorial prestige.'

(Andrews, I964, p.I65) And he continues to ask then answer the following question, 'How should an editor edit? He has several roles to play. He may be a trainer of an increasing number of journalists. He is a team leader in an industry needing closer and larger teams every year. He is inevitably a populariser of knowledge. He is a ruler of the people because he is a persuader of it. He is an industrial commander-in-chief whose planning and instruction bring either victories or attrition of resources. He is a key man in the earnings of dividends for the shareholders.' This contrasts sharply with the opinion of one Assistant Managing Director interviewed over a decade after the introduction of regional commercialism, who said that 'the charisma attached to the editor and his staff was now not as clear as it used to be.

The emphasis on news gathering leads to an increased importance of news selection both by quantity and quality. Of quantity Berrow's Newspapers Limited reported to the I947 Royal Commission,

> 'When in every daily newspaper office the sub-editorial staff receives daily from news agencies, correspondents, staff reports and from other sources, sufficient news to fill, say eight or ten newspapers of the size permitted, there must be a drastic sub-editing by condensation, summarisation and selection if a reasonable reflection of all news of importance is to be achieved.'
> (I949b, p.44)

Of quality Denis Hamilton maintains that

> 'Seventy percent of stories are the same. It is in the remaining thirty per cent that they differ; and this difference it is which gives individual newspapers their particular character.' (I950, p.2I)

Again these contrast with first a statement by one editor interviewed that he could not fill any more space in a newspaper even if offered it. And second by the size of newspapers which vary from day to day dependent on the amount of advertising secured such that a greater amount of news on say, Thursday and Friday of a regional evening is because of a greater amount of advertising. (3) If this is connected with the editor's statement then some form of institutionalised pressure has occurred, such that the editor only directs journalists to collect that amount of news which the level of advertising will allow.

4.3 THE VIEW FROM THE REGIONAL COMMERCIALIST

The ideology of regional commercialism centred on money and profit, and the means to achieve such ends, is encapsulated in that well-known phrase of Roy Thomson's, 'I buy newspapers for profit,' although any more recently he has unequivocally reasserted ...

'Most of the people who owned and ran newspapers in Canada and America and in Britain did so because they liked the prestige and the power that newspaper ownership gave them, or because they inherited that ownership and, without a great deal of personal enthusiasm or in any case without devoting a great deal of energy, were keeping a family business ticking over. I, on the other hand, was wholly profit orientated.' (Thomson, I975, p.6)

In applying this ideology changes were necessary, for the preceding ideology of publication of regional newspapers placed profit in a subsidiary position, as news, and thus editorial departments were supreme. The effects from the installation of this new ideology can be seen in the instigation of means to achieve this end, profit, and such means involve on the one hand more and more developed means of money-gathering, and on the other, vast cost-reductions.

For the first this could involve the increase of newspaper circulation and the sale of more advertisements. However, the level of advertising in any paper is related not only to quantity of sales but also the quality of those sales. This latter refers to the purchasing power of different sectors of the community. Therefore the profit ideology is not a total drive to sell, but a more subtle guidance of the news coverage and presentation (and thus gathering) to attract a particular sector of sectors of readers, (indeed the whole of the population of these sectors) that would appeal to advertisers with certain products. To elucidate, advertisers divide society into groups, ABC(I)C(2)DE, ranging from titled and professional, though to the sub-working class. The groups are arranged according, in some ways to their consumer tastes and their ability to fulfil them. Consider the advertising of a product bought predominantly by C(I) and C(2) groups. If a newspaper has a readership spread equally across all groups it has a distinct disadvantage in the advertising market against a newspaper with a high proportion of the C(I) and C(2) groups amongst its readership. For the first newspaper an increase in circulation would not bring an increase in advertising revenue, and, as an extra copy of the newspaper needs this revenue, this increase in circulation only lowers profits or adds to losses.

The second aspect, the reduction in cost, centres mainly on the reduction of personnel and more efficient working practices, and of course the definition of efficiency is decided by the profit-maker. Initially one small area of cost reduction can occur by printing only those number of copies determined by the readership - advertising balance. However this is relatively small compared to the costs savings in the two most heavily populated departments, production and editorial as shown in Table 4.8

The cost of paper and ink which is mostly outside the control of newspaper managers is a high percentage of total cost, and if this is ignored then the significance of editorial and production costs increases, and they can be controlled by management. (See figures in brackets in Table 4.8)

TABLE 4.8

THE COSTS OF EDITORIAL AND PRODUCTION DEPARTMENTS AS A PERCENTAGE OF TOTAL COSTS

	Editorial	Production	Total
Provincial Morning	22	2I	43 (59)
Provincial Evening	I4	I9	33 (5I)
Provincial Weekly	20	22	42 (53)

Source: I96I-2 Report, Royal Commission on the Press.

Of these two departments, a reduction in production costs would seem far easier because of restrictive practices and over-manning (4) which push up costs artificially high. However due to 'union demands and proprietor capitulations' (Thomson, House of Lords, Jan. I967) strength of trade unions has been sufficient, at least until the time of writing to rebuff any challenge to manning arrangements. Thus if costs are to be reduced, the editorial department may have to bear an over heavy weight. This neatly fits in with the expansion of revenue-gathering departments, with advertising in particular, and circulation and commercial activities in general, beginning to take on more importance. This rather simple, though in outline indicative, analysis provides the basis of any organisational conflict. For here it is proposed to demote in status, and reduce in numbers (relatively) that very department which was not so much important, but was the very reason why all other departments existed. After all you couldn't have a newspaper without news. For most, if not all, regional newspapers this demotion is relative as pagination levels have risen considerably, because of extra advertising, which concomitantly necessitated extra news. However editorial staffing levels have been reduced or remained static.

TABLE 4.9

THE COLUMNS PRODUCED PER STAFF PER WEEK IN THE EVENING OBSERVER (CENTRE A) FOR SELECTED WEEKS

Week	Editorial Columns	Editorial Staff	Col. per Staff per Week	Index
23-28 March I959	28I.5	200	I.4I	I.00
2I-26 March I977	439	22I	I.99	I.4I

If the work of the editorial department could be subject to work measurement techniques then there is a 4I% increase in work load between the two selected weeks as in the above table, and whilst such notions are anathema to journalists, the increase in work loads does mean less time for journalists to display any 'flair and artistry'.

From a management point of view the pre-existing organisational design was clearly inadequate to implement any new policies centred on the profit ideology. The organisation chart in Figure 4.I is of an organisation geared to news collection, selection and presentation, and to change emphasis to profit could not be achieved quickly at all, and even if planned would no doubt lead to a degree of conflict.

To a certain extent the organisational structure was maintained by the authority of either the editor or a proprietor with editorial leanings. Although not possessing the charisma of a Fleet Street proprietor, the regional editors (and/or proprietors) may have seemed important enough to the employees for such a news-orientated organisation to be ligitimised. The problem of the regional commercialist was how to re-orientate the newspaper organisation in the ways mentioned above. Thomson Regional Newspapers were the first to deal with this problem, and because they were essentially new press owners, their methods and influence can be traced.

4.4 THE THOMSON TAKEOVER

There were three distinct stages in the Thomson takeover: the organisation of the board and their policies; the introduction of budgets to control costs (particularly editorial); and the introduction of refined and developed classified advertising systems.

4.4.I The Change at the Top, a Different Ideology and Policy

Thomson Regional Newspapers are somewhat unique in the first aspect of the change at the top, as they were the first to introduce them. The other groups eventually followed in a similar vein. The Thomson Newspapers are here used as an example because they are clearly documented in the literature.

When the Autumn I959 Roy Thomson acquired Kemsley Newspapers, he inherited a nepotistic management structure 'Kemsley's four sons were staying on as directors of the firm, Lionel (Berry) as deputy chairman, Denis in charge of the Newcastle office, Neville in an indiscriminate capacity and Anthony at Cardiff.' (Thomson, I975, p.7I) Denis was also in charge of plant and machinery for the group. Immediately a new management structure was created. There was to be a parent board with Roy Thomson as chairman, which would decide the policy of the company and approve the main decisions of the executive board with Jim Colbart, the new managing director as chairman. Lionel Berry was conveniently left out of the board meetings because of discussion conerning the performance of his relatives in running what was now Thomson's company. Lionel was disturbed and still contacted his relatives and indeed decisions were taken by them. A directive from the parent board stopped this, which amongst other things led to some disagreement. 'Lionel was very nice about it. "This isn't going to work" he predicted, and two months later the sons all sent their resignations and departed.' (Thomson, I975, p.73)

With the entrails of nepotistic succession gone, the board could begin to implement a policy to achieve the commercialisation of their papers. In the next sections the internal measures of budgeting and classified advertising are discussed, however initially the board began to react to the external changing economic environment analysed in Chapter two. Elsewhere this has been termed rationalisation of the regional press, but for Thomson it was essentially commercial,

> 'What we needed was a sensible application of the one-paper solution which had worked very generally in Canada and the United States. A community of a certain size could only support one newspaper and that was almost always an evening paper. Readers grabbed a national daily ... when they were breakfasting or commuting or if they were housewives enjoying a mid-morning break, but in their leisure time they wanted to turn from national to more local news and to classified ads. as provided by the evening paper. In Edinburgh as in Winnipeg.' (I975, pp. 35-6)

This statement of Thomson's implies that there is a demand for classified advertisements, but also implied is the assumption that the British regional press is no different to the American or Canadian regional press, and thus, methods used over there can be used here. Notwithstanding that the American and Canadian Press is structured differently to the British Press, most especially in that the former do not have any truly national newspapers, Thomson himself sees no difference.

> 'In Canada and the United States we now own newspapers in I03 towns. Only three of them have a morning paper. None has two evenings. Because our operation (like other newspaper companies) restricted these communities to the service of only one newspaper, did not mean that these communities suffered. Two rural newspapers, each struggling to make ends meet and dragging out any scandal that this may sell a few copies, aren't performing the service that one prosperous and healthy newspaper could. You see them doing everything they can to please their advertisers, (even suppressing news, maybe.)' (I975, p.36)

Given these assertions by Thomson, it would be of interest to quickly review the state of the American regional press, particularly concerning its news content, as this was highlighted as a distinct advantage of the monopoly situation. The review should be seen in context to some of the theories outlined in Chapter three, in particular the libertarian theory of the press which held that the more papers the better. This with the current economies of the newspaper world has been transformed into the social responsibility theory, which whilst realising that increased concentration has become inevitable, suggests that monopoly newspapers have a social responsibility to communicate the news in an unbiased a fashion as possible. B.W. Rucker (5) has been one American commentator to consider the regional press in organisational terms, whilst others (6) have ignored this area in favour of analysing the effects of the mass media on the public. Although this area of study may be important surely a necessary grounding lies in the means (that is organisation of the press and its ideology) to communicate.

However, with reference to more impartial news coverage, B.W. Rucker (I968, p. 7I ff.) asserts that monopoly chain control produces less independence in news reporting because agencies who sell news rely on local newspaper reporters as a source. Thus little, if any at all, derogatory news concerning the 'home town' ever finds its way on to the 'wire', and inbuilt bias results which may also exist here considering the increasing use of the wire in this country. Indeed to pre-empt the empirical data, one personnel manager bemoaned this continual use of the wire, adding - 'They even use the copy word for word.' Because of this reliance on news agencies in America, Rucker comments concerning the First Amendment to the Constitution of the freedom of the press,

> ' ... on local issues the First Amendment is dead as far as millions of Americans are concerned ... They have no access to a local media voice, or receive only what a single owner of their radio station and newspaper and, in a few instances, television station, seem desirable. Thus those who have most invoked the First Amendment to protect their pocket-books have effectively killed it.' (I968, p. I88)

Thus the assertion of Thomson's that monopoly ownership as in America will be beneficial does not hold true, if the experience of the Americans is any base for evidence. Rucker also lists other areas of control or persuasion inhibiting the free dissemination of news. In general the policies, designed to force or price others out of the market, are to refuse to publish any advertisements from people or enterprises who have advertised on the radio, or in a different paper, although acceptances often mean advertising in the morning, afternoon and Sunday editions without question. Other policies are to compete unfairly by reducing advertising and circulation rates below cost, and members of one news agency (Associated Press) are excluded if they compete in supplying news indepently. (I968, pp. II-I8)

Elsewhere Rucker and Williams (I965, p. IO ff) have outlined some disadvantages of chain ownership in America. The manager or publisher may not feel compelled to promote the local community to the same degree as if he were in control himself, and readers may react to this by feeling that the paper is controlled from afar, that they cannot obtain any liaison with the editor and his staff and thus are somewhat alienated from the local paper. Also, because of chain ownership, managers promoted or moved to any one locality may feel that such a position is only one step in their career pattern, leading to a lack of a sense of permanence. This may result in a lack of commitment by managers or even editorial staff, although of more importance are the organisational changes that result.

Thus the policy of Thomson's, and eventually that of the other regional groups, was one evening newspaper, one town, although a morning paper may survive alongside an evening paper, particularly if the commercial template is not applied without question. Therefore besides rationalisation it could be conceivable that any new town (e.g. Milton Keynes) or indeed existing towns would require a newspaper. Thomson was alive to the possibilities,

> 'I had a hunch that there were areas in Britain which had never been appraised as possible centres for newspapers and which might be just the place for them in the greatly changed world I was now contemplating. No one in England had begun to think of running an evening paper with a small circulation and small costs as we do in America. We therefore set out team of experts to work and in due course they came up with certain places they had singled out as likely to provide an economic basis for an evening paper.' (Thomson, I965, p. I53)

New newspapers were started in Watford (I967), Luton (I967), Reading (I965), Burnley (I965), by Thomson Regional Newspapers, at Slough (I969) by Thomson in conjunction with Westminster Press, at Southend (I969) by Westminster Press, and at Doncaster (I966) by United Newspapers. However, whereas in the I930's when the press barons expanded into the regions, the basis for this expansion was to further their area of influence, it is now whether such a newspaper can make a handsome profit.

4.4.2 Budgeting

Prior to Regional Commericalism, newspaper management relegated costing to a subservient level, as their formula for success was news and the sales it would bring. The publish-at-all-costs ideology would find costing for editorial anathema, in the sense that budgets if introduced, would be redundant because to forfeit news or the 'scoop' because money was not available was to sign their own death warrant. Such an attitude finds legitimation from the I949 Report of the Royal Commission on the Press.

> 'As the time approaches for the first edition to go to press, the tempo of the office accelerates. Copy continues to pour in, reporting new events and modifying or developing items already in print. Up to the last moment copy is being prepared for the main page and items already set up are being altered or condensed to make more space for late news. As each successive edition goes to press work beings on the next. Late news, of which only a few lines could be given in one edition, is given more fully in the next ... When this happens the main news page, and probably a

second as well, must be entirely remade, replanned, rewritten, illustrated, set up, corrected, and fitted into the rigid limits of space - and all perhaps in less than an hour.' (I949a, paragraphs I3-4)

The E.I.U. noted (I966, p. 60) that it was unthinkable to place any commercial control upon the activities of the editor and his staff, however, the ideology of regional commercialism places profit above news in any list of priorities, and as editorial is one of the high-cost functions, any cost control in this area is bound to be beneficial to the profit motive, although it will reduce the quality or quantity of news. Moreover, in the monopoly situation the competition for the most exclusive and latest news does not exist and thus the editorial department can be more easily managed, as the news flow itself can be managed. Maximisation of sales through excellect news coverage is replaced by the deliberate selection of a readership which would appeal to certain advertisers. Again the editorial function becomes less important. Thus the special case of non-costing for editorial diminishes and budgets become more feasible, at least from the perception of the commercial side (the perceptions of the editorial sector are of course much different and are discussed later). Lord Thomson recalls,

'They tried to tell me in Britain that budgets did not really work with newspapers; editorial costs for instance, were bound to fluctuate widely, and sometimes could not be kept within pre-fixed limits. But I showed them that you could start with a wide margin, you would get more accuracy as the years passed, and that budgets would be a particular help to editors.' (I965, p. II8)

4.4.3 Classified Advertising

Before regional commercialism, display advertising produced sufficient revenue to balance newspaper sales revenue with total costs. Classified advertising had hardly been developed. The national press had a diet of nearly all display advertising, mostly originating from undertakings, as classified advertising would have been too expensive for most individuals to announce the selling of their wares, etc. The American and Canadian press had survived and prospered by the development of classified advertising, and Thomson saw no reason why this should not be the case for the British Press, regional and national. He first used it on the regional press, which he though could and should be the local market place for the exchange of goods and services. To this end he introduced an advertising consultant, George Pappas from the United States.

'He employed every possible technique of persuasion on the telephone and went through every kind of directory and list to find people who might want to advertise. He hired big staffs to do this, in most offices as many as fifty, mostly young girls, not because they were cheaper, though perhaps they were, but because they could learn better how to carry out his ideas. George taught them not only what

> to say but how to say it, to learn all over again how to speak in fact. Many of them went home in tears, but those who made the grade vied with their colleagues to win extra money for results.' (Thomson, 1965, pp. 160-1)

This development was highly necessary and, according to Thomson, did not affect newspapers and their news because such advertisements were a natural part of newspapers, even readers wanted them. Thomson legitimised the development thus,

> 'Newspaper people in Britain hadn't yet come to realise that a newspaper's primary hope of success was its ability to sell advertising space, and that this as much as the provision of a news service was the business of newspaper companies, a highly complex business requiring a whole range of skills and new techniques, and there was no call to go weeping about 'lack of support' and about newspapers going to the wall if these skills and techniques were not being used.' (1965, p. 159)

This was echoed by one news editor interviewed, 'At one time newspapers would sell themselves, now they have to be sold.'

In this way classified advertising emerged first as a powerful money-maker for regional newspapers, and second as a strong commercial voice within the newspaper organisation. Display advertising was also developed, and with the policy of commercialism, the non-editorial section of a regional newspaper organisation grew both in numbers and status overtaking and diminishing the role of the editorial department. However to examine such a takeover it is necessary to understand the perceptions of editorial and commercial managers of each other and it is to this that the chapter now turns.

4.5 EDITORIAL STAFF AND THEIR PERCEPTIONS OF NEWSPAPER ORGANISATIONS

In Gouldneresque fashion the editorial dominance before commercialism may be to the commercial manager an indulgency pattern characterized by flexibility and a lack of rigid rules and hierarchical offices. Whilst the commercial managers wanted to change this to more rational and efficient systems of operation editorial staffs saw the operation of a newspaper as normal and did not want to change it, apart from perhaps editorial independence from a Fleet Street proprietor. In what ways did the journalists and editors view the organisation as normal?

First journalistic supremacy was an important organisational characteristic, which was not only believed by journalists themselves, but was legitimised by, and was a result of the Fleet Street ideology. The Fleet Street proprietors were either journalists or information orientated and thus saw editorial as the most important department, and this was replicated in the regions. Following from this is the idea that the central function of a regional newspaper is to serve the community with regional news. To achieve this end all other departments were mere inputs to provide the news in newspaper form. Production printed the news, Accounts paid the wages, and there was no other department large enough to challenge the editorial hegemony. Production (50.6% of personnel), the largest numerical department in Centre (A) in 1959 appeared to have no viewpoint on how newspapers should be organised as long as they had control over their own working practices. This did not interfere with the news orientation of the paper as production was not concerned with news per se. Indeed in the previous twenty years or so the management of the newspaper had been prepared to give in to any demands of production almost without question, in order to preserve a news output.

A third characteristic was this emphasis on exclusivity and late news. In 1959 most regional newspapers had no competition of a like newspaper, although some competition for news did exist with national or regional morning newspapers and perhaps television and radio. Even so late news was still important to the newspaper, particularly if the story was locally significant, and for any such news, deadlines, if they existed, could be altered and working practices in the print and composing rooms could be accommodated likewise, even if it meant that nearly always there would be extra cost to the newspaper in increased wages. However, late news serves a larger function than merely its content. Because it can be inserted at a moments notice, and on the instruction of the editorial department, it is an exhibition of the power and supremacy of this department over all others. The fact that it costs extra only adds to this importance. The assistant to the Production Manager (Centre A) was in agreement with this argument 'We have 800 hours of overtime per week here. In part it's because editorial change the paper, especially late editions. They do it to justify their existence. After all any one person only ever sees one edition.'

The previous two characteristics lead to a fourth, that to provide this central item of news, 'early' or late, a fairly sizeable editorial department is needed, even though pagination was lower than today. The editorial staff comprised in Centre (A), 30% in 1959, but only 25% in 1976. One senior accountant complained of the lack of work measurement for journalists, but if this was introduced it would show that journalists, on average, were required to fill less space in 1959 than in 1977. In two selected weeks each journalist filled 1.41 columns per week in 1959, but this had risen to 1.99 in 1977. Any payment by results system would indicate the need for more journalists today, or proportionately higher salaries. Thus in number as well as ideology, editorial had supremacy.

These large numbers allowed the journalists to display their 'flair and artistry' in news reporting, whilst the intermittent nature of news occurrence, both in the timing of news and in the 'flair and artistry' needed to gather and present it, provided a circular reinforcement for the need for large numbers. Tunstall writing in 1971 calls this in relation to national newspapers (which at that time still displayed many of the Fleet Street ideology traits), 'innovation and creativity'. (I97I, p. 30)

Matejko, (I970) writing about the Polish national press discerns similar characteristics and Boyd-Barrett, in questioning journalists over their reason for choosing their occupation received the following replies -

'(i) Journalism seen as a non-routine, non-conventional, sociable occupation and hterefore attractive, - accounting for 35% of the respondents.

(ii) Journalism seen as the most desirable occupation available or possible for the respondent - 29%.

(iii) Journalism seen as a creative occupation - I6%.

(iv) Journalism seen as self-educational - 5%.

(v) Journalism seen as a bridging occupation offering good prospects - 3%.

(vi) Journalism seen as a public service occupation - I%.' (I970, p. I96)

The journalists in pre-commercial regional newspapers often had Fleet Street as the top of their career ladder, (Royal Commission, I962a, pp. 43-5) and thus to them editorial work demanded no less a commitment to 'flair and artistry'.

The proprietors of regional newspapers were either related to the press-barons of Fleet Street, or were locally important members of the community, a kind of regionalised press-baron. The legitimation of journalistic supremacy in national newspapers came from the authority of the Fleet Street proprietors, in Weberian terms, a kind of charismatic authority. In a similar fashion, by way of example, and of local press-barons, so journalistic supremacy was legitimised in the regional newspapers. In some cases there were the relatives of the charismatic leaders, for instance, the sons of Kemsley, and their authority would not be questioned: 'By the conception that charisma is a quality transmitted by heredity; thus that it is participated in by the kinsmen of its bearer, particularly by his closest relatives.' (Weber, I947, p. 364) Hugh Cudlipp illustrates Weber's concept when considering the paths into journalism,

> 'A few privileged young men, not all bright but some of them capable and diligent, became newspaper executives and later proprietors because their fathers were newspaper proprietors or, like the Harmsworths, because publishing was the family business and way of life and death. They practiced walking on the water in their nursery baths.' (I976, p. 33)

Where journalistic supremacy rests for its legitimacy on the authority of a proprietor interested in news and propaganda, then if that proprietor retires or dies, and the newspaper then has a proprietor whose interests are not in news and propaganda, (except where they are profitable) but are in money and profit making, then the basis of legitmacy is threatened, or even disappears. Newspaper organisations are therefore unlikely to continue to be characterised by journalistic supremacy, unless a new basis for its legitimacy can be found. It has already been shown that in the decade after I957, Fleet Street became increasingly bereft of the original propaganda-orientated proprietors, but to a large extent the organisation in Fleet Street still remained news-orientated, in part because of intense competition, in part on traditional grounds, in that successful newspapers could only be run in this manner, and in part because the nepotistic successors did not want to change methods of organisation.

In the regions, two of the three reasons inhibiting change in Fleet Street, do not apply. It has been shown that these newspapers do not have competition, and ownership has changed to ensure a strict commercial orientation. Only on traditional grounds could there be a continuing legitimate base for the authority of the editorial department, which in Weberian analysis is a natural tendency, and journalists in the editorial department clearly thought that successful newspapers were built on sound editorial.

The stability of the status of any department within an organisation depends on the perception of those in that department matching at least closely the perceptions by others in other departments. The editorial department claims importance because it has always been important, and it will maintain importance if others also believe it to be important in this traditional way. Thus even if, as will occur, the 'routinisation of charisma' by the journalists fails to provide their continued dominance, the fact they have always been dominant may succeed.

Traditionalism following the Weberian concept (I947, p. 34I) involves a high degree of strong leadership, which comes either from the editor or the publisher. If it has been the position that the editor is a strong enough character to persuade the rest of the newspaper enterprise to be directed by editorial, then a change of proprietorship and the commensurate change in ideology of publication, may not be sufficient to control the editorial function on commercial grounds. Traditionally a strong editor is required for a successful newspaper, but as this may not be accommodated by the new ideology, conflict will be the result.

Given the Thomson take-over and the associated changes in other newspaper groups, this solution can be seen as an attempt to base the legitimacy of journalistic supremacy on the authority of the editor. There are two problems here. First the new regional commercialist may not view editorial in the way editorial views itself. This dichotomy can be explained in the overall management, organisation and control of so-called artistic workers. Matejko comments 'in the case of highly qualified work, which seldom lends itself to standardisation, harmonious relationships are of paramount importance.' (I970, p. I68) Indeed some of the existing literature (7) on organisational theory has thought that the artistic worker could not be effectively managed in a rational-bureaucratic way. This therefore suggests that an informal network of relationships and communications would in the case of the artistic worker be more functional than any formal system. This informal system can only operate in the face of a single unquestioned authority, the editor. Matejko has found some empirical evidence

> 'As a rule the formal organisation of the office is simple loose, and fairly elastic. Sometimes the various sections are not even clearly demarcated. The same can be said about the demarcation of responsibility. The organisation is very pliable and the editor changes it as he goes along, as he thinks fit. This is possible because there is a distinctly crystallised informal organisation in the office, welding people together and bringing order to the human relationships. This organisation is obvious on all levels of the staff of these papers, but especially at the top, on the editorial level.' (I970, p. I23)

The regional commercialist will probably not see the journalists work as that artistic, and therefore he will consider it manageable by bureaucratic means. These differing perceptions of the editorial function and the way it is carried out lead to conflict within the organisation. This conflict takes place in those areas of interchange between editorial and non-editorial.

The second problem arises even if the regional commercialist agrees with the journalists view, and sees a necessity for an editor in the terms defined above. An editor who is too strong may inflict the editorial ideology on the rest of the organisational structure, and will conflict with the regional commercial ideology. Although this is a possible solution for the authority base of journalistic supremacy, the conflict it causes with non-editorial will provide a nearly endless struggle of ideological influences. The outcome of such struggles will shape the organisation, and the newspaper it publishes, as the stronger ideology becomes implanted. The conflict takes place in the area of interchange between editorial and non-editorial, an area of uncertainty in the words of Crozier. There are not parallel power relationships, for the commercial take-over suggests an inequality, which at first is biased towards editorial, in that they are more powerful as a result of the previous ideology. Eventually, though with the introduction of greater numbers of non-editorial, this area of uncertainty is bureaucratically managed by non-editorial. This process, a one-way influence of power, is analysed later under the headings of areas of uncertainty, and the problem of succession.

An alternative solution is to either appoint editors in sympathy with the new type of ideology, or to ensure that they regulate the working of the editorial department. The result has been a proliferation of administrative posts in editorial, staffed by once-journalistically ambitious journalists, whose ambitions now centre more on managerial careers than was previously the case.

To a certain extent the ownership of regional press, as it gradually became more commercially orientated, provided some legitimacy for the continued journalistic domination. Although some newspaper groups continued editorial control from the Centre, others allowed for regional autonomy and this appeared to provide for a continuation of previous practices. Editorial independence was often heralded as a benefit gained from the rationalisation and commercialisation of the press, but such independence was conditional on the newspaper being profitable. This would mean an editorial that appealed to all, and offended no-one, particularly potential advertisers. Editorial was not controlled, rather its independence had strictly defined limits, which were increasingly being set by those commercial departments which had the authority to do so, an authority legitimised by the ideology of publication held by the proprietor. There is an irony inherent here, for whilst such changes to commercial ownership would eventually destroy any editorial freedom the notion of editorial independence with its double-edged meaning, explains the faily quick and successful introduction and acceptance of commercialism.

This is reflected in the grudging acceptance of commercialism by editorial managers, particularly those with experience of pre-commercial days, at Centre A. The Deputy Sports Editor (morning) said, 'It's all financial now, but that's the way it has to be. I suppose we've got to make money.' The Assistant Editor (morning) felt there was a need to be 'commercially aware', whilst the Night Editor thought that commercialisation was 'a necessary fact of life'. The News Editor (morning) saw the dependence on advertising as 'a fact of life, with really little alternative', although the Features Editor (evening) whilst seeing commercialisation as a problem, particularly with regard to the spending of money by the editor, felt he now had more scope, if only because extra advertising had given more room to editorial. The legitimacy of the status of editorial can only be upheld if all departments have a belief in the tradition of strong editorial. In pre-commercial days this was fairly evident, but afterwards the regional commercialists questioned the authority of editorial to determine the structure and nature of the organisation. In the earlier period the editor was very much in control of the activities of other departments, in that they functioned for editorial. The areas of interchange between editorial and other departments were controlled by editorial, as they had traditionally done so, and there was no one to question this state of affairs. Post-commercialism the authority of editorial to dominate other departments was questioned, so therefore was the tradition. The perceptions of the advertisement, circulation, administrative managers towards the status of the editorial department was now distinctly different from those of the editorial managers. These other department managers wanted to control their own departments, and even question the editorial contribution to the success of the firm. The commercial managers defined success in a different kind of way to editorial, profit against news in a clash of ends, which leads to a conflict of means to ahcieve those ends.

4.6 THE PERCEPTION OF THE COMMERCIAL MANAGERS

To a commercial manager in a newspaper organisation success is defined as a healthy return on capital invested, which involves maximising revenue and cutting costs to the minimum needed to produce a saleable product. That product must have sufficient quality to maximise sales, or alternatively there may be a trade-off point between the level of quality of the product and the number and quality of sales, the latter being most important, because of advertising revenue. The amount of 'quality' is perceived by editorial as being necessarily high, whereas the commercial manager could only justify such a high input given the type and number of sales. Thus editorial becomes a cost to be controlled. Moreover, the commercial manager begins to define the areas of required journalistic input, which is an input and is not the central aspect of the organisation, and is an input that can be bureaucratically managed.

The commercial manager views a newspaper organisation as being no different in structure or management style to any other organisation.

TABLE 4.IO

ANSWERS TO THE QUESTION: DO YOU THINK NEWSPAPERS NEED A DIFFERENT KIND OF ORGANISATIONAL/MANAGEMENT STRUCTURE BECAUSE OF THE NATURE OF THE PRODUCT?

	Yes	No	Undecided
Editorial	64.3%	I4.3%	2I.4%
Advertising	9.7%	7I.0%	I9.3%

The above table is significant in that 7I.0% of advertising managers who saw the production of a newspaper as not dissimilar to the production of any other manufactured goods. Typical comments were, 'That it is a newspaper is irrelevant; the managerial standards or style is no different.' (Personnel Officer), and 'The system of organisation and management is good for any industry as far as I know.' (Production Manager).

The one function that is notably different from other industries is of course editorial, which in many ways can be viewed as the research and design end of the organisation, however, there is one major difference. With a car or similar manufactured product, the research and design process is fairly long and complicated, and produces a blueprint which can then be copied in thousands or perhaps millions. Although a research and design team are constantly working, their perceived output occurs only once, say every five years, whereas with a newspaper the research and design occurs every day. Many studies have shown how research and design teams are ignored or ostracised by other managers from the main organisation (7) and while this is not too detrimental to some organisations in the short term, as integration is perhaps only needed once every five years, the editorial department has to be totally integrated every day. It is also a costly item and therefore needs control in the terms of the commercialist. However the nature of journalistic input according to the journalist is not capable of the type of commercial control envisaged by the commercial manager. For instance, although the commercial manager recognises the importance of news, he sees nothing magical or artistic in its gathering, interpretation or presentation. Once perhaps, managers in newspapers were motivated by competition, in exclusivity and late news (scoops) however such scoops are comparative, and not absolute. To obtain a scoop, news is gathered exclusively, or interpreted from a new angle, always in relation to what other newspapers have done or are doing. Where competition disappears, so does the scoop. For regional newspapers the day of the scoop has passed.

Thus news gathering, according to the commercial manager, can become ordered and even governed by strict rules. The hectic sprint for the scoop is replaced by the orderly dissemination of the news from regular and certain sources. Thus news in the main can be efficiently collected from the institutions such as the courts, council meetings, police stations etc., and from the 'wire' (news agencies), and to a large extent this is'static news' which requires no large journalistic staff to acquire it. Indeed there is no competition to be first or even totally up-to-date, for news that is not reported, of whatever significance, is not news because it is not reported. It may become news the next day and because there is no competition, it is seen by the readers to be up-to-date.

Non-institutional news can still be reported but the commercial managers' demand for it is low, if it exists at all. This is for several reasons. If the paper has sufficient news from institutional sources, then there will be no need or room for further news stories, which are costly in time and manpower, a cost which is not offset by any significant improvement in the newspaper. For instance where saturation selling exists, there can be no increase in sales revenue. And the type of news reported in this way will not increase advertising revenue, either because the news story in its investigative way, is anti-commercial, that is, it may show up the 'unacceptable face' of capitalism or the council. Or alternatively, if extra advertising is collected, the cost of producing that advertising either outweighs or is significantly costly to obviate the revenue gained. This is because of increased overtime to obtain the advertisement, to print it and the cost of the paper, which is needed for any accompanying editorial. (8)

Thus the commercial manager when asked about the artistic input of journalists was either derogatory or talked of the unrealities of newspapers. Many mentioned the mythology surrounding journalism,

> 'Once you have removed the mystic of journalism the making and selling of a newspaper involves the same function as making or selling anything else.' (Managing Director)

> 'There is too much of the newspaper mystic. Its purely a manufacturing operation, with editorial just one of the raw materials.' (Assistant to the Production Manager)

One Accountant even suggested that their work output be monitored as he maintained that the 'output of journalists has not been questioned. They have been given the aura of the academic too long. They need to be put in their place, to be able to produce something.'

The previous chapter remarked on how editorial were pre-eminent in pre-commercial newspapers. The Key Accounts Manager in Centre (A) commenting on the pre-commercial pre-eminence of editorial thought that this tradition, which had led to editorial insulating themselves from other departments, was hampering the development of a fully effective organisation. He continued

> 'The results are good so I suppose we are an effective organisation. But we need team spirit - it very much depends on individuals. Newspapers are usually departmentalised, full of insular groups. I think this may be due to editorial for historical reasons, in that they always in the past thought of themselves as the number one department. But now the emphasis is to commercialism - a changeover to produce money. We've been profitable, but we've spent a lot as well. We need to stay and consolidate. In fact you'll find many editors making good commercial managers - we have some in this building.'

Apart from a few managers with a curt affirmative answer, most disagreed with the last comment of the Key Accounts Manager. Typical of the answers was this from the Deputy Production Manager at Centre (B),

> 'Its a big mistake to promote editorial staff to senior management positions. Its evident from events here. Editors are naive in the ways of the world. They're not interested in the commercial side of the job - they're a race apart - reporters are just not aware of, or involved, with the pressures of commercial life.'

The news editor (evening, Centre A) thought along somewhat different lines, 'If a journalist becomes a successful manager, presumably he would have become a manager in the first place.' However he did concur

> 'A manager's job is completely foreign to an editor - although we do have management courses. For instance I do not think in terms of ordering, say, thirty-four

reps about. If I became an A.M.D. I would have to learn the job. This is wrong, I should be tip-top at the start. Why should the paper have men learning the job?'

These comments reflect the isolation of editorial mentioned by the Key Accounts Manager. Indeed many editorial managers welcomed this isolation because little control could be exercised, although many of them were blinkered in their outlook towards the rest of the organisation. Most, for instance, as reported in chapter one, were in ignorance of the function of the personnel department, and had limited knowledge of the workings of other departments. The Assistant Editor (evening, Centre A) thought 'reporters ought to spend more time in production - then they might understand problems in that dpeartment.' Others thought this ought to be reciprocal, that the rest of the organisation shoudl understand how editorial works. Some, however, were adamant such communication was unnecessary. In answer to the question, 'Do you think it would be better to know more about other departments' the Sports News Editor (Centre A, evening) said, 'There's no real need, as they do not affect the job. Anyway people tend to keep in their own departments.' The Key Accounts Manager (Centre A) was worried over contacts with editorial. 'Communication, this is where the insular bit comes in. Little communication with editorial, nothing formal ... in fact I've never had a meeting with them. This will have to change.'

This was worrying to some commercial managers because with such isolation the exigencies of editorial could not be controlled. The areas of interchange are gradually controlled by commercial managers, but to end the isolation of editorial some areas of interchange had to be developed. One such area is that between editorial and display advertising. At the time of interviewing, relationships here were informal, (along with the wishes of editorial) but the Display Advertising Manager at Centre (A) wanted to formalise them,

> 'We have meetings with editorial, but they're informal rather than formal. Now I know and respect editorial independence, but you cannot have complete editorial freedom. We need more co-operation at senior level between editorial and commercial. We should have a type of committee, this should be more formalised - most decisions are made informally after informal discussions with various departments but we need the official rubber stamp.'

The evidence given in this section is from a period or decade after the introduction of regional commercialism. Two observations, first the comments of the commercial manager were fairly extreme, suggesting that their view of the early 1960's (when editorial dominance was more prevalent) would have been more extreme. Second, this perhaps can be tempered by suggesting that by the time of the interviews 1972-75, they saw themselves as sufficiently powerful to fully, rather than partially, control the activities of the journalists.

4.7 CONCLUSION

It is now obvious that there is a conflict of views as to how a newspaper enterprise should be organised. The ability of either viewpoint to be interpreted into action depends on the basis of authority to make decisions affecting the performance of editorial and non-editorial departments. The analysis of this conflict can be interpreted in two ways, both inter-related. First, continuing in the spirit of Weberian analysis, the conflict develops between traditional authority and rational-legal authority as a basis to organise the newspaper. This can be couched in terms of areas of interchange which become areas of uncertainty, as each department attempts to control such areas. Before commercialism these areas are controlled by editorial with an emphasis on flexibility where rule-breaking is the norm, whereas afterwards there is a development of an ethic of commercial efficiency with an emphasis on rules with strict adherence. The areas of interchange now become areas of uncertainty as flexibility vies with rigidity as the conflict of the sources of authority develops. As the commercialists gain control, so the imposition of rules in these areas of interchange begin to shape the activities of the journalists. The emphasis on the rigid adherence to more and more rules is reinforced by the quick succession of managers, who add to the rules to, in part, justify their own position. Newspapers eventually, and perhaps inevitably, become bureaucratic organisations.

> 'The development of the modern form of the organisation of corporate groups in all fields is nothing less than identical with the development and continual spread of bureaucratic administration.' (Weber, 1947, p. 337)

The second approach to this development of bureaucracy arises because of doubts expressed in the first way. Organisational goals, departmental goals, boundary interchanges, environmental determination, etc., all seem elements of a systems approach to organisation theory. This then leaves the investigator open to the familiar criticism of reification and homeostatsis, the concentration on eventualities and not process, the neglect of people and their perceptions which form reality etc. To overcome these objections the argument is developed in terms of power, the ability of one person, or a group of persons to inflict their will on others and thus divert their action.

This avenue is arrived at in other ways. For Weber legitimacy to authority within organisations came from three sources. To him this authority was only one form of power, that commands or instructions would automatically be obeyed, because of charisma, of traditional or because of legality of rules. Where this authority is challenged a fuller discussion of power is required. In many ways the areas of interchange are areas of power struggles. This power can be treated in a variety of ways but briefly in relation to newspapers, the editor for instance will have some kind of power within his own department, and outside his department in controlling the activities of others. The two are related, but the problem remains for the commercial managers who may easily regain control within their own department, but are they powerful enough to control editorial, and if so, how do they achieve such control.

NOTES

(I) Figures in the tables in the text following this note refer to changes in the regional press from the pre-commercialist period to the post-commercialist era and stop at the mid-I970's when the commercial changes have for the most part been completed. Changes after this time whilst resting on similar methods were concerned with the introduction of new technology.

(2) The Leamington, Warwick, Kenilworth and District Morning News has no evening paper in competition and is published by Courier Press (Holdings) Ltd. in Leamington Spa. The Irish News and Belfast Morning News published by Irish News Ltd., with a circulation of 57,000 is in competition with the News Letter published by Century Newspapers Limited, (75,000) The latter company also have a Sunday newspaper, The Sunday News (97,000) and The Thomson Organisation publish an evening newspaper, The Belfast Telegraph (I86,000).

(3) For a fuller discussion see Chapter 7 and also R. Boston, I970 p. II ff.

(4) This was found to be 40% of the production payroll in a survey of four national newspapers undertaken by Personnel Administration Limited, in February I962, for the Royal Commission on the Press I96I-2, see report p. 220. In the regions 40% would probably be on the high side because it was generally thought that overmanning etc. was not so prevalent.

(5) In particular see B.W. Rucker: The First Freedom. See also F.W. Rucker and H.L. Williams: Newspaper Organisation and Management and B.W. Rucker: Newspaper Circulation: What, Where and How.

(6) Examples can be found in

M.L. De Fleur:	: Theories of Mass Communications
J.D. Halloran	: Control or Consent
M. Janowitz	: The Community Press in an Urbansetting
L.A. Dexter/ D.M. White	: People, Society and Mass Communications.

(7) See in particular, C. Perrow: A. Framework for the Comparative Analysis of Organisation, American Sociological Review I967; Homans: The Human Group, ch. I6; Burns and Stalker: The Management of Innovation; G.F. Thomason: The Management of Research and Development; R. Likert: The Nature of Highly

Effective Groups in New Patterns of Management NY I96I.
N.R.F. Maher, J.J. Hayes: Creative Management.
H.W. Gabriel: Techniques of Creative Thinking for Management; Tunstall: Journalists at Work.

(8) See G. Cleverley: The Fleet Street Disaster; Chap 2.

5 Ideology, mobility and bureaucracy

5.1 THE AREAS OF INTERCHANGE

The editorial department is only part of a larger media organisation, the newspaper, and although they perceive themselves as the central activity, with all other functions being service departments to allow them to print the news, they naturally must have relationships with these other departments. Recognition of this will lead to an investigation as to the nature of those relationships, as well as to who controls them. It is this communication between departments which is called the areas of interchange, and as this analysis is concerned with the commercialisation of the regional press, which involves the demise of editorial dominance, only those interchanges between editorial and other departments will be considered.

The other departments can be broadly conceived of as advertising (classified and display), circulation, production, accounts and personnel. Prior to 1960 classified advertising was a separate function and personnel did not exist. For instance, in Centre A, in 1959 (See Table 5.1) there was no personnel department (only introduced in 1964), no classified advertising section, and only seven people working in the display advertising department, and transport for distribution of the paper was considered to be a service function, which could be sub-contracted to an outside firm. At a senior level, interactions between departmental heads in 1959 would be fewer than in 1977. Again at Centre A, in 1959, the two editors would deal only with a works manager and company secretary, whilst in 1970 the editors could deal with five other departmental heads, Production Controller, General Advertising Manager, Personnel and Training Officer, Commercial Controller and the Company Secretary.

TABLE 5.1

PERSONNEL IN CENTRE A 1959 AND 1977

Department	1977 No.	1977 %	1959 No.	1959 %
Editorial	221	23.7	200	32.4
Production	281	30.2	312	50.6
Advertising[(a)]	119	12.8	7	1.1
Circulation[(b)]	138	14.8	30	4.9
Sales Promotion[(c)]	26	2.8	0	0
Accounts	75	8.1	52	8.4
Others[(d)]	71	7.6	16	2.6
Total	931	100.0	617	100.0

NOTES:

(a) This includes classified, display, and advertising administration. 1977 Figures given with 1959 in brackets. Classified 60 (0), Display 45 (5), Advert Administration 14 (2).

(b) This includes transport as well.

(c) Transport in 1959 sub-contracted.

(d) This includes Personnel, Canteen, senior management and establishment (security, labourers, etc.)

Some of the main areas of interchange between editorial and other departments are deadlines for journalists copy (Production), the ratio of news and advertisements (Advertising), the allocation of advertising in the newspaper (Advertising), the recruitment of personnel (Personnel) the control of editorial costs (Accounts), and the type and amount of regional news (marketing and newspaper sales). Each department has an interest in controlling these areas of interchange. For instance if the production department control deadlines, then the work routine within this department is more easily managed. Also if advertising control the advertising/editorial ratio they can maximise current advertising revenue and plan for future advertising revenue. However the ability to control the areas of interchange rests on the authority to do so. The Fleet Street ideology gives editorial pre-eminence, in the sense that newspapers exist because of, and for news, and therefore all other departments are merely service agents for editorial as the ideology in action is demonstrated. Thus the editorial department has the authority to control these areas of interchange, because editorial is necessary for a paper to succeed, and it is therefore rational in the economic sense. Moreover the editorial form of organisation is more informal than formal, more flexible than rigid, and more irrational than rational. The other main departments, accounts and

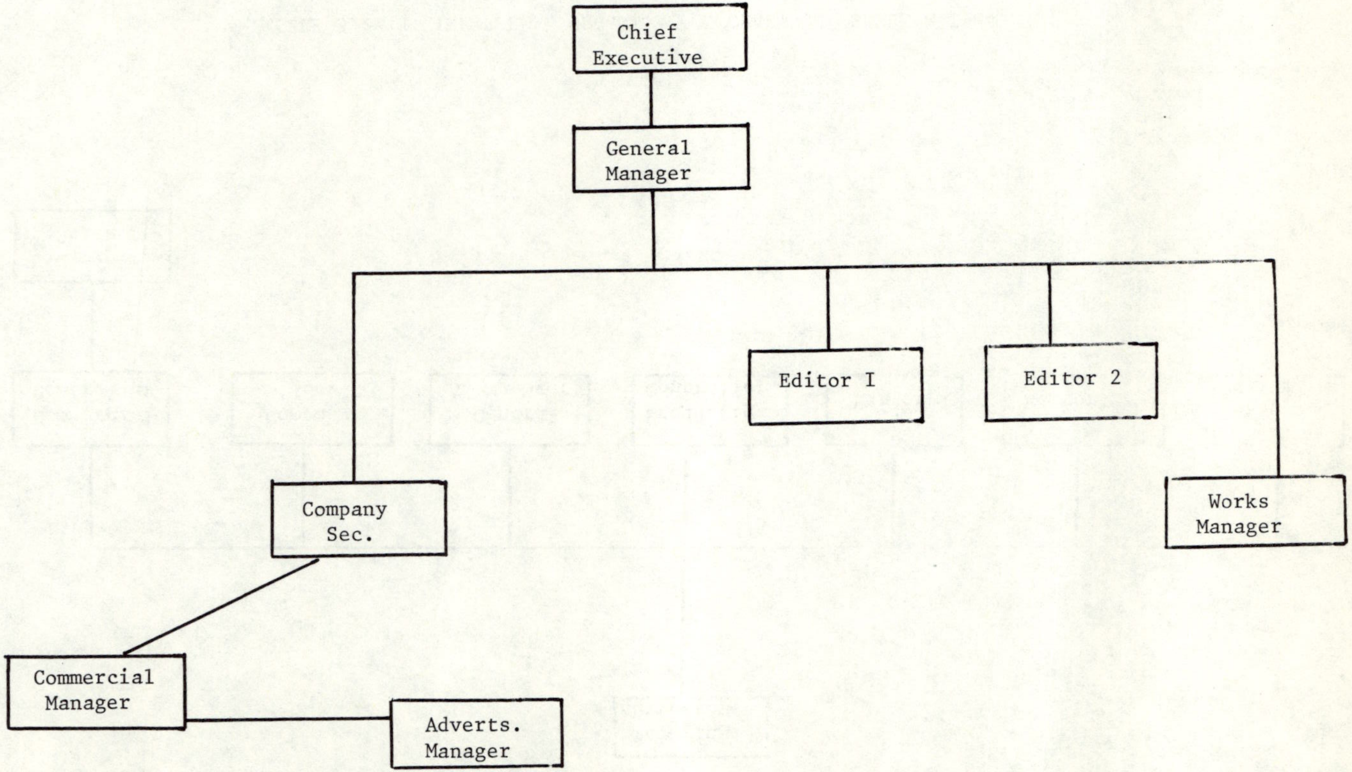

FIGURE 5.I : THE FORMAL ORGANISATION CHART OF CENTRE A PRE-I964.

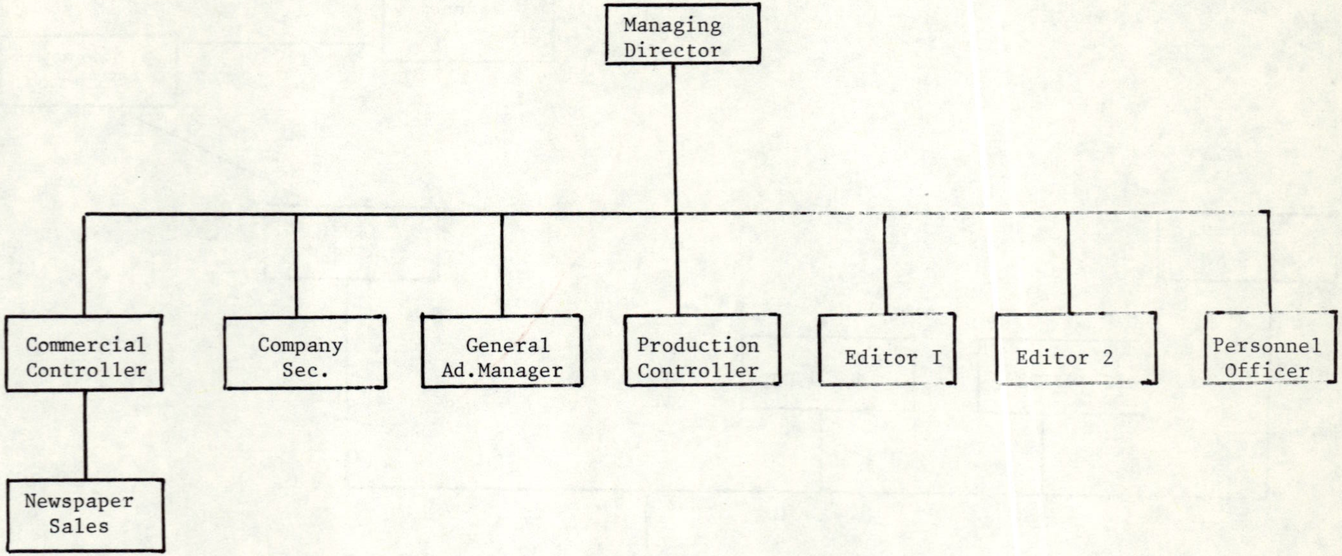

FIGURE 5.2 : THE FORMAL ORGANISATION CHART OF CENTRE A I964-72

production believe in editorial domination, thus reinforcing the editorial authority.

Before 1964 in relation to the organisation chart, several areas of interchange were non-existent because within the Fleet Street ideology some functions (departments) did not have any role in a newspaper enterprise. Thus the recruitment of personnel for editorial is controlled without question by editorial, who decide the criteria for recruitment, and interview or engage personnel without recourse to any other department (apart from overall staffing levels), which in Fleet Street are drafted under the influence of the proprietor. Therefore if editorial require a specialist correspondent, then they engage one if this is necessary for the proprietor to see his ideology in action. In the regions the traditional authority of the editor or publisher allows him to do the same if and when required. The ability of the newspaper to sell is determined by the actual news content and its presentation. To market a newspaper pre-1959 is a redundant occupation, for it markets itself, and thus there is no interchange between editorial and marketing.

Certainly the production department were physically strong (over 50 per cent of staff in 1959 in Centre A), but one major area of interchange, the deadline is controlled by editorial. Tunstall maintains that deadlines are 'rigidly fixed' (1971, p263) but often this has not been the case when editorial had decided that late news warrants an extension of the deadline. In these cases the production department has to change working practices to get the paper printed at all. There are 'absolute' deadlines beyond which it is not worth printing the paper, because it will arrive at the selling points after most potential buyers have gone. The normal deadlines are set some time before the absolute, and thus some flexibility is catered for. However this flexibility is costly, because it involves changed working practices resulting in increased manpower utilisation over and above that normally required. This has to be paid for and it disproportionately increases costs as the craft unions see editorial enthusiasm combined with the 'absolute' deadline as a strong basis for bargaining. The more it is done the greater the bargaining strength, the higher the bonus, and thus the costlier it becomes to print the newspaper. The assistant production manager (Centre A) was aware of this situation,

> 'There's a tradition here that if there's some big news - the normal points of friction disappear and we get the job done. But the chapel is usually ruthless afterwards to obtain money.'

As mentioned earlier the breaking of deadlines by editorial is an exhibition of their power within the organisation, and the more they do this the greater their power, seen both by themselves and others, especially production. It is of course reinforced in this instance of breaking the deadlines, by the pecuniary advantage to the members of the production department. The editorial staffs frequently engage in such exhibitions because they see late news as crucial to the continuing success of the newspaper.

A second reason for the unchallenged authority of editorial from production lies in the status of the works (not production as post-1964) manager. Traditionally he was the time-served craftsman, who has climbed the promotion tree to be works manager by the time he was 60, through the principle of dead man's shoes. Because of his experience the works manager would be imbued with the tradition of editorial supremacy, and would view his department as purely a means to allow editorial to print its news and views. He and his department were servants to the editorial master and perceived no other function. The Assistant to the Production Manager at Centre A summed up the position of his department, 'We are isolated as a department - we are just a service department for Editorial, Advertising and Circulation.' Similarly editorial perceived the production manager, in organisation chart terms, as 'somewhat below the level of the other executive managers.' It was not until the 1970's that production managers were recruited from areas other than the traditional one. This new genre of computer-trained printing specialists had been installed at Centre B in 1967, but not until 1974 at Centre A. Thus the deputy production manager could still say in 1973,

> 'Editorial sometimes try it on, and change page layouts for late editions. This often involved the breaking of deadlines, but its a bit of a battle. I don't know why they do it, after all people only see one edition. I suppose its their self-importance.'

The advertising department in 1959 was numerically and in status, weaker than editorial. Their function was to provide extra revenue for the excesses of editorial, which could be justified by the very ideology of publication. The areas of interchange centre around the ratio of advertising to editorial, the ability to change that ratio, and the placing of advertisements in the paper. It was mentioned earlier that in 1959 the advertising content in Centre A was 6.62 pages (53.7 per cent), whereas overall for regional evening papers it was 6.46 pages (49.07 per cent) (Royal Commission 1962a, p.185) of the total paper on average. This in itself is an indication of the influence of advertising in recent years, as in 1977 the levels were for Centre A, 12.87 pages, (61.3 per cent). Advertising as a function was not developed, because it had not been allowed to, and it is not an unfair assumption to believe that more advertising could have been included in the paper. However if sufficient revenue was accruing, further advertisements would demote the status of the newspaper to that of an advertising manual. Again it may be useful to stress that it is a <u>news</u>paper not an <u>advertising</u> paper, although ironically if advertising had increased then extra editorial would have been allowed.

Thus editorial controlled these areas of interchange between itself and advertising. The ratio of advertisements to editorial was decided by editorial, but of greater importance was the control of the day-to-day ratio, and the physical placement of such advertisements within the paper. For instance, advertising content is normally known a day or days in advance, and it can thus be determined within the newspaper earlier than can the news. The bulk of the latter is only finalised on the day of publication and its quantity will vary. Given a fixed number of broadsheets to fill, it is the level of advertising which has to vary to allow editorial to place within the newspaper the amount of news etc. it alone thinks is necessary. There is a great deal of interchange here, for a newspaper can only expand in either two-page or four-page steps, which means that given a planned 14 page evening paper of roughly 7 editorial and 7 advertising, if on the day of publication editorial requires any increase up to 8 or 8½ it is advertising which has to drop. The Deputy Editor (morning, Centre A) recalled the days of the 1950's when the editor was in control,

> 'In those days the editor decided what went into the paper. If an advertisement was in the way of a big story, it was the advert that went. It's different now.'

The movements are probably of a lower order, however what is crucial is that it is editorial who control this area of interchange. A similar control exists in the area of the placement of advertisements, these being moved to give news and other editorial input a better place on the page make-up. Editorial also determine which advertising-sponsored articles if any are inserted, a distinct difference to the regular 'puff' form of today.

The final important area of interchange pre-1959 exists between editorial and accounts. By the very fact that budgeting did not exist until the middle 1960's suggests that the accounting department, far from controlling, or even monitoring the spending of money in the pursuit of news, merely added up the costs once spent. There was of course an overall spending limit, derived more from commonsense than from cost control, but in the main editorial spent what it thought necessary to produce the newspaper it wanted.

All the areas of interchange were thus controlled by editorial, which results in two complementary sets of influences. First, the staff of the editorial department were not constrained in their activities by the influence of any other department in its activities. The control and management of journalists in their work was directed by the editor, who decided the kinds of ways his department would be organised, which, as has been mentioned, is informal rather than formal, non-routine rather than routine, and flexible rather than rigid. The second set results from the influence of the editorial on all other departments. They control the areas of interchange, which in part reflects on the ability of each department to organise as it seems fit. These influences are the informality, non-routine, flexibility (etc) and act on the departments whose operations are more easily organised, in a rigid, routine, and formal way. Thus accounting which becomes more efficiently organised the more the rules are adhered to, finds several of its rules necessarily infringed by editorial, which requires the accounting department to re-assess many of its principles in its conduct. Thus not having budgets in the editorial area makes nonsense of any strict budgeting, the hallmark of good accountancy. This influence restricting the efficiency of the accounting department and making it operate in certain areas, in ways anathema to its principles, will itself be a cost. Similar influences exist elsewhere, such that advertising may be lost because it is not printed at the right time, in the right place, and of course, that production costs ceaselessly rise. It has been shown that the authority of editorial is legitimised by the 'charismatic' proprietors in Fleet Street, and that strong editorial becomes a feature of all newspaper organisations. Two changes occur post-1959. First already mentioned, the demise of 'press barons' removing the basis of authority for editorial dominance of Fleet Street newspapers, questioning the authority of editorial departments in the regions. Second, the introduction of new leaders with new ideologies, in some cases changing overnight, gives authority to the administrative staffs of the non-editorial departments to act with the assistance of impersonal rules, more commercially, as this is the goal of the leadership. The way these departments act in controlling uncertainty both within and outside their departments clashes with the editorial control based on traditional authority. Post 1959, editorial's authority, if it exists at all, is based on traditional grounds, whilst the non-editorial section by way of rational-legal authority creates a bureaucracy to control uncertainty.

5.2 NON-EDITORIAL AND RULES

The work of non-editorial departments is normally routine, that is few exceptional problems occur which require intuition, experience or personalised knowledge to solve. Where there are exceptional cases the departments or organisations seek to minimise them, by, as Perrow (1967) argues, standardising their raw material. Whilst Perrow is undoubtedly reifying the existence of an organisation as such, his idea warrants investigation. A crucial assumption of his is that the organisation has control of some degree over the raw material it has to process, and relating this to the action of individual members of a department produces some understanding. For instance the raw material of a newspaper organisation could be said to be news (and advertisements), although to individual departments and their members this is not the case. The Accounts department has raw material of budgets, costs and revenue, Personnel of interviewing, Circulation of unsold newspapers etc. To follow Perrow is to follow an open system approach of input, work and output, of environmental determinism, and boundary exchanges, but to do this may misdirect analysis to the raw material, and to its eventual saleable nature, often ignoring the process of the work done on that material, although the type of raw material does influence the type of process that the department uses. It has already been suggested that the perception of editorial work by non-editorial people centres around the myth that journalism is in some way a mystical art. However they feel it can be rationally organised because news can be considered routine, certainly for regional newspapers. These perceptions arise because non-editorial operate themselves in this kind of way, because the material they deal with is capable of being administered in that way. Their work is routine, in that a finite number of rules, which once followed, solve most of the problems that arise. If a problem arises for which there are no rules, then a certain disruption occurs to solve it, which eventually leads to a new rule so that if such a problem occurs again it can be routinely solved, and this is one way in which the department can reduce the exceptional problems.

Another way is to control the incoming raw material. For instance the Accounts department in budgeting expects all other departments to work within the agreed budgets. For editorial this, according to the journalists, is difficult because of the nature of journalist's work. The open system begins to break down as the input for the accounts department is controlled by another, editorial. One wants budgets, the other does not, one wants rigidity and rationality, the other flexibility and informality. It is an impasse, an unresolved conflict, or as the system theorists suggest, an imbalance rectified by the homeostatis process. 'When parts of the system are pulled out of balance, or when some of its essential operations are blocked or threatened, the system reacts and mobilises to restore the system to its prior balance.' (Dalton and Lawrence, 1970, p.292). This unfortunately is of no help, for it cannot be decided what are essential operations' and for whom are they operating? Is the Accounts department to forfeit budgeting or is the editorial department to be under cost control decided by others? What is significant for this argument is the nature of the work process within the accounting and other non-editorial departments, where emphasis is on routine work, the use of rules to govern this routine work and the minimisation of exceptional cases. In short, the rational-legal bureaucracy in the way discussed by Weber, with an emphasis on 'rational solution' for 'efficient administration', and although these terms are rarely defined they are assumed to be certain processes which provide pathways for the attainment of certain ends. To Weber such a bureaucracy was highly functional in allowing the administrative staff to achieve the ends laid down by the leadership. The administrative staff would achieve such ends by impersonal rules, and the members would obey the orders, because of a belief in the legitimacy of the legal authority of the bureaucracy. It must be remembered that the legal authority necessary for the bureaucratic administrative staff to operate is derived from these beliefs in its legitimacy.

This outline describes the growth of a bureaucracy in the non-editorial departments, through the structure of a leadership, an administrative staff and then the members of the organisation, although here it is of more relevance to apply the analysis to departmental level. The leadership of regional newspapers, changed in ideology either because of a physical change of person or because of a realisation of the need for commercialism, embarked on hiring a qualified administrative staff to efficiently administer advertising, classified and display, marketing, personnel, and to re-order production and accounts. They operated from the beliefs mentioned earlier, and were characterised by a rigid set of rules and offices, with hierarchically arranged career patterns. The success of such administrative staff to achieve the commercial ends laid down by the leadership depends in a belief in the legitimacy of such a bureaucracy. Within the non-editorial departments there is little to doubt this belief, however within editorial there could be no belief on such rigid and formal office procedures. Editorial further have little agreement with the stated purpose of the organisation, that of profit-making, apart from the very basic need to survive. Thus there is a conflict on two levels, dependent on each other, one over the process to achieve certain ends, which leads to the second, the ends themselves.

5.3 THE AREAS OF UNCERTAINTY

Interaction between individuals in different departments is more likely to generate conflict than any interaction between members of the same department. Thus the perception of two journalists about how best to produce their desired newspaper will have more common ground than the perception of a journalist and an advertising manager about how to organise a newspaper enterprise. The two journalists will probably agree on the paramount importance of journalism as a necessary art, whilst the commercial man will perceive artistry as unnecessary to the pursuit of, what is to him, the more relevant ends of money and profit. Thus areas of interaction are more likely to be areas of uncertainty when they occur between individuals in different departments than if these individuals were in the same department. Often this becomes an area of uncertainty between departments, and can be justified if it is over an issue where there is consensus amongst the members of each department. For instance the issue of deadlines and their extension may not have the total agreement of all editorial staff. However because the act of breaking through a deadline is a reinforcing exhibition of editorial authority, then the act becomes functional for all journalists.

The analysis in the previous section talked of areas of interchange controlled by editorial. These areas would be perceived by Crozier as areas of uncertainty, even though the analysis here suggests there is one element of certainty, that is, that editorial will control these areas. This could be said to have a degree of stability if the nature of editorial intervention was predictable, and rational. Because the organisational structure within editorial bears neither of these two characteristics, the nature of the editorial intervention must have a high degree of uncertainty. That it is always controlled by editorial is legitimised by the ideology of pre-1959 regional newspapers.

Once the ideology has changed so too does the basis of legitimacy, and thus editorial needs to embark on a search for new sources of legitimacy for them to continue to dominate these areas of interchange. The ideology post-1959 gives legitimacy to the commercialists to improve commericalism. According to Crozier, 'Individuals or groups who control a source of uncertainty, in a system of action where nearly everything is predictable, have at their disposal a significant amount of power over those whose situations are affected by this uncertainty.' (1964, p.192).

Pre-1959 Editorial have a basis of legitimate authority to control these areas, but after 1959 when this base is withdrawn a conflict develops between the authority of editorial and non-editorial. A conflict in many respects over control which for editorial would result in uncertainty but for non-editorial rationality in the form of guidance of impersonal rules. Areas of uncertainty can also be defined negatively by the areas of certainty, or indeed control. For the moment the non-editorial departments are assumed to control their own internal operations, and following Weberian analysis this is not unreasonable, as the administrative staff in their offices have authority to govern by clearly-defined rules. It is also assumed that the administrative staff act with one purpose in mind, as defined by the leadership, through the rules. Thus areas of uncertainty as defined by the non-editorial departments can only arise where either there is a disagreement with the rules, or a situation arises for which there are no rules. The former naturally occurs with editorial, but initially it will be better to discuss the latter.

Pre-1959 it could hardly be said that there was any administrative staff in non-editorial departments, with the two largest in this section, production and accounts being merely service departments. With the change in ideology and leadership provoking a growth of commercial staff, there must have been the development of a system of rules to govern everyday routine situations. Initially the number of rules would be small, but eventually there would be a rule for all conceivable situations, enabling the commercial staff to function efficiently. The growth of rules would occur because of the mobility of managers which is fully examined in the next chapter. However there will be a growth of more rules to deal with unexpected cases, and indeed recurring exceptional cases. With the latter the commercial staff will try to change operations to produce rules to make administration more efficient. Two examples illustrate the point.

i) Advertising may be thought of as an occupation full of non-regular work. For instance the salesman when approaching a potential customer, is of course, unsure if the client will advertise, and if he does, how much, for how long, and in what form. Advertising is determined by the client and will be, from the advertising manager's point of view, irregular. This inhibits efficient planning of the work of the department, and has its effects on the future pagination levels. The work was full of unexpected cases, indeed there were 5,500 separate accounts, most of whom were just selling once a year, incurring high costs purely in liaison with the clients. To regularise this work, the administrative staff changed the routine of work. No longer would the client wholly decide, but now in conjunction with the newspaper's advertising representative who would begin to act in a consultative way, suggesting advertising campaigns, the style of advertising and the days in which to do it. For instance the General Advertising Manager said that many of the infrequent advertisers should really be advertising elsewhere, on billboards, magazines, radio or television. The local press was not maximising the expected return from the advertising. Although the manager thought this would lose some accounts, it was those which were costly to produce anyway, and it would enhance the department's reputation, enabling it to secure greater amounts of profitable advertising in the future. In this way the number of accounts was reduced to 2,500 once a year customers, with 470-80 regular customers. The unexpected cases were reduced, and the expected ones increased. Of course the administration of the latter is easily conducted by a set of impersonal rules.

ii) The second example follows on from the last. The advertising department was gradually 'bureaucratising' the expected cases, but the two departments of classified and display had too many types of cases to administer, so that the amount of rules needed was too high. So re-organisation occurred primarily along the expected and unexpected dimensions. In classified this was achieved by splitting the type of advertiser into regular and irregular, the former being perhaps the local garage, and the latter the householder wishing to sell an item of furniture. The regular accounts are thus easily administered by its set of rules, whilst the irregular accounts have their own rules. In Centre A the evening newspaper had approximately one million potential advertisers, as this was the total population of the circulation area. Assuming a fairly equal distribution of customers throughout the year(1) the administrative staff only have to have a set of rules or pigeon-holes, into which drop the different types of advertising. Thus a call to the newspaper to advertise will begin with the tele-ad girls asking for the category (up to 100 of these), the type of advertisement (blocked, spacing above and below), the days of insertion, and finally the words. By following the rules the different types of advertisements from cars to cabbages, can be efficiently administered.

5.4 MOBILITY AND BUREAUCRACY

A major problem for the regional commercialist is the hiring of an efficient administrative staff to organise the commercial aspects of newspapers in a rational way. Administrative staffs and senior management in many cases had to be hired from outside of newspapers. Naturally they brought the methods from their respective industries, as less than 10 per cent of the non-editorial managers interviewed thought newspapers to be any different from general manufacturing industry. Given this these managers would expect a mechanistic rather than organistic organisational structure. Following Burns and Stalker, they would want stable hierarchical control with specialised work functions, because in the systems terminology, they are operating in what they perceive to be a defined and predictable market. These perceptions are of course different from the editorial members, who see news gathering as non-routine. However, such managers had little experience in newspaper management, something Roy Thomson was aware of,

> '..... experience was a very important element in the management side of business .... for management to be good it generally must be experienced. To be good at anything at all requires a lot of practice, and to be really good at taking decisions you need to have plenty of practice at taking decisions. The more one is exposed to the necessity of making decisions, the better one's decision making becomes.' (1975, p.104).

To obtain the necessary experience senior managers were placed in as many different decision-making situations as possible. This was done by moving the managers either between newspaper centres, or between jobs at the same centre. Thus the non-editorial managers interviewed had had an average of 2.90 posts in the last five years, had been at their centre on average only 5.41 years, and had only been in their present position for 2.10 years. This constant movement of senior managers provides a major continuing problem of succession. Gouldner in one major study has highlighted the characteristics and consequences of such a problem. First Gouldner observes how rules became introduced, and why they became more rigid in enforcement. In investigating the Gypsum mine he discovered at first what he called an Indulgency Pattern, where formal rules had been ignored or only partially observed by the workers in factory and mine, and had been replaced by other rules or norms.

To rectify the situation, the owner, following Weberian terms appointed a new administrative staff. This began with a new plant manager, who immediately replaced some of the supervisors with his own choice of men, who had a specific directive.

> 'The main office personnel who determined his promotion reminded Kean of his predecessor's inadequacies and expressed the feeling that things had been slipping at the plant for some while. They suggested that the old plant manager, Godfrey, was perhaps getting over indulgent in his old age and that he, Kean, would be expected to improve production quotas.' (Gouldner, 1952, p.342).

The pressure on the new manager and his supervisors increases by their perception of their own position. Individually they want to succeed to either maintain their present position, or to obtain future promotion, and they also feel the need to be successful in order to repay the faith placed in them, by those who have promoted them. To succeed in the terms defined these new managers would have to rationalise production methods, and because of their newness and alien nature, that is coming from outside, these new managers would not be aware of any informal system of operation, so therefore to succeed at least initially they had to use the formal channels.

The indulgency pattern was in part characterised by few rules, and even fewer that were strictly enforced. Thus to increase production these non-rational aspects of the organisation would have to be eradicated and more rules would have to be introduced for the manager to achieve these new production targets. This tendency towards a proliferation of rules is reinforced by the managers feeling that their subordinates were unwilling to fill their expected role-obligation, and introducing more rules to achieve such an end. The credibility of these rules, and indeed their successful enforcement depends on their legitimacy. Although seen by managers as legitimate - that they provide for rationality and therefore efficiency, they may not be seen in the same light by those whose work is governed by the rules. There may be a reaction to the rules, the unanticipated consequences of a bureaucracy, outlined by Sleznick, Merton and now Gouldner, which may only produce a need on the part of managers for more rules, thus exacerbating the situation.

5.5 SUCCESSION, MOBILITY AND RULES

Whilst delaying until later a fuller discussion of these unanticipated consequences it is important to note the effects of succession and apply them to newspapers. Gouldner has found that 'a high rate of succession is one mechanism among others, apparently functional for the development of a bureaucratic organisation.' (1952, p.351). It must be added that the succession is of managers, who have the authority to introduce the rules, a bureaucracy developed in pursuit of rationality and efficiency. It occurs because of succession, and in turn allows for succession. The pursuit of efficiency is legitimised by the ideology of publication of the regional commercialist, and this is reinforced by the legitimacy of the rules in that they are rational. The high rate of mobility in the newspaper centres investigated, in the terms of Gouldner, would provide for a highly developed bureaucracy in which informality or indulgency patterns would not have time (2-3 years) to emerge.

The development of a bureaucracy is hastened and reinforced in newspapers in two ways. First, career patterns in the regional newspaper group involved a great amount of physical as well as job movement. Particularly on the commercial side where established management was lacking, the route to experience was achieved, as Thomson said earlier, by being placed in different sets of decision-making situations. The Chief Accountant in Centre A commented on this pattern,

> 'The organisation as a whole is always seeking ways to develop managers. For instance, I feel at present I am only to 60-65% of my potential in controlling my line function. By giving new structures we hope to develop more managers and give them more responsibility. For instance, we had one A.M.D. up to January of this year and several departments involved with that A.M.D. But the organisation is constantly changed and now central office suggests two A.M.D's. This is good practice because an A.M.D. with responsibility for management development, could then become a managing director ... ... sometimes moving managers around helps to avoid a clash of personalities if people are vying for the same senior post. But really its the best way for management development. There may be some ill effects for individual firms such as no forward carrying of responsibility but the whole organisation benefits. There was a shortage of manager material and there was a need for a big development to get away from the previous aristocratic type of management practised by the old proprietors. There's a need for professional management development - to develop themselves - need ability to control, to manage - human relations .... to get the best out of your workers - need a man to motivate his workers to offer promotion and give them pride - this previous to autocratic style. Moving people about helps to create this.'

The Projects Executive, Centre A, was more forthright when asked about the movement of senior managers,

> 'New personnel could impel one to reorganise as one could say that the structure is born out of personalities. This means when people move the organisation changes. For instance, two people here have left and this will allow us to reorganise more effectively, particularly in relation to advertising, circulation and marketing ... All of this moving of managers provides a physical succession. They're all promotions, rarely have sideways movement.'

The fact that career patterns are characterised by this movement suggests that individual managers will not allow any indulgency pattern to emerge. There is a belief in the adherence to rational rules to produce the increased efficiency needed for a manager's further promotion, and along with this strict adherence comes the second reinforcement of bureaucracy. Because career patterns are seen by managers to be constructed around 1½ to 2 year steps, the time to achieve the increased efficiency is naturally short. Thus the manager introduces new rules rather quickly, and enforces them strictly in an effort to be seen to be achieving the increased efficiency.

These two ways lead to a further reinforcing tendency applicable for all succession. The above discussion has been couched in terms of one of the ideal types of imperative co-ordination outlined by Weber, but this is not wholly realistic, as these ideal types are rare in practice. It can be assumed that the base of authority is derived from mixed sources, although primarily the rule orientated bureaucracy. For instance, each new manager will want to 'stamp his authority' on his new department, and whilst he can do this by merely overseeing the enforcement of the existing rules, he may wish to introduce newer, extended or updated rules, that bear his authorship which, as Weber outlined involved the use of expertise, in introducing and enforcing these 'better' rules. However, the outcome is to reinforce bureaucratic patterns of organisation.

The phenomenon of succession is exhibited more in non-editorial than editorial, and indeed for several departments it was the means to physical growth of the department as a bureaucracy. For instance, the appointment of many managers during the 1960's decade would have been the first appointment in such a post, initiating the same tendencies towards formal rule making, even though an indulgency pattern centred on informality could not have existed.

However, with every change of manager came new procedures and working practices, and of course more rules, which were far-reaching, and given the changes in the structure at Centre A, the appointment of new posts led to further rule-making. For many of the advertising managers co-operation with (and indeed control of) certain areas of editorial were essential, and with these changes editorial would have to succumb to many of the wishes of advertising. During the interviewing schedules working practices were constantly changing with, in Centre C the Classified Advertising Manager introducing a third supervisor to increase efficiency, and at Centre B the Circulation Sales Manager developing a home-delivery service in conjunction with normal retail shop outlets. In fact the three centres were geared to successive managers and fresh working arrangements. Even during the time a manager was in one position there was constant pressure to change, to upgrade targets, to cut budgets, to rewrite job specification etc. The Classified Sales Manager at Centre A explained,

> 'My job description is a company one, but I plan in advance the objectives of the department. This is initiated by myself on a monthly basis - I set key tasks for each person and for each department. There are quarterly objectives on revenue for the company and I try to meet these. Therefore my principle objective is a pre-determined level of revenue per quarter. This gives me a basis for

'the budget - and here we can be realistic up to three months. It's significant and manageable - a remarkable consistency.'

For other non-editorial departments, production and accounting, a bureaucracy existed pre-1959, but with the introduction of new managers, new working practices and the associated rules were introduced. At Centre A the Chief Accountant changed the internal structure just after his appointment.

'The organisation of my department before I arrived was terrible, with thirteen section leaders reporting to me. I used family trees or organisation charts so everyone knew their position and to whom they had to report. We changed in one day, and had job descriptions as well ... ... In many ways the growth and development of the company and the office are linked to this changeover.'

When asked to explain further he continued,

'Well the office was taken as the scapegoat for much of what was happening or going wrong. The previous man's ideas of structure were so far behind. He had no pride and there was a great level of turnover. The new system was explained department by department .... we checked the flow system, and worked through departments very gradually. Now the conditions are much better and there is a change of atmosphere.'

In fact these changes heralded the start of more precise and, rigidly held to, budgets, one of the rules of interchange, and the subject of a later section.

Two years later a new Revenue Accountant was appointed and his changes were no less drastic. He even convinced the Chief Accountant of a further reorganisation.

'When I arrived I wasn't satisfied with the organisation chart given to me, so I changed it to the present. I had to persuade the Chief Accountant, he isn't a systems man, and at first objected, but since we've had this better system he was very grateful. In fact I'm a systems man. With systems you check prices before you order then to supervisor 2 - buy here we are six days behind in checking the day's ads, ledging the accounts, sending off etc - 6 days!'

When asked about the advantages he said,

'The salary structure has gone down, and the whole department is now running under the budget allowed. We changed the basic system from mechanical accounting, this had led to 180 hours of overtime per week, and we have reduced stationery costs by stopping duplicating. Now by the end of the day we are on top of the day's paper, and have finished ledging accounts. The January figures are out by the 5th Feb. for example.'

This manager was due for promotion very soon and began to outline the changes he would introduce.

> 'First I would introduce micro-filming for invoicing. We need them with V.A.T. and save all invoices for three years instead of one year - we have 800 invoices a day. Then the Customs and Excise can see the company every three years. Second we need mini-computers. This is justified by a report which stated that these would save £7,000. I know there may be union opposition, but any job loss can be achieved by natural wastage.'

To complete the picture, a third senior accountant talked of the changes he would like to make.

> 'This department is top heavy. There is no need for five senior accountants, two would suffice, together with efficient section leaders. For instance if I was Company Secretary I would not have a Deputy Chief Accountant, nor an Assistant Company Secretary. One of us is redundant but effectively I do his job. Technically the Company Secretary could operate this simple operation with only secretarial assistance - with four people reporting to him - The Revenue Accountant, the Management Information Officer, the Wages Supervisor, and someone in charge of secretarial duties.'

During the interviewing schedule this manager was promoted to Chief Accountant in Centre B, where he immediately began to put these ideas into operation.

In production the work routines are heavily loaded with rules; however, there is an exception - that the printers have organised themselves sufficiently strongly to have an immense influence on the making of the rules, and as a consequence production has largely been overlooked in having a high mobility of managers, that is until the 1970's decade. The typical production manager pre-1970 was the time-served craftsman who by a series of 'dead-mens shoes' promotion found himself at a late stage in his carrer, as production manager. Far from introducing any changes he is so engrossed in the ways of the department he actively seeks to preserve them. In Centre B there were changes in the status and role of the production manager because of the new technology, and his importance is discussed under deadlines in Chapter six. At Centre A a new production manager had been appointed, at the time of the change in official organisation structure, and had begun to introduce new rules to gain control of the production process itself, 'Control is in the hands of the overseer, although a joint control with him and the FOC (father of the chapel), of course the overseer is official and the FOC is unofficial - it was the latter who was gaining ground before I came, we are slowly reversing the position.' He saw his immediate tasks in achieving this reversal as first to change the wage structure, and second to change the equipment to photo-composition, which would involve a new list of procedures and rules as it was a change in technology. Although the bulk of this change occurred after the interview schedule, the wage structure had begun to be tackled by the new manager,

'We have a P.A. scheme in operation here to measure performance, but it is now six or seven years old and most of the times and schedules have fallen by the wayside. With new methods introduced there had been no retiming due to the chapel putting pressure on the management, and therefore the times remained very loose. The men have a £30 minimum, now if you have a superman he can get a bonus of 165-66 which will add £20 to his packet. Now because of loose times all our men are on 166 with a practical guarantee minimum of 165. As we have a labour shortage about another £25 overtime making up to £75 in earnings.'

'Now I want to change to a group incentive scheme. We have stopped the measurement now and are negotiating the basis of a new one. What I propose to do is take out £20 of 165 and give them a basic of £40, and have part of that £10 as a bonus - for instance getting the paper to print on time every day. This will balance cost and stabilise things because an individual scheme during the changeover to photo-composition will see men back to basic as they retrain for the new job. Therefore it must be introduced before the new technology.'

As a preparation for the new technology he had accelerated the five-year plan. 'I have contacted the corporate production controller over the five-year plan. I had to rectify the plan to push photo-composition through, after seeing that with present labour force we could not expand our volume through composition. I would need 20 extra men with conventional equipment.' Further changes were envisaged outlined by the Assistant to the Production Manager, who had also been recently appointed,

'In twelve to eighteen months we are introducing new technology. We have to because of the growth in advertising. It will also cut down overtime - we have very high-earnings because of overstaffing. It will be the most up-to-date equipment, and will make our department more versatile - particularly in handling advertising and different news for different regions. Deadlines will also have to be sorted out.'

The outcome of this analysis is to demonstrate the increasing bureaucratisation of most of the non-editorial departments, whose managers abhor non-rational methods of work organisation, of the type that the journalists used to control the areas of interchange, and it is to the rationalisation of these that the analysis now turns.

5.6 THE CONTROL OF EDITORIAL WORK PATTERNS

In many ways the following discussioncould be sub-headed the management of artistic workers, the definition of which is very wide, ranging from the artist per se to the person working with irregular material. It is the latter end of the spectrum which is of concern here, and Perrow's (1967) notion of 'exceptional cases' and the search process, delineated by March and Simon (1963) to deal effectively with such cases, seem of relevance. The management of such workers has been the central aspect of several studies, in particular Arensburg and McGregor (1942), Burns and Stalker (1961) and Thomason (1970). The first two studies are concerned with the integration of creative workers (Design engineers and research and development staff respectively) with the rest of the organisation, and how their work is controlled by the managerial staff. Such workers often having work of an exceptional nature, and needing informal rather than formal procedures to carry out such work, create a problem for the rationally orientated manager or executive. For him the more formal, and the more rigid, become the more rational, and thus the work process is more efficient in achieving his defined aim, but the nature of exceptional work does not generally fit such a bureaucracy. There is little problem if both managers and 'artistic' workers agree on the nature of the work, but conflict naturally occurs when each perceives the nature of the work differently. The outcome from this is that if a company has to handle exceptional cases to survive a different organisational structure and management style will be required than if cases are routine, and the relative importance of perceived definitions of the exceptional cases will produce survival at different levels. In many ways this may be a discussion of the power of one group to enforce its views on another.

In regional newspapers the editorial departments treated the development of vast commercial areas as virtually necessary for increased revenue to maintain editorial contributions. However, once established the commercial departments which perceived editorial work capable of rationalisation for efficiency, began to use their authority to control the areas of interchange. The non-editorial then attempted to regulate the work of the editorial department, and thus rather than a process towards organic styles of management and organisation it is a movement towards a mechanistic one, following the terms used by Burns and Stalker. It is very much a case of perception of different departments of the level at which survival can be achieved, and further, as mentioned earlier, the authority for one set of views to be more important in decision-making than any other set. In this way editorial who view news and the vast deliberation in its collection and presentation as important, have little authority derived from the ideology of publication, whilst non-editorial do. Of course, their perception of the nature of news and its collection centre on ideas of rationality. For them a newspaper has to have news, but the monopoly position suggests that for them the news is different.

First, an analysis of news will reveal that it occurs in the main from a set number of institutions, diary events or regular occurrences. When a newspaper is in competition these types of news are open to all either from a reporter or from a news agency. The newspapers, to exhibit their differences and individuality, have to report something unusual based on these sources (follow-up, in-depth survey, etc.) or report on events outside of these sources. A distinction can be made between the two types of sources, and using Tunstall's words they are routine and non-routine, or in Perrow's terminology expected or unexpected. Where a newspaper is in a monopoly position the question of differences or individuality does not arise, except in relation to national morning newspapers or local radio and television. The national newspapers are not competitors for regional news, and local television and radio has normally to work within prescribed budgets. Further, newspapers can deliberate on regular expected news far more than can a radio or television news broadcast. News can thus be redefined, in the commercialist terms, as emanating only from regular and expected sources. Any other news outside of this area either is not news because it is not reported, or is communicated to the newspaper by a member of the public or police, etc., and it thus falls into the regular and expected category. The notion of the scoop is now redundant. The scoop is a relative not absolute term, in that exclusivity is no longer required where competition has been virtually eliminated. Indeed, it could be said that all news is exclusive and all items of news are scoops.

The collection of news can be rationalised, although part of the news will have to be presented sufficiently well to maintain a higher enough level of sales to justify advertising. Thus, non-editorial, particularly advertising, do not perceive the nature of editorial work as artistic, needing flair and intuition, and requiring a flexible informal style of management and organisation. The Display Advertising Manager at Centre A exemplified this opinion when asked about the nature of a newspaper business. 'It's not a unique business at all. The time element is merely a constraint with which we work. I would not accept this unique theory, it is merely that decision-making is done much more quickly. Other businesses have to work within other constraints.' The Manager was then asked if he felt there were any differences in the method of organisation and management between editorial and non-editorial departments. 'There are to a certain extent. There is some conflict between editorial and commercial. This I think stems from the fact that editorial make the paper and the commercial side sell it. And it is bad if the commercial side has little or no influence on the style of the paper.' However, perceiving editorial work is not the same as controlling it and non-editorial, although having authority via the ideology of publication, to achieve efficiency in pursuit of profit, do not have power to run editorial departments, but they do have the authority to make decisions in the areas of interchange.

Tunstall conceives of these areas of interchange being as Crozier describes the areas of uncertainty with parallel power relationships, 'Just as the non-routine editorial (or design) department, by redesigning the product so frequently, influence what happens in the encompassing media organisation, this relationship operates in two directions. The routine media organisation with its production, distribution, and finance problems requires that the non-routine organisation arrange its operation to meet very rigid deadlines.' (1971, p.28-9). Tunstall is talking of the national media which as earlier chapters have indicated is in the throes of traditionalism, but in the regions the strength of the non-editorial department in status and in numbers has substantially increased during the 1960's, for such areas of interchange to be characterised by increasing commercial dominance.

The process to achieve this dominance has been by the introduction of rules to govern these interchanges. Earlier it was indicated that the internal workings of non-editorial departments has been bureaucratised, and that the succession of managers has given a boost to the proliferation of rules which are dicatated by efficiency criteria, and are rigidly enforced by those commercial departments whose authority is legitimated by the prevailing ideology. An organisation of whatever kind requires some co-ordination between the activities of members of different departments, for after all, activities are organised because they are inter-dependent. To distinguish between the rules governing the activities of members in one department with those of another, with a further distinction covering the rules governing the interchanges may be too precise. Even though rules, by their very nature will apply to certain activities, they will have influences on the activities of others. For instance, a rule in the accounts department concerning deadlines of costing requirements, will have an effect on other departments. In editorial this will mean the preparation of a budget, which may not seriously affect the working of the department, as one person (the Deputy to the Editor) will merely be assigned the task, and thus an accounts rule has some influence elsewhere.

A rule concerning an area of interchange, for instance, the deadline of editorial copy for certain pages, could be changed and moved earlier allowing a more even distribution of work in the production department. This will have great affect on the operation of the work of editorial, for some re-organisation will be necessary to produce the required copy much earlier. Either the editor decides that yesterday's unused copy can be used (he uses extra material), or he alters work routines to provide up-to-the minute copy. The former two are easier decisions to make, as the latter involves taking journalists away from collection of news, something he will find hard to do. One thing however is certain, he will not get increased staff.

5.7 THE SIGNIFICANCE OF INTERCHANGE

Interaction between two parties, for example over deadlines, involves some benefits for both, although in pre-commercial days areas of interaction were not characterised by this mutual benefit exchange except in the sense that editorial needed, say a production department to print and publish its news, and in this way the editorial department exercised its authority in any dealings with production, and indeed other departments. With a change in ownership and/or emphasis in the objective of newspapers, the nature of these areas of interchange alters. With a changing economic environment, where advertising and sales revenue are decreasing, and paper, ink and labour costs are rising, the newspapers have to either close or rationalise their budgeting to achieve survival, and within this framework editorial can no longer use all other departments as service agents for its purpose. Editorial only exists because advertising has increased and advertising exists not so much because of editorial, but because, given a minimal editorial input a survival can be assured at a high level of profitability.

Thus there is a relationship of dependency between commercial and editorial departments, but, however, the relationship has limits, in that editorial is necessary but only to a certain level of scope and depth. By itself it cannot survive, for it cannot generate enough sales revenue, and indeed advertising revenue (without some advertising drives) to exist. In isolation it can increase the price of the paper but this will decrease sales, and it can reduce staff, and thus reduce the editorial quality or quantity (again decreasing sales.) The editorial department has thus to eventually recognise the dependence on advertising, and this belief becomes another source of legitimacy for the authority of commercial departments to regulate affairs of the newspaper. A similar position exists for advertising, in that as a department it needs an editorial format within which to place its advertisements. The advertising managers do not perceive their function as a service one to allow editorial to continue domination, for they believe their effort is central to the new objectives of commercialism and profit. The prevailing ideology gives credence to their authority to introduce commercial methods, a change of balance as the Classified Advertising Manager, Centre A remarks, 'Advertising has saved the paper, particularly classified. Without it there would be no morning for certain.' Thus the newspaper primarily exists because of advertising, not to provide a news service.

The commercial managers are faced with regulating editorial work and its associated costly activities. However, journalists are one group where their present size, importance and power is not legitimised by other groups, in particular the commercial side from which senior management is primarily drawn. Moreover,commercial management cannot control the internal activities of editorial simply because an editorial input is required and commercialists are not capable of undertaking this function. Indeed, part of commercial philosophy is to use experts where needed, thus justifying use of journalists to produce the editorial input, although this has to be controlled, and more important the manner of its collection needs some rationalisation. There is a further argument grounded in the widely accepted notion of freedom of the press. Whilst the definition of freedom is undoubtably restrictive in this instance, it suggests that the editor and his staff in gathering and presenting the news should do so independently of the influence or authority of others, a position supported by the law and reiterated by one of the editors interviewed. Both arguments, editorial dominance to provide news, and commercial rationality for survival, find legitimacy in the theories of the press outlined in Chapter three, but the commercialists have the authority and have to rationalise and control work activities of journalists.

The first move to control occurs in these areas of interchange. Previous to commercialism, flexibility and informality governed them, with rules, if they did exist, being regularly broken. Therefore, the control of such areas, in regard to editorial, is first to rigidify the adherence to the existing rules, and second to introduce more rational rules in the pursuit of efficiency. The first occurs merely because of the introduction of commercial managers bent on rationalisation, and for whom the adherence to rules is essential if organisational efficiency is to be achieved. The second set of rules occurs from the phenomenon of succession.

The types of rules can be ordered into four categories. First, those that regulate the flow and nature of work that occurs because of the environment within which the organisation is located. Second, there are rules which order the work processes, primarily within a department. Third, rules are introduced to control the areas of interchange, although this is dependent on the authority to introduce such rules. Finally, given the corporate/plant organisation pattern of the newspaper under study (and indeed of industry in general), there are rules generated from corporate level to be introduced at plant level. These are very impersonal, but add to the increasing bureaucratisation of newspapers. Rules that are introduced may fall into more than one category, in that whilst they are rules to control certain activities, by doing so they affect working arrangements elsewhere. For instance, rules of interchange will almost always affect working arrangements in various departments and require a re-appraisal of the rules governing such work. The introduction of budgets by the Accounts department, requires editorial, (and other departments) to keep spending within required limits. This rule of interchange however, affects the operation in the editorial department in that each section has to regulate and control its spending.

The advertising/editorial ratio, controlled by advertising also affects the internal workings of editorial. The amount of news to be published is determined by the amount of advertising available, and as advertising varies with the day of the week so must news, which means that the editor and other editorial managers must be fairly precise in arranging job rotas to collect sufficient news to fill the space available. Further, the relative balance of regular to irregular news stories or reactionary to investigatory reporting is altered because of the advertising/editorial ratio. When a large amount of editorial is required then regular and expected news will have a higher proportion than if only a small amount of editorial is required. However, it may be that job rotas are altered to provide the same regular/irregular balance each day. What is certain is that the interchange rule of advertising/editorial ratios, affects and perhaps introduces rules in the editorial department to govern internal working arrangements, and to regulate the flow and nature of work that occurs because of the environment. The following section therefore considers some interchange rules, but perhaps of more importance assesses their effects on working arrangements, and the rules that have to be introduced there as a consequence.

NOTES

(1) This is not an unreasonable assumption, for different categories of classified advertisements vary in opposite ways in relation to economic conditions or the times of the year.

6 The rules of interchange

6.I INTRODUCTION

The informality and flexibility of the editorial style of organisation derives from the nature of journalistic work which is non-routine, centred around exceptional cases, needing some form of flair to accomplish the collection and presentation of the news in an acceptable form, a view however not held by the commercialists. For instance, the accountant at Centre B remonstrated when asked about the flair or artistic nature of the journalists' work.

> 'There is nothing like that in their work - it's the same as everyone else's.'
> Question: 'Do you think you could pay journalists on some kind of incentive scheme, say words in the paper?'
> 'Certainly! Their work is no different and could be made in some ways amenable to some form of productivity basis.'

The Features Editor of the morning paper in Centre A reacted strongly to such views, particularly when a senior manager had been placed in the editorial department to assess their work. She first referred to the constant problem of reconciling management and editorial.

> 'Neither understands the work of the other. There is a cold war type of attitude. But we've had a new Assistant Managing Director around each department so that he can understand the process. Well, that's a good thing, but he talks of rationalising the features department, of efficiency ratings, of measurable rates for work loads, and articles, etc. Well, this is not realistic. It's not comparable with other types of work, although the mystic of the job is too extreme; it is not possible to measure and produce in a certain time a certain type of feature.'

The Advertising Manager for Special Features even if not agreeing with all the above, certainly saw a need for change.

> 'The industry is divided into the new and old guard. Editorial is now out of step, but I suppose it's historical, it's the way editorial view their own jobs. They're not commercially aware, they tend to go their own way, all this ethical nonsense, the morality aspects. It's quaint all this

creativity, but with their standards and image try to make the paper look one thing and it doesn't always succeed.'

Thus, non-editorial does have the objective of rationality, for instance a planned newspaper, say 65% advertisements, 35% editorial, and 13 pages of advertisements, 7 pages of editorial. The cost of producing the advertisements and collecting and publishing the news can be predicted to a fine degree, whilst revenue from advertisements can be regulated from sales of a minimum figure to provide a reasonable profit. Increased sales then become a bonus. The editorial sources are regular, thus making news collection routine, and editorial organisation rational. The process of achieving this starts in controlling the areas of interchange.

6.2. THE ADVERTISING-EDITORIAL RATIO

6.2.I The Ratio

Among regional commercialists there is a belief that regional newspapers can exist with a lower level of editorial content than hitherto. Therefore they had to determine what level would be both acceptable to the editorial staff, and necessary to maintain sales, which legitimises advertising rates and inpart determines volume. This level has to be governed by advertising, so that costs spent in collecting and presenting news can at least be related with advertising revenue. This leads, not unnaturally, to an advertising/editorial ratio. The scales in the ratio are constructed, at one end around the relationship of the lower level of advertising and the lower level of editorial space required by the editor and his department. This always occurs on the same days, Monday and Saturday and sometimes Tuesday. At the top level the ratio is concerned with how much advertising can be acquired together with a sufficient amount of editorial for the newspaper not to be classified by its readers as an advertising manual. A study over two weeks of the evening newspaper at Centre A showed a pattern that as advertising increased by 200 per cent, editorial increased by a maximum of 50 per cent, given that at the lower ranges editorial and advertising occupied equal areas of space in the newspaper. Table 6.I illustrates the ratio in action. The crosses in the table move from top right to bottom left, as the size of the paper increases, but the different scales show that the percentage increases in advertising are far greater than those in editorial.

Further evidence is shown in the relationship of editorial and advertising space to the total space available. Correlation coefficients are shown in Table 6.2 for both relationships, the higher the figure the greater the degree of cause. The conclusion is that the paper increases in size because there is a greater amount of advertising.

The figures for 1959 Centre A evening newspaper suggest that an increase in editorial is nearly as influential as an increase in advertising in providing an increase in total pagination. The situation at Centre B where it was a 'tight operation' was somewhat different to that at Centre A. Here a certain amount of editorial was included as of policy, but hardly varied as the advertising manager tried to increase the amount of advertising. Thus the newspapers returned figures for one week in I973 as in Tables 6.3 and 6.4.

The amount of editorial varied by only I0 columns, whilst the pagination varied by nearly four times this number. Indeed,

TABLE 6.I

ADVERTISING AND EDITORIAL CONTENT FOR TWO SELECTED WEEKS MARCH I977 FOR EVENING OBSERVER : (CENTRE A)

(Number of columns - 9 per page) (Av. pagination 20.5)

		Editorial					
		60-64	65-69	70-74	75-79	80-84	85-89
	60-79	XX	XXX	X			
	80-99						
Adverts	I00-II9	X					
	I20-I39			X			
	I40-I59						
	I60-I89				XX	X	X

TABLE 6.2

CORRELATION COEFFICIENTS FOR RELATIONSHIP OF ADVERTISING AND EDITORIAL SPACE TO TOTAL SPACE

		Ad./Total	Ed./Total
Evening Paper Centre A : W/C	I4 March I977	0.9954	0.88
" " "	2I March I977	0.9952	0.79
" " "	I6 March I959	0.9979	0.98
" " "	23 March I959	0.9954	0.92
Evening Paper Centre B :	I9 Nov. I973	0.9985	0.87
" " "	26 Nov. I973	0.96	- 0.27

editorial space was negatively correlated with pagination, although the relationship was of a low order (- 0.27). The other paper returned similar figures for the same week.

In only one case does the editorial rise above the 50% level. Elsewhere it is closely related to advertising, which when low, Saturday and Tuesday, determines a lower than average sized newspaper. By way of comparison, figures are also supplied for Centre A for 197I and 1959, again showing only one week, which for present purposes is indicative of the situation pre- and post-commercialisation.

These figures exhibit the dominance of advertising in the newspapers, a reflection of their control within the organisation of the advertising/editorial ratio. Without dwelling on the figures, which are self-explanatory, a comparison between Monday and Thursday figures for I977 of the Evening Observer in Centre A (Table 6.6), shows an increase of I03.5 columns of advertising, whilst editorial only increases by 4.5 columns. The editorial managers were aware of these changes and the concomitant control of their working practices. An Assistant Editor of the morning paper in Centre A talked of a battle for control in the organisation.

'It had been between editorial and advertising, but during the I960's there had been a change, a fantastic leap by the commercial side, who now had much better prestige.'

A Deputy Features Editor of the same paper complained that

'the editorial department has had a raw deal, pushed and squeezed into a corner. Many have forgotten that the basis of a newspaper is editorial, but people do not see our side of the case.'

A Deputy Editor saw accountants and accountability as being the centre of the commercial pressure.

> 'We have accountants breathing down our necks - a good thing; need to be accountable. Pre-I959 editorial were fairly heavily in control, but since that time qualified accountants have been introduced. We have now slowly evolved to a position with a paper size based on advertising content, and strictly controlled budgets.'

A Deputy Sports Editor conceptualised the process, 'Money rather than principles is now the governing factor.' The conclusion of this analysis is that the advertising/editorial ratios, having been in existence pre-commercialisation, are now determined solely by commercial reasons and are rigidly adhered to.

TABLE 6.3

ADVERTISING AND EDITORIAL SPACE FOR
EVENING TIMES IN ONE WEEK IN MARCH 1973

	Pages	Col	Total Col	Ad	Ed	% Ad	% Ed
Evening Mon. Oct.29	I8	9	I62	93	69	57.4	42.6
Tues. Oct.30	I6	9	I44	76	68	52.7	47.3
Wed. Oct.3I	I8	9	I62	98	64	60.5	39.5
Thurs. Nov. I	I8	9	I62	98	64	60.5	39.5
Fri. Nov. 2	20	9	I80	II3	67	62.7	37.3
Sat. Nov. 3	I6	9	I44	70	74	48.6	5I.4
Total	I06	54	954	548	406	57.4	42.6

TABLE 6.4

ADVERTISING AND EDITORIAL SPACE FOR
EVENING EXPRESS IN ONE WEEK IN MARCH 1973

	Pages	Col	Total Col	Ad	Ed	% Ad	% Ed
Evening Mon. Oct. 29	I6	9	I44	83	6I	57.6	42.4
Tues. Oct. 30	I4	9	I26	66	60	52.4	47.6
Wed. Oct. 3I	I8	9	I62	99	63	6I.I	38.9
Thurs. Nov. I	20	9	I80	II6	64	64.4	35.6
Fri. Nov. 2	22	9	I98	I30	68	65.6	34.4
Sat. Nov. 3	I6	9	I44	8I	63	56.3	43.7
Total	I06	54	954	575	379	60.3	39.7

TABLE 6.5

ADVERTISING AND EDITORIAL SPACE
FOR EVENING OBSERVER IN ONE WEEK IN MARCH 1959

	Pagination (8 col)	Total Col	Ad	Ed	% Ad	% Ed
Mon 23 Mar I959	I2	96	47.5	48.5	49.5	50.5
Tues 24 Mar I959	I0	80	37	43	46.3	53.7
Wed 25 Mar I959	I2	96	52.5	43.5	54.7	45.3
Thurs 26 Mar I959	I6	I28	75.5	52.5	59.0	4I.0
Fri 27 Mar I959	I8	I44	89.5	54.5	62.2	37.8
Sat 28 Mar I959	8	64	24.5	39.5	38.3	6I.2
Total	76	608	326.5	28I.5	53.7	46.3

Average pagination I2.33, 6.62 Advertising, 5.7I Editorial

TABLE 6.6

ADVERTISING AND EDITORIAL SPACE
FOR EVENING OBSERVER IN ONE WEEK IN MARCH I977

		Pagination	Total Col	Ad	Ed	% Ad	% Ed
Mon	2I Mar I977	I6	I44	7I	73	49.3	50.7
Tues	22 Mar I977	I6	I44	74.5	69.5	5I.7	48.3
Wed	23 Mar I977	22	I98	I25.5	72.5	63.4	36.6
Thurs	24 Mar I977	28	252	I74.5	77.5	69.2	30.8
Fri	25 Mar I977	30	270	I85.0	85	68.5	3I.5
Sat	26 Mar I977	I4	I26	64.5	6I.5	5I.2	48.8
	Total	I26	II34	695	439	6I.3	38.7

Average pagination 2I, I2.87 Advertising, 8.I3 Editorial

6.2.2 Control of the level of the ratio

The control of the level of the ratio, and its enforcement is now the prerogative of the advertising manager. Although the editor is, in law, responsible for the content of the paper, this is but a small limitation on the ability of the advertising manager to determine where advertisements and editorial are placed within the paper. For any day's paper the size is roughly determined one week in advance, by expected advertising space bought or booked, but this may vary by up to two pages dependent on late advertisements which can be accommodated. The day before publication the advertising managers produce a page plan, of where the advertisements are, and of course indicating the space for editorial, and this is then passed to the editor for his approval. Normally this is given, but he can change the placing of advertisements if he thinks this affects the design of the newspaper, and if these changes bring brighter and better appeal then they are agreed to by the advertisement manager. Thus the editor is told how much news there will be for any one day. It is not news occurrence or its gathering which is the determining factor, but rather the level of advertising.

The editor can, given a set amount of space, provide what he thinks is the best blend of news stories, features, sportsnews, etc. If a news story of importance occurs its inclusion will mean the exclusion of other news stories or even regular features. The latter can occur when, even given a set advertising/editorial ratio, advertising, at a late hour increases by say four columns (just under half a page). Given that this is when the newspaper is already planned at 28 pages, the marginal ratio of advertising to editorial would be at least 3, 4 or even 5 to I. Thus, as a two page extension is the minimum possible (I8 columns), at least I4 columns of advertising would have to be generated to allow such an extension, but as there are only four columns this eats into the editorial space. Many of the editorial managers were aware of these quotas and resented their operation.

A Deputy Editor of the morning paper at Centre A commented, 'In the early I960's the editor demanded the size of the paper, but now it is determined by the advertising content. We have a strict quota system, but it works unfairly.' A Deputy Features Editor was more adamant,

> 'The advertising/editorial ratio is unfair. I understand there is pressure on newsprint, but its wrong to cut out things as we provide a service. Weekly items are sometimes omitted. The advertisement department gives to editorial the page plan. But we have no control over the ratio. Advertising oversteps the mark sometimes - once a week, for instance the farming page. It's because they do not have an early enough deadline.'

This pressure from the commercial side seems to be exacerbated in the Sports Department. A Deputy Sports Editor commenting on the advertising determination of paper size said, 'It's a cock-eyed way of doing things ....sport sells the paper - look on any bus, and seven out of ten people are reading the back page .... but the amount of space we have depends on advertising.' At Centre B, the so-called tight operation, such pressures had resulted in regular cuts in space. The Sports Editor complained,

> 'I have a great feeling of dissatisfaction of not seeing things in the paper. For instance, each week we try to cover the local football and publish their league tables. It helps to generate a local feeling for the paper. But these tables are only printed occasionally. They should go on the inside back page, but where classified advertising encroaches up to three of four columns, which happens very often, it is the tables that are sacrificed.'

The News Editor (morning, Centre A) was also concerned at the increase in classified advertising, particularly in occupying traditional editorial spaces, 'It's quite frightening to have small ads. on the middle pages.'

Thus, the second aspect of this rule of interchange is that at the margin the advertising/editorial ratio can be changed by the advertising managers, and those in editorial have little or no influence to stop their space being occupied by advertisements.

6.2.3. The Use of Editorial Advertising.

The level of advertising in the newspaper can often be increased by its direct relation to editorial content. This is the phenomenon of the advertising feature or the 'puff'. They can range from the generally well received in-depth supplements seen in the quality newspaper to the prostituted feature written to attract advertisements. The former usually take a central theme; a country or an industry, or a geographic area, and devotes to it several pages (or page) of feature articles, often very informative. To justify such articles advertising relating to the subject is obtained, but it is open to conjecture whether it is the advertising which justifies the feature or the feature attracts the advertising. As the articles are often highly informative, well written and analytic in character, the supplement is thought to be credible.

At the other extreme, features are written, blatantly mentioning the desirability of certain articles, and advertisements of these articles are placed prominently around the feature. This type of 'puff' has virtually disappeared only to be replaced by more subtle forms of the advertising feature, which, however, are similar in that their prime objective is advertising and not any informative editorial. These are of four types and are extremely common in regional newspapers. The first is a derivative of that type found in quality press, except that its editorial content is subsidiary to the advertisements. Sometimes they are informative, in that they centre on a tour guide, or a major event in the locality, but this is only a welcome by-product and not wholly intentional.

The second type concerns the opening of a new factory, restaurant or shop. Besides being a plug for the shop itself, who naturally advertise, everyone who has helped to design, build or refit, is asked to participate in the advertisement feature. Most do and the feature is very profitable, which is its aim. However, the editorial content is poor, and really is a reflection of Thomson's phrase that it is 'the bit between the ads.' This is highlighted in two further categories. Third, advertisement features appear because of no reason other than for the advertisement revenue gained. The topic can range from personal music tastes to deep freezers, and the advertisements are accompanied by a piece of editorial of dubious heritage. An extract of one illustrates.

> 'The real hi-fi enthusiast would probably have on his list a record player, casette recorder/player, cartridge player, stereo microphone, reel to reel tape recorder, plus FM aerial for stereo tuner and amplifier in addition to left and right hand speakers and headphones.'

The final category combines editorial with the advertisements. The feature is heralded as a shoppers page, with some fictitious woman talking of her tastes for certain services or goods and of course recommending a certain brand. Again an example illustrates.

> 'Drink delicious wine - from a bottle that has only cost 56p! No, it's not home-made, it's just free from alcohol. Quite honestly I find this a refreshing change from drinking ordinary wine - you can still enjoy the natural flavour of the grape - since these wines are made from pure grape juices - in fact they taste just like wine - but the juice has not been fermented, only the natural sugars from the fruit used. Being a health food fanatic I really appreciate the benefits of the delicious wines .... They can be bought from ....'

These advertisement features affect the area of interchange between editorial and advertising, as the features involve some editorial content, generally not more than one third of the total space which fits in between the advertisements. The advertising managers decide what type of feature they want, this being dependent on the relevant advertisements they can secure. To editorial this is an exhibition of commercial pressure on their work routines, and more importantly, on the ethics of journalism. The ideas concerning freedom of the press and the editor's responsibility in law are also relevant whenever the editor and his department is ordered to do something against its member's wishes. The editorial content of the feature is not news, nor an article of interest; it is merely a filler to generate advertising revenue. As such it is anathema to the journalists, for they become the agents of commercialism, something they have been resenting. Their first reaction is therefore to reject such practices, or if they take place to refuse to write the relevant content.

However, there are opposite pressures for them to become involved. Within a commercial newspaper enterprise the editor no longer has the authority to order other departments in their work routines. Indeed, where revenue is concerned the editor has little or no power at all, to even influence any activities in its gathering. Authority now resides with the commercial manager, and their decision to print or extend advertising features cannot be questioned. The editor if ordered, by say the managing director, or indeed the group editorial director could possibly refuse to participate in allowing one of his subordinates to write the editorial content. This is unlikely given that the editor is ultimately responsible for all that goes into the paper, not only in law, but also in terms of self-respect. Given that such advertisement features are to be printed, then the editor might at least have control over the quality of the editorial content. If it is written by other non-journalists, journalists will define it naturally as poor; it will nevertheless reflect on the editor and his staff, as readers will think that, because it is editorial, it will have emanated from them. Thus the editor will want one of his staff to write the editorial content.

The editors were questioned on the imposition of 'puffs' in the paper and their contribution to them. As a background, all the editors said they were commercially aware, perhaps because of their position, as the Editor of the Evening Express at Centre B said, because 'the editor is only part of the management team.' He further commented,

> 'Puffs? - we've got to live with them. The editorial content comes from the editorial staff but I don't like it."

The Editor of the Morning Mail had a similar ambivalence when asked of his attitude to puffs,

> 'Well, there are good and bad puffs and good ones are fairly informative, if on the standard of the Times and Guardian, etc. In fact we have done some on the restaurants in the locality, a bona fide study in which restaurants were visited. But bad puffs are a disgrace and merely money grabbers, for instance when a garage or a shop opens. We write the editorial content but the journalists are paid extra.'

(It is of interest that this editor had previously been an editorial manager (originally administrative manager) on a Fleet Street paper, where he was responsible for staffing, budgeting, union relationships, pagination and other administrative duties.)

Thus the editors have, in some cases reluctantly, concluded that 'puffs' are here to stay, and that the editorial content should be supervised by journalists. The editor in making such a decision on behalf of his staff may be wearing his manager's rather than his editor's cap. So it is to the perception of those journalists involved in 'puff' writing that the discussion now turns.

Two editorial managers in Centre A were involved, and it is some indication of the authority of non-editorial managers, in that these puffs were dealt with at managerial level in the editorial department. The two were the Assistant Editor (Special Features) and the Deputy Features Editor. The Assistant Editor (SF) had been with the evening newspaper for twenty-five years, and whilst rising to his present position had seen vast changes, most occurring after and because of a change in ownership some time before from a family to a newspaper group. He said at present

> 'the firm lacks warmth and it is very impersonal. Editorial now only played a minor role, and was less effective than it used to be because of poor coverage of events. For instance, there are only half of the district reporters that there used to be. The Editor also takes less care. You rarely see him out of his office, let alone in the case room. The commercial (advertising) department is now all important. What they say matters.'

To him therefore advertising features were inevitable given the strength of advertising, and his perception of the diminished role of the editor. However, this only served to increase his distaste for puffs. He said,

> 'This job's been in existence for some time but is now growing. But this is an ad-man's job. I've always been a newsman. The newsman is trying to stop it. I'm really filling in for advertising. These have been going on all the time over many years and are now increasing. No journalist wants this job."

He then gave details of the process by which these puffs come to fruition.

> 'The ideas usually come from the advertising people. I give the editorial content to the advertising features manager. I sometimes get a reporter to write it. It's usually two-thirds ads., one-third editorial. The puffs are very costly for the customer, but they're always initiated by advertising. We have three or four a day sometimes, but the average is eight or ten a week."

Unfortunately this Assistant Editor had no control over the timing or content of the puffs.

> 'Sometimes I reject an advertising puff as being too vague, and some are so corny, they're very bad. But it's difficult to refuse because of losing cash.'

The size and timing of the advertising features rested solely on the ability of the advertising representatives to obtain the necessary advertising. If they couldn't they would at the last minute alter the plans,

> 'I get a brief (memo.) that a page in the newspaper is wanted on such and such at a particular time. I get the copy, and the picture and then advertising cancel saying

that there is not enough advertising, or postpone, or bring forward. Some alteration of some kind happens every week. It's either change date, forward or back, change size, up or down, or scrap altogether.'

The Assistant Editor not unnaturally hated his job and definitely saw it as one not for a journalist.

The pressures on the Deputy Features Editor (morning paper, Centre A) acted in more subtle ways. Advertising did not totally control his work because it was primarily editorial and thus the prerogative of journalists. However, the work of the features department was usually known well in advance and thus advertising representatives knowing this could sell space to customers whose products had some relation to the feature. He saw that,

'On features the editor is conscious of pressures for advertising and circulation. What mileage can be gained from a feature in terms of circulation and advertising. Peculiar - readers were once the main concern.'

He then began to list the ways in which advertising could limit the scope of their activities.

'First we sometimes have to write puffs, we're forced to write them but don't like it.'

His immediate superior, the Features Editor echoed his comments,

'On ad. features we usually get outside people to do this, but it must be vetted as many are too shallow. The Supplement editor can ask the junior staff to do these on a freelance basis. Some ad. features are in-depth and need extra staff, but that's up to the supplement's editor. I disagree with straight puffs.'

'Second, our features often appear to be related to adverts, but this is because we give the advertising department our list of features and they go and get the ads.'

'Third, advertising has begun to ask the features editor to produce features from ideas suggested by them, so that advertising is easier to secure.'

'We are against ad. features in general. They usually have a very low form of editorial, and are placed in prominent positions. All of this does not give the paper a good image and this reflects on editorial.'

In several interviews with editorial managers at Centre A the fourth type of advertisement feature was discussed, this being the personalised shopping page. Most were against it in principle, but an interesting division of interests arose with the editorial managers of the morning paper. First the editor (the one who had been an administrative manager) thought it to be an excellent development; when asked what his opinion of the column was he replied,

'I wouldn't mind having it in the paper, especially as one page of the women's section with some aspects there is genuine interest.'

This reaction compares sharply with the Features Editor and her deputy on the paper. The Features Editor thought it dishonest and her deputy said,

> 'I would not write it. It's not a high standard of editorial, it's not journalistic writing and in any case it's purely for advertisers.'

These opposite views suggest that the Editor as part of the management team is more conscious of the commercial aspects of the newspaper than the preservation of editorial standards. Perhaps it is an indication of the success of regional commercialism, notably as the preceding evidence suggests, in directing editorial feature work towards the needs of advertisers, but also in producing editors (the morning newspaper editor was recently appointed), of a managerial rather than journalistic ilk.

6.2.4. Can Advertising Control Editorial Content?

A final area of advertising influence on editorial space centres on the editorial content itself. The discussion on advertising features has shown one large area of influence. Another was outlined by the Sports Editor of the evening newspaper at Centre A.

> 'In yesteryear it was the Editor who had the power. He decided what ads would go in. When A.B.Smith* was the editor and a half-page ad came along, which might destroy his story, it was the ad that went, and the story was printed. But now the Ad people draw up the page plans and give it to the editor who will then advise if ads clash with bad news - for instance car ads with car crash - have to give ads more suitable place. Or, for instance, editorial might have a story which will lend to the ad.' (*fictitious).

An area of influence often discussed is that of direct or covert control of editorial by advertisers. When asked blatantly "Do advertisers influence editorial?", the managers, not surprisingly, played Caesar's Wife, and the answers were unanimously in the negative. However, a few managers did refer to the withdrawal of advertising following derogatory reports of that particular company's activities. A manager at Centre A explained the story in response to a question on the possible influence of advertisers because of the newspaper's heavy reliance on advertising as a source of revenue.

> 'It's difficult to answer - we have just recently encountered pressure from a major nationwide department store. Their butcher's section was fined for infringing certain regulations - it was a dirty shop. Well we printed this opposite one of their ads - a half page one. They reduced their advertising budget by fifty per cent, but they soon were back to normal levels.'

He then added a rejoinder,

> 'But we will not be answerable to advertisers although they may withdraw ads.'

Another manager expressed concern at the incident but felt it could have been avoided if editorial had put the story on a different page.

From all of the discussion over this issue, two arguments emerge. First that editorial is independent of all outside pressures, and further ought to demonstrate that it is so. From this editorial decide on editorial content irrespective of whether it reflects badly on local business, interests or institutions. This is a somewhat 'tongue-in-cheek' attitude if held by commercial managers, for they realise that anyone wishing to advertise locally in a newspaper has no choice but to use their newspaper. The monopoly position puts a certain power on the side of the newspaper. This argument may have some truth in it, and indeed it will be the one publicly stated. However the second argument builds on the analysis of this study and thus has a greater degree of credibility. The manager who expressed concern over the placing of the advertisement was probably truthful. Advertising managers have a fear of losing customers, particularly important ones as in this case, and although the monopoly position may force such large advertisers back to the newspapers, such events create uncertainties. Previous chapters have concentrated on how commercial managers wish to reduce uncertainty in areas of interchange, and with the environment in which the organisation is located. Indeed theories of organisations have been developed around the concept of controlling uncertainty. For the commercial managers here, who have gradually reduced uncertainty, to actually allow development of it, is a retrograde step. Therefore although they desire certainty, the achievement of it in instances such as this, is directly very difficult as editorial independence must be seen to exist. The achievement of such certainty occurs through the areas of interchange. Previous chapters have discussed the relationship of editorial and advertising, and the lack of communication between them and many commercial managers wanted this formalised, possibly at a higher level. Control of this area of interchange would allow advertising to inform editorial of the nature and type of advertisement, not only to avoid incidents such as the one described but to facilitate greater co-operation over the advertising features mentioned earlier in this chapter.

A more fundamental point arises from this analysis, and concerns the ability of regional newspapers to adequately report news. Mention of this was made in the opening chapter of the study, in relation to David Murphy's study, and is most easily summed up as the ability to report the unacceptable face of local interests, capitalism, or whatever. Editorial now have more space to fill and proportionately fewer journalists to fill it. The nature of many journalists' work is such that the only news they can obtain is from institutional sources, investigatory reporting being a luxury that cannot be afforded. Therefore 'unacceptable faces' are rarely seen. Further, and in relation to the 'butcher's shop' incident, court or council reports unfavourable to the major advertisers, can easily be replaced by more mundane 'failure to park correctly' reports. Through the areas of interchange advertising may only need to persuade editorial to use one story rather than another or to put it in a less prominent position in the newspaper. Given the increasing control of these areas by advertising the probability of such events happening is increasing.

The evidence also suggests that advertising control any area of interchange between itself and the features department. In many ways it can be said to have created that particular area of interchange, which since commercialism was introduced has grown larger. Indeed, control of this newly created area, along with control of other areas of interchange, has led to commercial pressures within the editorial department. To the effects of these on work routines, and the change in character of editorial appointments, the study will return later, but now another area of commercial inway must be analysed, that of the budgets.

6.3 BUDGETS

A budget is another rule of interchange and in an earlier section, the introduction of them by the Thomson Organisation was discussed in relation to increased commercialisation and the newspaper centres visited were no exception. Strictly imposed budgets are a way of getting the editorial staff to control its own activities in terms of finance. Given that they adhere to the budget and produce an acceptable level of editorial (both qualitatively and quantitatively) then the process of control is complete. Most of the commercial managers interviewed saw a necessity for cost-control of editorial, with budgets as a primary means to achieve it. Some others thought that either the process had gone, or was going to go, too far, and that cost-squeezing would affect quality. This latter opinion is relatively new, and has had little influence although in the conclusion its significance will be assessed.

Most commercial managers saw the production of a newspaper as no different to that of any other product. Indeed many managers had originated fairly recently from outside newspapers, and had instilled in them, the norms of working practices elsewhere. The Features Editor of the morning paper at Centre A was aware of these changes.

'The outside managers who came in were more of the businessman type, and this naturally perpetuated or even widened the gap between editorial and management which has always been big. They don't have newspapers in their blood.'

The General Advertisement Manager had only left two years previously a large marketing company, and quite forthrightly spelled out his objectives:

'1) To provide the company the necessary budgetal resources to allow a satisfactory return on capital used.

2) To resource the Departments in such a way to provide jobs of a certain calibre, and filling them with individuals who are capable of assuming responsibilities in the future.

3) Equip and develop individuals through training on the job. Enable them to progress more easily in their careers......'

To this manager budgeting was not only normal but highly necessary. The Chief Accountant (Centre A) was responsible for installing and policing the budgets. His job description is quite clear

'Section 2(iv) The maintenance of detailed accounts and necessary support documentation on the total conduct of business and all financial transactions, required to satisfy the company's auditors.

> Section 4 To engage in profit planning by means of the budgeting process with departmental managers and subsequently in detail with the Managing Director.'

The Chief Accountant when interviewed referred to the budget for editorial.

> 'The newspapers here exist for commercial reasons only. But editorial have tended to get their own way to a certain extent and this may be a constraint on commercial and financial business. But now the creative side of things is beginning to be costed and the budget is being imposed on editorial. This produces a strain, but not too much. It is only a problem really of education of the editors and their staff. But they must realise that even though they provide the input to the paper, the money must come from somewhere.'

The Display Manager (Run of Page) saw the commercial influence somewhat more harshly.

> 'There is some conflict, in fact they (editorial) at times, have been dragged along screaming to make it a more marketable product. To a certain extent they are academic, but editorial should be how they are and I respect them for it. Yes, there is some conflict, sometimes we've used the whip-hand to show that this is a commercial organisation.'

Finally the Assistant Company Secretary was somewhat more pragmatic.

> 'We certainly need to have budgets, and editorial is no exception. But if we have reporters available, and there's a possibility of a good story, then they have to be used.'

Thus it seems budgets can be broken, and probably initially they were by all departments. This was expected as the Assistant Chief Accountant remarked that the budget levels were under-estimated. That they can be broken is a mere technical detail compared with their effects on work practices. Undoubtedly certain work practices would be constrained, and the editorial managers, although reluctantly seeing the need for some form of costing to make management easier, and decision-making more predictable, disliked the control aspects that the budgets naturally had. Given the need to control costs, budgets became very effective, for the editor has now to make choices of different kinds of work, rather than allow all work to proceed, and then choose which stories are to be included. It produces a greater relationship of work completed and stories included. It means journalists when reporting must be sure of a story, rather than hope that something 'big' will emerge. This is one aspect of routinisation of their work, to which the argument will return later.

The Assistant Editor (morning, Centre A) thought budgets were 'philistine operations' and the budgeting process was "a diplomatic battle, with the editor arguing like hell", but "the budgeting is a control system and its tightened things up." This led him to qualify his enthusiasm for his job "its a fantastic job, within financial constraints." The Deputy News Editor saw the budgets as an important area of interchange, and one that the editor always lost.

'Cost-control is really an inter-department argument, traditionally a lot of tension between circulation, advertising, editorial, when in fact they should work together. We've had many squabbles over the budget, but journalists are always the poor relation. The rest of firm merely see us as an input. Well, perhaps its not quite as extreme as that - we're regarded as a necessary evil.'

The Night Editor thought 'it would be nice to have no budgets' but these in their turn were necessary evils 'but with quotas and the dependence on advertising it's a necessary fact of life.'

The Features Editor of the Evening Observer (Centre B) saw the budgets as making the operation 'tight', whilst his Editor saw it as a means of greater managerial control. 'We have a budget now which is decided by the new Assistant Managing Director, but I'm not fully responsible to him, especially on editorial matters.' The Deputy Editor of the sister paper at Centre B saw budgets as a move towards 'compartmentalisation', something which the Features Editor (morning, Centre A) expanded upon,

'We're going to have budgets which is going to bring greater commercial control. Budgets help you to become more commercially aware, especially with a balance sheet. But I don't really know how the budget is going to be based. I will have a tighter financial control. Have to think twice, on way, a big trip for a solus feature. It may mean a change of work routines, because we run out of money.'

In the evening paper at Centre B, the Editor had given the Deputy Editor the task of preparing and maintaining the budget. It was becoming a burden upon him.

'I'm conscious of being a manager, and I think I've come to terms with the commercial pressures. I leave most of the afternoons for administration, particularly the budgets. At first I was a bit lost on this. I even spent some time in a small corner trying to figure out budgeting. I don't like figures. Budgeting is damned hard and requires some training in managerial skills, because although frankly its fairly tedious, non-commercial people are often groping in the dark.'

The Display Advertising Manager (Special Publication, Centre A), wanted to go further and was in the process of introducing works costing, but at present he couldn't do so 'because of too many gaps. For instance house agreements are a problem, because you cannot apply the clock in the studio - not that I would want to, even though I am a workstudy man.' In part his problem was a communications one, 'Not the information existing to do such things.'

Many editorial managers had been on training courses, either internally or externally at management training centres, such as

Ashridge. The Assistant Editor (evening, Centre A) saw this as a way out of his problem with budgets,

> 'Budgets are anathema to journalists, especially myself. As you go higher there is more and more administration, you can't get rid of it. I have previously stayed clear of figures, although I've been on management courses at Banbury and two at Bedford. These were on communications and motivation for middle management.'

At least both editorial and non-editorial agree on the need for training of editorial managers in management skills. However as this training will be controlled by the commercial side it is just another aspect of their control, which derives from the control of the areas of interchange. The Assistant Editor continued,

> 'The courses are of use as a framework for the rationalisation of things. We have job description and job appraisal etc. Although I try to resist this compartmentalisation of journalism - it can destroy us - these management tools are taught with that in mind.'

Further, given the acceptance of budgets, and the need to understand them, the legitimacy of authority to control editorial, comes not only from the ideology of regional commercialism as held by the owners of the regional press, but from the editorial staff themselves.

6.4 DEADLINES

An area of interchange that has always existed has been that of deadlines. The strict adherence to deadlines is essential for the success of any newspaper, not only that the newspaper arrives at its point of sale at the most appropriate time, but also in relation to the organisation of work. The rationalisation of newspaper production undertaken by the regional commercialist has involved a consideration of deadlines and their effect. A deadline in theory should be the last possible moment when copy goes to production. Moreover it should also influence the pattern of work routine in the time before the deadline. Thus display advertising may have a two-day deadline, which means the organisation of advertising copy on a planned basis. Similarly with features. Classified advertising may be more up to date, although here the deadline should be set to allow copy to flow at off-peak time in the composing room. General news coverage is that which is most difficult to organise and plan to provide a steady flow of news copy. However some of it can be planned, certainly the institutional news from regular sources, for instance, for an evening paper, council meetings of one day can be prepared for the next, and filtered into the composing room to maintain a regular flow of copy. Court reports can be used as fillers, increased or decreased depending on the irregular sources of news.

At Centre A deadlines for editorial copy existed but were often breached, which caused overtime, and higher costs, in the production department, and often the cost was proportionately higher as production workers, in their bargaining relationship have a great deal of power. Management, particularly production, imbued with traditional values of late news, exclusives, etc. gave way. The Assistant to the Production at Centre A commented,

'The reason for their power is the weakness of management - always giving way to publish at all costs. Management is now getting stronger although the Boardroom still believes that the paper must come out at all costs.'

He continued to give an example which occurred some time before when this centre had been selected for one-day strike action.

> 'At the end of the week the men were paid, but their wage and bonus for the one day was stopped. And then they went on strike. As it happened on that day the M.D. of the central board was here and he intimated to our M.D. that the paper be published at all costs - but although we had this pressure, we were determined to fight against the men.'

This new breed of management in production, the graduate engineer rather than the time-served craftsman, was beginning to change the character of the rule of interchange, the deadline. At Centre A there had been both a new production manager and an A.M.D. to co-ordinate production activities with the rest of the firm, and the result was that deadlines were restructured and strictly adhered to, at least for editorial.

Advertising however, because of its importance in revenue terms, still had sufficient authority to break deadlines. The Deputy Production Manager (Centre A) said,

> 'Twenty years ago editorial were all powerful, but the position is different now. Editorial are being dictated to, and they know it. The Production Department is aware of the factors affecting the deadlines, but other departments are not. The overriding consideration is the sale, and the deadlines are not adhered to rigidly - this creates production problems. Copy comes late, especially from display.'

The Assistant to the Production Manager continued,

> 'Production is just a service for Editorial, Advertising and circulation. I suppose it all depends on the product and we must be a sales orientated company. The Production Department is only good when it is versatile. We have a say but really we're sales orientated. Well we're really revenue orientated, rather than profit. We never refuse advertisements, we never ration the volume. This means that production must produce, and we must have a tremendous production capacity - we can never turn down an advertisement. If we eradicate this problem for production then we create a problem for advertising. And the general opinion is that you get as many ads. in the paper as you can. The Ad. reps. will always try to sell up to as late as possible and then the production manager has to bend over backwards.'

Thus the advertising department could dictate its terms to production, as once editorial did, but the costs of keeping the production capacity and the overtime needed may not be balanced by the additional revenue received from the extra, though late advertisement. This explains the revenue rather than profit maximisation as an underlying characteristic, which was mentioned by several other managers. With the new production manager this problem was beginning to be rectified, as although the flow of display advertising was not strictly controlled by production, that for classified was, by the introduction of new deadlines. The new production manager was rather pleased with himself,

'With this change of deadlines, we're more consistent in the policy. The firm is more effective now than it was six months ago.'

A strict adherence to deadlines is essential for planned and stable work routines. If advertising levels, both display and classified are known sufficiently in advance, then the amount of editorial required is pre-determined, even though some of its pages are last to be type set. If deadlines are not adhered to then either editorial content is reduced as last minute advertisements are accepted, and thus editorial costs are higher than would be as copy is not used, and overtime in production increases. Or, there is sufficient last minute advertising to justify a slip page, requiring more editorial, which if it is to be available, will require additional staff waiting by for such an occurrence. With strict deadlines such costs are avoided.

At Centre B where the production manager was more influential because of the changed technology, he felt he had sufficient authority to control areas of interchange, particularly with editorial.

> 'Editorial give me late copy deliberately - they see it as their function to get the paper with late news content. But the paper depends on me. I resist such late copy, but there's a lot of resentment with editorial - and its led to stand-up rows with the editor.'

His deputy endorsed these views, 'Editorial is not what it was fifteen years ago. The value of a story is not quite so much, and the pattern has changed.'

He continued by referring to the influence of budgeting, 'Composing is now run from the balance sheet, as production costs have risen so much. We have imposed deadlines and its a strict system. If there's late copy then it means overtime and increased costs, so we try to avoid them.'

The production manager at Centre A was in a unique position to compare both centres, as he had recently been promoted from Centre B. Referring to Centre A he said, 'Production is very low down here because of past personalities, but at Centre B they were production orientated, and nothing was done without the production manager's knowledge.' He was concerned at the lack of communication between departments and again he referred to Centre B. 'To my mind they have a much better system than here. Problems are solved on a committee basis from all departments.'

Given the production manager's authority he was able to influence and begin to control this area of interchange with advertising in order to reduce further the costs of production by, for instance, avoiding late copy which produces the overtime. Indeed the costs of providing late advertising copy may be more than the revenue gained.

> 'For instance the deadlines on classified. They always used to object to deadlines before, they said it would lose business

but it hasn't. It's made them more organised. For instance, firms don't suddenly decide to advertise, they have a prepared budget. Besides advertisers would rather have accuracy than a quicker insertion. Before the deadlines classifieds were not proof read.

6.5. THE IMPERSONAL RULES

A fourth category of rules emanates from the corporate or group level. The legitimacy of such rules is found in their efficiency and where they affect non-editorial they are most often agreed to, although differences do occur concerning the most efficient way to profit-making. For instance, in the Accounting Department, certain procedures were not thought to be efficient by the senior managers in that department, who wanted to introduce computing and micro-filming immediately, but were constantly over-ruled by the group headquarters (who controlled most major spending of this kind) on the grounds of cost and the repercussions on staffing levels, of which the unions were most concerned. To the corporate level a sufficient level of efficiency had been achieved. The conflict between the two levels had arisen because of the enthusiasm and the initiative of two managers, the Revenue Accountant and the Deputy Accountant. Within three months they had moved to higher positions, one inside and one outside the group of newspapers.

Impersonal rules introduced for the regulation of editorial work would not be greeted with such enthusiasm as in non-editorial departments. If such rules were a move towards efficiency as defined by the corporate group, they would be perceived by journalists as implements of control. The legitimacy of such rules, at least from the editorial managers and journalists, would be in question. However, the increasing managerial consciousness of the senior editorial staff makes it more certain that any such impersonal rules will be carried out rigidly, and the impersonality of the rules is further guaranteed by the action of editorial managers. They at the same time can implement the rules in their position as manager, but support the journalists in their frustration over the rules, by maintaining that they are powerless as they are not the authors of the rules.

During the period of interviewing, staffing policy was the concern of nearly everyone in editorial. It was not just that more staff were required because of higher average pagination, but there were complaints, at the margin, of staff who had left and were not being replaced. The Deputy Features Editor (Centre A, morning) explained how wuch a situation had arisen, 'because we had not been able to replace them.' His superior, the Features Editor, saw it as being imposed, 'At present there is a clamp down on getting new staff for economic reasons.' At Centre B, the staffing problem was more acute. The Deputy Editor of the Evening Observer saw some consequences of fewer reporters, 'We don't have enough reporters, and so I have to rely on the diary a lot.' The diary is concerned with routine new stories, and the trend towards this will not stop. His editor was more phlegmatic. 'There is no more staff because of the budget.' The journalists took a sterner view of the run-down of staff, and to many of them the non-replacement of staff leaving was sufficient a grievance to become the basis of strike action. The Deputy Sports Editor (Centre A, evening) said that the present disputes 'had built up over staffing. The management wouldn't allow any additional staff on reporting, only replacements for sub-editors who had left.'

The Editor of the morning in Centre B was the recipient of one impersonal rule which had produced the situation as described.

> 'Recently there has been a recession and the Central Board communicated to our M.D. that a 10% cut in costs was necessary to maintain profit margins. Therefore we've had a ten per cent cut across the board, although it can be negotiable between departments.'

This editor, more a manager than a journalist, would implement rather than question this instruction. And as to the split between departments, it has already been shown that in relation to the commercial departments, editorial have little power.

Perhaps the most important areas of control by the central board were the change of structure, the appointment of senior personnel, and the movement of staff. Centre A had recently undergone a change of structure, pre-determined by the central board, and the movement of staff has already been documented. The appointment of the editor of the morning in Centre A illustrates the central control. 'My appointment here was done on a very secretive basis, with interviews conducted outside of the office - maybe to stop internal members knowing.' The mechanism for making impersonal rules, and therefore for control, was well developed between all three centres and the central board. Most managers had to make reports to a director on this board, although at varying intervals. For instance the Display Advertising Manager at Centre C kept in constant touch with the central board.

> 'I have monthly reports to the regional controller, this is direct. I contact my central sales manager daily and my controller three times weekly. In addition I contact the central features department weekly when they usually give leads to us, and I contact the central marketing division weekly.'

The relationship between the Classified Sales Manager at Centre A, although less contact was made, was of greater depth. 'The classified controller comes more than once a year because we can get committed to things, develop habits, which will need correcting. Well he comes twice a year and we spend a week going through the system thoroughly.'

Even editorial had to report to editorial directors. The Editor of the Observer at Centre B remarked when discussing his organisation chart, 'I report to the managing director on commercial matters, and to the editorial director at the central board on editorial matters. Indeed many editorial managers placed this relationship on the organisation chart, and at Centre A, this in spite of perhaps, an organisation chart which the News Editor of the morning said 'had been floating around the office during the last two or three days.' Although independence of the centres, and of course, editorial independence, were often talked of, it was conditional on the individual centre being profitable. Any deviation was quickly dealt with by a central director or controller.

There were other impersonal rules emanating from group level that affected the work of the journalists, and the editorial managers, acting as managers duly implemented such rules, and by doing so these senior editorial staffs had further administrative work. Expenses for journalists were increasingly limited, even routine claims for travel were carefully checked, and at Centre B, any expenses after 5.30 p.m. had to be authorised by the editor first. This in reality meant that reporters, who may do some investigatory reporting of their own, for instance, in public houses, where they exchanged a beer for some information, or a quote, have to pay all of their own expenses after 5.30 p.m. Thus, given the fairly low salaries of reporters, little if any, reporting was done after 5.30 p.m. and reporters began to have to concentrate more on the institutional routine news sources in the 9 a.m. - 5.30 p.m. period. Payment for working rest days was a form of institutionalised overtime, which regularly increased the wage for reporters, but to cut costs group management had decided to give days off in lieu, rather than pay overtime. This had two effects, first, the number of journalists working at any one time was reduced, and given the size of the paper, this meant a greater output from each journalist. This was another influence towards routinisation, and certainty of news sources. Second, the journalists began to grumble about pay and conditions, which will be discussed in the next chapter. Many editorial managers saw this reaction as simply an industrial relations problem. The Editor of the Evening Express said 'the days off rota and pay etc. is part of the crisis of editorial thing - really an I.R. problem.'

These were a few of the impersonal rules imposed during the time of the interviews. To adequately describe the control that the commercial managers had over the general work activities of the journalists, it is necessary to describe their working conditions, of which non-replacement of leaving staff, controlled expenses, and non-payment for days off is only a part.

7 The effects of commercial control on editorial work practices

7.I THE ORGANISATION OF NEWS

As outlined earlier the rules of interchange affect working practices in associated departments, usually requiring further rules within such departments to ensure that practices meet the requirements set by the rules of interchange. In the development of commercialism it has been editorial that has had to become more rule-dominated to ensure it can fulfil its role, which is couched in terms of filling the space in the newspaper with sufficient editorial, and, to journalists, of a certain standard. It has been shown that the amount of space for editorial to fill is pre-determined by advertising, to a degree of certainty for each day of each week, although there may be last minute alterations in the amount of space for editorial, again determined by advertising. News space varies throughout the week according to advertising levels, and thus to ensure that enough news is collected and processed the editor (and his deputies) must arrange for more journalists at peak advertising times, and fewer when advertising levels are lower. This in itself is an arduous task, normally undertaken by the news, or deputy news editor. The News Editor of the evening at Centre A comments, 'I must generate ideas, organise news coverage to control the working lives of the journalist'.

There are more implications from this comment of the news editor, particularly over his terms 'generate', 'organise', and 'control'. The organisation is to enable sufficient news to be available at the appropriate times, as indicated above. However the term 'generate' has more sinister implications. Chapter four described the 'flair and artistry' traditionally associated with journalists and their work, and this presumably also includes the writing of news stories, and of finding fresh sources for news. This appears to contradict the news editor's comment of generate. The contradiction can be explained by reference to the amount of news required, and the types of journalists now employed.

First, the amount of space for editorial to fill has risen considerably since pre-commercial days (over 55 per cent in the study in Chapter six) much more, in proportion, than the rise in the number of journalists, thus leaving each journalist on average to fill 40 per cent more space per week. To ensure such an output journalists need more direction than before, by the editor and his deputies, such that their news sources will have to be organised on a routine basis to ensure that sufficient news is generated. Boyd-Barrett in a survey of junior reporters found that expectations were not met by the type of work done.

> 'Analysis of time consumption would indicate a greater degree of routine and conventiality than the expectation of respondents alone. On average, the most important single category of work in terms of time consumed is desk work (25 per cent of work time), or office work. Well over a third of all respondents spent between a quarter and a half of their time in the office and a further quarter spent between a half and three quarters of their time in the office. The second largest category of work is that of 'diary reporting' which involves coverage of fairly routine, predictable events. This is followed by coverage of court proceedings, council affairs, annual general meetings, dinners and so forth. Such work is likely to become quickly familiar to most trainees, tedious sometimes, predictable often, a shorthand exercise always'. (Boyd-Barrett, 1970, p.197)

Investigatory reporting, costly in terms of time and manpower, becomes a luxury used less and less frequently. Indeed news, to ensure the appropriate supply, comes from regular and routine sources, and in this way news becomes managed in a rational way, and as the commercialists desire, with order and bureaucracy replacing flexibility and flair.

Second, the type of journalists have changed. They have better initial educational qualifications and perhaps higher expectations, which as has been shown are unlikely to be met. One consequence of this is that district reporters, once a well-known local man, content to make a career in the district, is replaced by perhaps a graduate trainee who sees the job merely for training purposes. Thus his news must come from institutional sources, the courts, council etc, as his stay is temporary inhibiting any development of a network of contacts. The news is regular and ordered, his job can be managed, and the need for flair and artistry diminishes.

The editorial department may initially welcome commercialism, for after all it does provide more editorial space, although with no commensurate increase in staff, news has to be managed in such a way to provide the 'filler between the ads'. This gradually makes editors and their deputies, managers rather than journalists. The following evidence provides substance to this outline analysis.

7.2. THE ADMINISTRATIVE RESPONSIBILITIES OF SENIOR EDITORIAL STAFF.

It is generally agreed that direct control of editorial abrogates the freedom of the press (as defined by owners, and editorial staffs), so therefore it becomes a process of controlling their exigencies in relation to the rest of the enterprise. At the same time, the rest of the enterprise, for various reasons outlined above, introduces new regulations to which editorial have to conform. Of these the preceding analysis has highlighted the editorial/advertising ratio, the advertising features, budgets, and the impersonal rules.

One major effect is that all editorial managers said they were commercially aware and that their work was now accountable. The Features Editor of the evening paper at Centre A confirmed this. 'Editorial has more accountability and cost effectiveness'. They perceived commercial pressures in general, by the very increase in advertising content in the paper and the number of advertising staff. One Deputy Editor (Evening paper, Centre A) said, 'the new owner is a businessman' and 'there are more reps on advertising than I've ever seen before'. A News Editor (morning, Centre A) commented

> 'Suddenly there's a distinct change in the office. There were black suited gents with attache cases just wandering about. I said have you seen him - the suited gent: yes, was the reply, that makes four today'.

The Features Editor on the same paper saw the managers as 'plastic moulds sent from London, not people really - they can walk sideways'.

The editorial managers, because of the increasing number of regulations, particularly budgets, began to think and act more like managers than journalists. At Centre B where the operation was 'tight' the Editor of the Observer was forthright on his managerial function,

> 'I'm a managing editor with 60 people to organise. An editor has less discretion now than ten years ago. There's more bumf, I supposed based on Parkinson's law. The admin side takes more and more of my time, and I suppose the budget is a challenge. Although editorial independence is supposed to be sacrcsanct the management have nearly taken everything over. Its a management orientated outfit, and the editor is only part of a management team'.

The Editor of the sister paper talked of changing managing techniques and added 'The editor has more power now as a manager than as a journalist'. At Centre A the editors felt that the position had not deteriorated that far as yet, for the Editor of evening paper said, 'more and more I am a manager, but essentially I'm a journalist. I once said 25 per cent manager, 75 per cent journalist, but I feel the balance is changing.'

He realised that he had to conform to commercial standards, 'We have to be commercially aware, and not produce in isolation. We have a need to sell and we must gear our content accordingly.' His Assistant Editor confirmed the trend, 'The editor is not a true editor any more', but saw some consequences, 'there is a reaction against this commercialisation. We fight it and attack it on their ground.' The last phrase sums up the extent of the influence of commercialism.

The amount of management necessary in editorial is also produced by, and produces a need for, the appointment of editors (and other senior editorial positions) with managerial as well as editorial qualities. Such editors will not find budgets and other strict working arrangements anathema to them and the Editor of the morning in Centre A is an obvious example. He had worked for a national news paper organisation praised by the E.I.U. for its efficiency, where one of his posts had been as

Editorial Manager and when questioned as to the nature of his duties he replied,

> 'Well, the paper had a very efficient management structure, but my title was really only prestige, the previous one was called the Admin. Manager. My functions were staffing, budgeting, union relationships etc. All administrative rather than editorial.'

The process also works in the opposite direction for several editorial managers saw their promotion possibilities as much in general management as in journalism. Indeed the Assistant Managing Director in Centre B had previously been a deputy editor.

The News Editor (morning, Centre A) saw promotion only as a manager, and not as a journalist.

> 'In Fleet Street you are paid on ability and may stay on as a reporter. But in this group it doesn't happen - they have the big promotion kick. You don't get on here as a reporter. So most people go through the promotion game. It's all working against the reporter. We train journalists, who then leave to earn more money if they want to stay as journalists and reporters. Here, the good journalist to get on, status and salary wise, must promote to managerial status, but they may not make good managers, and we lose good reporters this way. We've people in this department who are not good enough to be editors or general managers - the Deputy Editor and Assistant Editor.'

It is of course no accident that such integrative movements are made possible by the commercial pressures and the reaction to them in the editorial department, as in the following evidence. The Deputy Editor of the morning paper at Centre A saw 'the organisation of editorial as very rigid. The editor with ad quotas, expenses payments, budgets etc, and I myself, have a whole range of administrative matters.' The Deputy News Editor of the sister evening paper thought,

> 'I manage too much of my time, but if the organising is not done properly then the journalist function cannot carry on. The managing is very easy but boring. I sometimes long to be a full-time journalist again. I'm too desk bound.'

The administrative duties arising from the commercial pressures were restricting the Features Editor of the morning paper at Centre A, 'I need a better secretary to do all the administrative chores, but the budget does not allow for such people.' This editorial manager realising that administrative work was increasing, and that no extra secretarial help could be obtained because of the budget, saw herself more and more as an administrative head of her department. She increasingly had to delegate, and whilst delegating had to impose her own sets of regulations on her subordinates. Their work became more routine because of this. The News Editor (morning, Centre A) was in a similar position, as his time was increasingly taken up with 'more and more admin every day - budgets, petrol chitties, memo-writing etc. I've got 15 districts and have to control them, but the budget is involved in that anyway.'

The delegative role was also outlined by an Editor at Centre B, (Evening Times)

> 'There used to be and probably still are, some shirtlsleeve editors, but I'm different. I'm a manager of journalists on a day-to-day basis. It's a new attitude, and being a manager its my business to understand new techniques. I delegate work and let people get on with it, that is after I've picked the right people. It is a very hierarchical department, they all know to whom they report. Different departments have different work routines as laid down by objectives, in fact there's a lot of management by objectives here.'

7.3 THE ROUTINISATION OF EDITORIAL WORK ACTIVITIES.

As editors and their senior staff become more competent as managers, so administrative duties, such as budgets, become easy to accomplish, even second nature. They also increasingly take decisions concerning the effect of the commercial pressures, for instance, the advertising/editorial ratios provide a stability in planning future pagination. As revenue is the deciding factor in what costs are allowable, so it is the level of advertising which decides the level of editorial. At Centre A, the management team were engaged in 'pre-determined levels of revenue per quarter', which classified and display advertising managers used as targets. From this the level of editorial is also determined, and the editors are informed of this.

Advertising varies throughout the week for economic reasons, and although advertising representatives try to sell advertising for the traditionally poor days, Monday, Tuesday and Saturday, the amount of advertising space sold on these days is always lower. In fact it is predictably lower, to the extent that advertising levels themselves are predictable, and given the quota levels, the amount of editorial is known, and the gathering of news can be planned. News sources can be placed on a routine/non-routine continuum. At the routine end are the news stories emitting from the courts, councils and regular meetings, whereas non-routine stories are centred on scoops, whilst in between there are the car crashes, fires, murders etc, which always happen but not in regular places, nor regular times. Within this continuum features can be placed as a routine editorial supply, for although a feature is by its nature more investigatory than mere council reports, it is planned ahead. (The Feature Editor talked of a two day deadline.) Stories from Council meetings and court hearings can also be planned to fit into the paper on certain days. With other regular features such as the television and radio column, cartoons, the editorial, and more important the agency news, the amount of non-routine news stories is very low if it exists at all. With news broken into these categories, and the increasing managerial orientation of the senior editorial staff, the planning, collection and writing of a newspaper increasingly becomes highly routine, indeed even bureaucratised. The Editor of the morning at Centre A confirmed this analysis, when asked about the different sizes of newspaper during the week.

> 'With the different ad quotas on different days we produce

'different levels of editorial for these different days. We are geared to a certain size paper per day, and if suddenly an extra two pages is given to us on a Monday we will probably not have enough news.'

Much of the preceding analysis has suggested, at least by implication, that editorial would never have extra space to fill, other than that planned for. However, there are instances when such space may become available. If advertising, which has a late deadline, (as it is a revenue source) obtain late advertising, say 14 columns (9 columns per page) then this will justify an extra slip page. To complement, editorial needs to produce four columns of news. This occurrence was curtailed with the arrival of a new production manager, who began to regulate the informal area of interchange between advertising and production. To him, later advertising, even though a revenue earner was costly, and such advertising could often be placed the following day with no detrimental effect. Deadlines were now strictly adhered to as the production manager would not accept any advertising past a certain time. The opposite occurrence, that advertisements are cancelled, may also force editorial to provide extra news columns. One Deputy News Editor, (Centre A, morning paper) saw a solution, 'When adverts increase we can manufacture news by getting people's opinions on events and their effects.'

During the same interview he suggested that the sister evening paper would in the same circumstances, use any unused diary story, or news from the wire, both routine news sources. The Deputy Editor was more adamant about the editorial policies on news and its gathering.

'Journalism closes on a Friday, no one does anything, and so there is a shortage of the gathering of news. Saturday's paper is only 12 pages because there are so few advertisements, and indeed we have a difficulty filling it, because few journalists are working. Journalists are not finding the news, its not that it doesn't occur. You see, if we had more journalists over the weekend they would generate a lot of news. We want more, but we cannot.'

This is because the advertising quotas only justify a set amount of editorial space, and indeed the budgets set limits based on that ratio. The Deputy Editor continued, 'When we had two more pages, we could not fill it with hard news stories, we had to manufacture milk and water stories.'

7.4 MORE SPACE, FEWER JOURNALISTS

Another inevitable move towards routinisation of editorial work can be found in the increased pagination. During the last fifteen years pagination for editorial had increased by over 50 per cent whilst staffing levels in the same period had only increased by 10 per cent. Indeed many editorial managers complained bitterly of staffing shortages. Besides the Deputy Editor just mentioned, the Deputy Features Editor of the same paper mentioned that there were 'fewer staff than before, compared to the size of the paper.' The Sports News Editor of the sister evening paper complained that 'staffing levels should be higher.' The Deputy News Editor, in charge of district news for the same paper, remonstrated 'In this department now there is too much work done to the size of the paper - it has increased enormously, and the staff hasn't increased enough. Need more staff for the general news.'

These complaints are indicative of the problem for senior editorial staff, which is how to fill larger and larger editorial spaces given the same (or nearly so) complement of journalists? The solution can either be found in increased us of agency material, or to move reporters away from investigatory reporting to reactive or regular reporting, in effect a switch to routine as against non-routine news sources. This is not to say that all news is dull, boring, and from institutions, but rather that it needs to be presented in a more interesting way. Thus the evening paper in Centre A, goes at great length to find flavour and interest in a story that emantes from the courts or the council. Of the latter, the headline, 'Disgraceful Damp in Houses' can often be traced (in the article itself) to a complaint by a councillor at a regular council meeting. This increased pagination has not so much benefitted editorial, in that it has more to say, but rather that all of what is says arises from regular and most institutional sources. The Deputy Editor at Centre A, morning paper said that commercial pressures could result in a storage of unused stories,

> 'Commercial pressures have resulted in fewer and fewer non-institutional stories. We have a problem of getting the basic information for them. So now we are prepared to compromise and build up a "stock of new stories." Unfortunately we lose credibility because of this.'

There were other effects on the journalists work activities including the lack of outside writers. The Deputy Features Editor (Centre A, morning) said he 'could do with more writers, but we had no money to pay them. If I want to spend over £10, I have to contact the editor, and if it is over £100, it has to go to the M.D. (Managing Director).'

In the sports section the budget had resulted in the 'Last of the travelling cricket writers.' (Deputy Sports Editor, Centre A, morning.)

The Chief Assistant Editor (Centre A, morning) saw work activities curtailed as well as fewer specialists being employed.

> 'We are cost conscious. It is impressed upon the staff that money doesn't grow on trees, that there must now be a reason for every penny spent. With large scale projects we must persuade the managing director. This is a crucial development over the last ten years. There must be a limit to spending. But things needed, for instance a newspaper artist, but because he is not budgeted for, then we cannot have him.'

The News Editor (Centre A, evening) wanted a picture editor, 'but here he is called the photographic manager, but he does not report to the editor, he is the head of a commercial business, which is part of the organisation.'

7.5 COMMUNICATION: PROBLEM OR CONTROL?

On traditional grounds editorial have a legitimate claim to dominate the organisation. However, if other departments or the proprietor do not agree conflict, as outlined, will result. One way to either avoid conflict, or to rectify it in their favour if it occurs, is for the editorial department to convince others of their strategic importance. This can perhaps be achieved by communication. Most text books on management or writers on organisations stress the importance of communications, in order that decisions may be correctly carried out, control achieved and objectives met. Communication as a general question was included in the interviews, in terms of how people communicated, with whom did they communicate and their opinion over their answers. An overview of the answers and opinion would be that most conceived of communications as a problem, whilst some were quite satisfied so that they never contacted anyone outside of their department.

At the highest level in Centre A, Executive Management, meetings were infrequent, though at Centre B they were more regular, where the Managing Director was accessible while at Centre A he was a distant figure. The News Editor said, 'Half of my staff do not know the name of the M.D.' and a Sports Editor said, 'Many people would not recognise him.' One Commercial Manager, the Personnel Officer talked of being unable to see him to resolve certain problems, a statement echoed by others. Given the perceived conflict between editorial and commercial it may have been a deliberate management ploy. This policy allows such conflicts to resolve themselves, and given that commercial departments now have more authority it is they who gain control, often through the areas of interchange.

At the next level, that of the majority of managers interviewed, communication did occur through the areas of interchange, but for many this was not enough. They had a desire to know more of the work of other departments and for them to understand their work. This seems a reasonable suggestion given the growth of certain departments in the previous ten years. The requests came from both editorial and non-editorial departments. The Deputy Chief Accountant remarked that 'the rest of the organisation is appallingly badly run. A bad lack of communication between executive level and M.D. This delays many decisions.'

The Advertising Manager (Special Features) at Centre A was more specific,

> 'We have a limited awareness of each others responsibilities and jobs. Would be better if everyone knew each others jobs and frustrations. Would help if Ads and Editorial knew why circulation was down 2,000.'

Formal meetings with the Managing Director were ruled out by this manager as 'everyone is inhibited. After I was promoted I was never spoken to, nor spoke for four months. So we withdrew.'

Their request was for more inter-department meetings especially with editorial, so that the commercial policies could be explained.

The reaction of editorial managers to the growth of the commercial departments and the rules they were imposing was a call for more information. The Features Editor (Evening Observer, Centre B) thought, 'We should know more of other departments', and the Editor (Evening Times) complemented his statement 'Other departments should know more about us.' The News Editor (morning, Centre A) remarked, 'I do not know how advertising works.' The lack of contact and communication (apart from that necessary in areas of interchange) lead to a lack of understanding according to the Chief Assistant Editor (morning, Centre A), 'There is a tendency for advertising not to have a feeling for the paper and for editorial, although circulation do have this.'
The Deputy Editor (evening, Centre A) saw the problem with production, 'We have a rivalry with production, we try to understand their problems but they not ours.'

The Assistant Editor (morning, Centre A) thought more communication, perhaps more regular inter-departmental meetings might provide a forum for editorial, in particular to expound on their grievances, he said,

> 'A present gripe of editorial is that the paper is too small. After all we do have to compete with the nationals. At present everything is related to advertising, we need ads, but the organisation could make an investment and expand.'

Given the increasing commercial control such an eventuality was highly unlikely. Certainly editorial staff could voice their opinion, but commercial reasons, given the authority of commercial managers, would outweigh any editorial objections. The more likely outcome would be another area of control, an inroad opened by editorial themselves. The Chief Assistant Accountant conjectured on the possibilities,

> 'The Management Information Office and the Financial Accountancy Office should be set up to produce all information in the firm. No manager will have his own department for producing information. There is too much information that is duplicated. Various managers overlap. In this way we can maintain adequate control and produce saving, particularly in staffing.'

On the latter he saw a 10 per cent cut everywhere, particularly in production and editorial, whilst the trade union opposition was great, in the former he saw no problems in achieving his aim in editorial. 'For instance, take the output of journalists. They have been given the aura of the academic for too long. They need to be put in their place to be able to produce something.'

At Centre B many of the pressures apparent at Centre A had come to fruition, and control of communication was one of them. The production manager at Centre A, had recently moved from Centre B and could give comparisons, particularly as to the efficiency of the communication process. He said,

> 'The style of management here (Centre A) is very different. It is autocratic, whilst there (Centre B) it was very much on a committee basis, weekly at least, where questions could be asked and decisions taken as a whole. There was a formalised information flow, which doesn't happen here.

'You become familiar with, and had an understanding of, the problems in other departments. This was confined to the more senior heads, and the lower ones came in on a monthly basis, and thus became more integrated in the firm.'

This manager's attitude is quite clear. Further control to achieve cost reduction is highly necessary, and management meetings with the editorial staffs might be the means to implement such policies. Communications may be perceived as a problem, but its solution is only to increase the routinisation process of the journalists work activities.

7.6 THE WORKING CONDITIONS OF THE JOURNALISTS

The following comments cannot be taken in isolation, they must be related to the previous working conditions and also those of similarly placed workers within the enterprise. Indeed the viewpoints of the editorial managers were couched in these terms.

7.6.I Cars

The journalists had had their expenses for travelling restricted. Traditionally reporters were expected to use their own cars or public transport where necessary for editorial work and claim back the expenses, although at Centre B this freedom was limited after 5.30 p.m. This in itself does not seem to be a constraint on their ability to collect news, that is of course if they owned a car, but the enforced use of public transport would naturally limit a reporter's scope for news collection. Of course the institutional and routine news sources would be available, although follow-up stories might be difficult. If news is held at a high premium the management would provide company cars, but as the management feel sufficient news can be collected without providing company cars, company cars were not provided. This is not exactly true at Centre A, there were 230 company cars, the editors had one each, and there was one for the editorial pool. At Centre B, there were 150 company cars of which each editor had one, and there were two, one each for the different journalists on each paper. These two cars however were really those of deputy editors, who allowed them to be used during the day, as long as they were returned by 5.30 p.m. for the deputy editors to go home. The Deputy News Editor explained the position,

'Most journalists have to use their own cars, the management prefer us to, although for years we've grumbled that we need them. They regard journalism as a vocation, profession, no need to give perks or financial rewards because of this. The ad reps get cars and we've been left behind, and used. Only the editor gets a car. We've tried the N.U.J. but we're up against higher executives who think its traditional for journalists to use their own cars. We ask for company cars merely because of the basic economics of the thing, although we get a reasonable mileage rate. We've put forward all the obvious sorts of arguments, we negotiated with the Managing Director over this, rather than the editor as he has no say, although he's sympathetic.'

The last phrase is indicative of the impersonal rule. The editor still retains his credibility with the journalists, as they see that it is not him who is imposing conditions on their working activities. The Sports Editor at Centre B (Evening Observer) thought is unavoidable that the non-editorial executives should have cars. 'To them its part of the job - the company needs to give a car to attract the right sort of manager. If no car he can go elsewhere, but a journalist can't.' However even with this, he was highly dissatisfied.

7.6.2 Office Conditions

Most editorial managers thought that office conditions for the editorial staff were both worse than several years ago, and worse than those for similar staff in other departments. As management has placed a lower priority on news and its gathering than hitherto, it was not unnatural that privileges and conditions should be considered more applicable to non-editorial staff. The position was perceived as approaching crisis point at Centre A, particularly in comparison with the past. In Centre B, with its short history such comparisons could not be made, and grievances centred on direct pecuniary matters, such as expenses, cars, pay for working rest days, wages, etc.

The most apparent change at Centre A, was the increase in commercial staff, and as the newspaper had been in the same building for the previous 10 years, there were accommodation problems. A Deputy Features Editor (morning paper) remarked, 'We used to occupy the whole of this floor, but now we only have one third. And we have to share it with the evening paper. Other departments have taken over physically.' He continued with grievances over other conditions. 'They keep us last in the pecking order. We have low pay and conditions in comparison with other departments. Take machines (typewriters) we've got 1932 models - they're poor typewriters, but look at those in the tele-ad department, they're new.' The Deputy News Editor of the same paper took up the theme,

> 'Journalists are regarded in this group as the poor relation. Circulation is the traditional one here (maybe because the Managing Director had graduated from circulation). For instance you find when the place is re-carpeted, it is the circulation, then advertising who get it first. Then new furniture its the circulation and ads. From this you suspect that circulation and advertising are more important. Take the machines (typewriters) we have a 30 years old one, theirs are brand new.'

7.6.3 Pay and Status

These two are often related, in that if a mangement team views a particular function in high esteem, because it is necessary to the functioning of the newspaper, then high wages are paid to attract and keep the best personnel. When the Fleet Street ideology gave prominence to editorial, because it was thought that the better editorial, the better the paper and the higher the sales, so journalists commanded high salaries. However where management perceive the editorial input in a newspaper to be no more than the 'bit between the ads' , that bit being easily collected from routine stories, then high salaries do not need to be paid, because virtually anyone with basic skills can fulfil the task. Thus journalists, in the management's opinion, do not need to have high salaries. The Deputy Production Manager (Centre B) summed up the position, 'It's the fault of management - they've allowed journalists to fall behind production workers.'

There is an opposite argument that centres on the content of the job involved. If this is one of high enjoyment, or indeed perceived status, then this may, in the management's opinion be part payment for the job. Some professions have these characteristics, for instance, the vast majority of actors, musicians, university lecturers. The realisation of such a position, does not stop such groups grumbling about pay, yet it does not, usually, stop them continuing in their chosen field. This kind of argument can be used in the case of journalists, and indeed together with the previous one was often mentioned in interviews. As a background most interviewees saw some relation to low pay and low status, from the general commercial pressures outlined above.

The Deputy Editor of the morning newspaper in Centre A, thought that

> 'The status of the journalist has gone down and this is because of the commercial pressures. Editorial is less important - the journalist is just a fact gathering instrument, he isn't allowed to say anything. Certainly he cannot be offensive and upset anyone, because of ad pressure and the wide market they have.'

The Deputy Editor of the Evening Observer - Centre B, said that 'Journalists taken advantage of - often taken for granted. The journalist never asks what's in it for me. We're frustrated by the apparent lack of editorial awareness from the rest of the organisation.' This lack of perceived status was of concern to the Night Editor (morning, Centre A), 'Journalists no longer have the status imposed upon them as they used to. When I was a copy boy I would obtain great respect from say, Accounts.' Similarly at Centre B, the Chief Sub-Editor on the Evening Express said, 'The journalist has less and less status. For instance here the journalist has never had to stop the paper, and is always treated with contempt.' The Features Editor of the same paper, 'The status of the journalist has gone down, before the war it was high, but the N.U.J. are reacting to the loss of status.' The Chief Assistant Editor (Centre A, morning) was largely in agreement,

> 'We have been used by management because of the lure of the job, the intrinsic value etc. Pre-1959 the journalist was rich, high status, car, paid £5 when an agricultural worker was paid 28/-. Since then wages generally and of production workers in particular, have risen by industrial action, but journalists always put the paper first. Other wage rates have increased - the production worker on £120/£130 (1974 figures), its not regular, but its not unusual.'

The Assistant Editor (morning, Centre A), thought that 'From the view of editorial its probably a problem of perks - look at the perks that are obtainable to say, Ad people, circulation etc.' Low pay was a reflection of low status, and indeed the pay grievance provided a focus for all journalists' grievances. 'Tele-ad girls get more than a trainee journalist - trainees are graduates in responsible jobs,' (Deputy Features Editor, morning, Centre A). Within this statement lies the seeds and the cause of discontent. Whilst the status and pay of the regional journalist has been dropping, the standard of entry into the occupation has been rising. Entry into journalism has now to be via the regions, as the N.U.J. try to stop direct entry into Fleet Street.

> 'Under a recent agreement between the N.U.J. and the Newspaper Proprietors Association (representing national newspapers), no national newspaper may now recruit staff who have not had three years experience on non-national publications, (two years for graduates), although exceptions are allowed for in certain fields of news gathering.' (Boyd-Barrett, 1970, p.186).

Tunstall (1971, p.60) reports that in 1967-68, of the recruits to provincial newspaper journalism, 12.1 per cent were graduates, 11.5 per cent had three or more G.C.E. 'A' levels, 17.6 per cent had two 'A' levels, and 8.5 per cent had one 'A' level. In both centres there were a vast number of graduates who were discontented with their job, and reacted to it in terms of militant action. This is not surprising when comparing the standard of entrants, and the quality of reporting required, from these routine, institutionalised news sources. The Assistant Editor, (Centre A, morning) dwelt on the nature of reporting, the difference between investigatory or reactive.

> 'The difference is between graduate and non-graduates. The training of a university education leads to analysing ideas. The graduates are resentful of the low wages, low status. They have realised that the commercial accent is here to stay, but there is still this degree of alienation. It is reflected in the high turnover of training staff.'

There are consequences from the perception of this low status, and the reality of low pay. For instance, militancy, work-to-rule, strikes, etc, but also there are consequences on the work practices, particularly on the turnover of training staff. Regional newspapers rely on the public in part to notify them of any newsworthy events, which is done either by phoning the newspaper or by contacting a reporter. In Centre A, the two newspapers served fairly wide areas, and many district reporters were employed. The News Editor (evening) continues,

> 'At one time the district reporter was a native of the area in which he worked. Everyone knew him, and he knew everyone. If there was a fire or an accident, the police and the fire people would be contacted, but so would the reporter. He knew everything that was going on. Now the situation is much different, we have to use graduates for these areas, and they don't like it. They want to get to Fleet Street, and they view such posts as temporary training. After three months they want to come back to the main town. Well they find nothing in three months.'

The Deputy Editor continued in the same vein. 'Journalists are not prepared to chase after news. They merely go to any P.R.O. (Public Relations Officer) and get company views. They accept anything and serve up half myths.' The Deputy Editor on the morning, saw a lack of commitment on the part of these graduates, 'When you're a district reporter it should be a 24 hour a day job, but these graduates just do 8 hours now.' Given the commercial pressures towards routinisation of news collection, this attitude of journalists becomes a reinforcement to the extent that such routinisation is self-perpetuating.

This chapter, so far, has suggested that editorial work has become routinised, and commercial departments have achieved some measure of control over the activities of journalists. This has been achieved by control of the areas of interchange and the imposition of impersonal rules, and the reaction of journalists to them. There has been a greater reaction, that of a series of strikes in the regions in the early 1970's, and these will be considered in the next chapter, particularly in the context of the editorial manager's reaction and opinion of such action. However before that it is necessary to include a final section which might redress the balance in favour of editorial. Many editorial managers still saw the editor as the most important and powerful man in the organisation. Because of the foregoing in the chapter, the disucssion of such viewpoints is entitled, "False Perception."

7.7 FALSE PERCEPTION

An indication of how editorial managers viewed the position of editor in the organisation came from blank organisation charts which the managers were required to fill in during the interview. (See methodological appendix for such a chart.) At Centre A, of those editorial managers who gave the editor a superior, nine said that it was the Managing Director, but four gave a variety of answers. One, the Features Editor, saw the editor as responsible to himself in all matters, crossing out the box where she would write the name of the Editor's immediate supervisor. In the interview she qualified this by saying the Editor has to report to the Managing Director on managerial matters and to the Editorial Director of the group, based in London, on editorial matters. The Editor also saw this division of duties and drew the organisation chart as in Figure 7.1. He went on,

> 'These relationships need explaining. I am appointed by the Editorial Director, but I must be able to work with the Managing Director. I justify what I do with both the Managing Director (in the commercial sphere) and with the Editorial Director (elsewhere). If the M.D. wants me to change the style of the paper I squeal and go to the Editorial Director.'

This is little comfort for the journalists and the routinisation of their work practices, for many of the impersonal rules emanate from the Editorial Director. Indeed the Editor has little freedom to do as he chooses and he is responsible in his activities to commercially-orientated senior managers. However many perceived the Editor to have a great deal of freedom, and that he was the most influential person in the organisation. Even the way the Editor talked suggested he was aware of his freedom. For instance his ability to determine the "style of the paper". Earlier on it was recognised that the

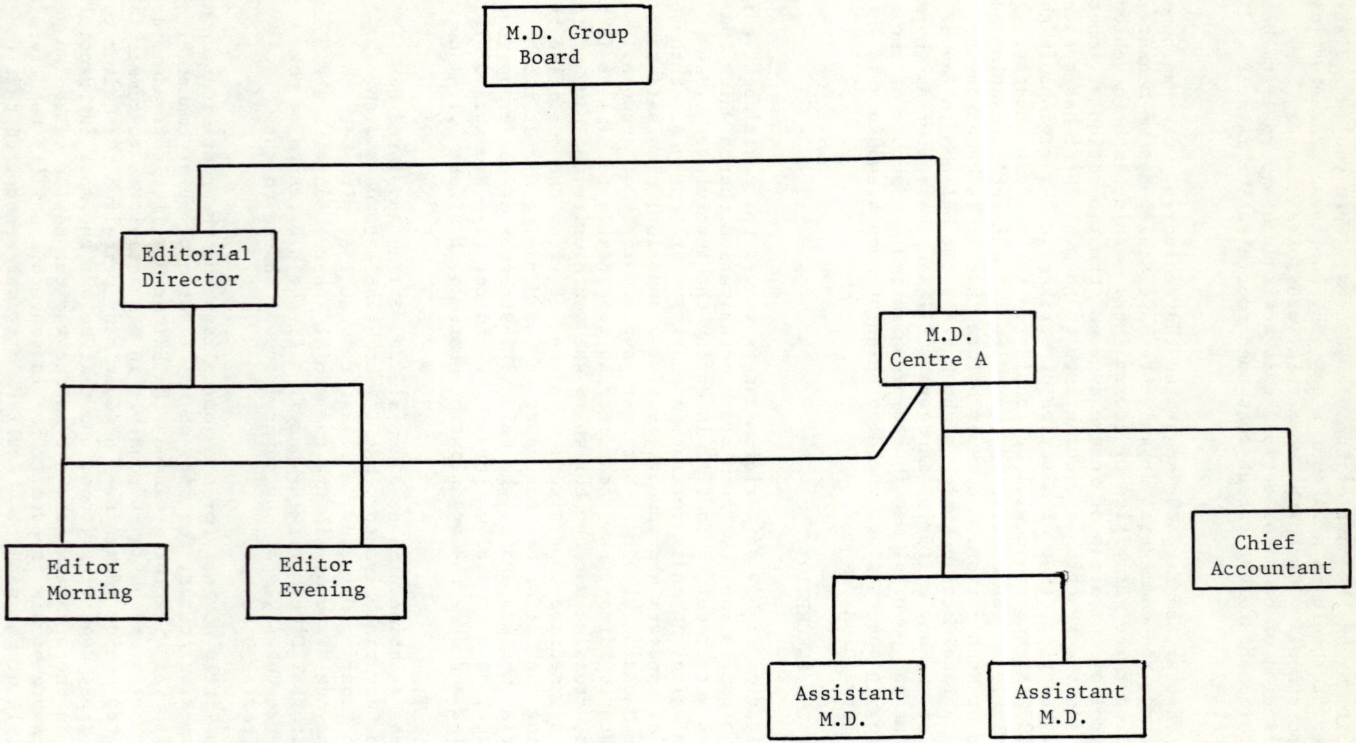

FIGURE 7.1 : THE FORMAL ORGANISATION CHART OF CENTRE A AS PERCEIVED BY THE EDITOR OF THE EVENING OBSERVER

Editor had such a freedom, but it was a hollow one, because commercial influence via the areas of interchange had forced the Editor and his staff to change that style, for instance, more news from routine sources, little news gathering after Friday, and the proliferation of advertising features.

This false perception of the Editor's own position was echoed by others in their organisation charts. The Deputy News Editor saw that the editor was responsible to himself, although he perceived a relationship of some sort to both the Managing Director and the Editorial Director. The Sports News Editor was adamant that the editor was responsible to the Editorial Director (although he called him the Editor-in-Chief), and the Night Editor was confused, whilst having some agreement with the Sports News Editor. Others also commented on the position of the editor, the Assistant Editor (morning) said, 'The editor is above all others', and the Deputy Editor (evening) 'The Editor is revered although not as much as he used to be'. This was in agreement with the Assistant Editor (evening). 'The Editor is still in command but only just', and the Chief Assistant Editor (morning) 'The Editor has less control of the content of the paper.' He then went on to suggest that all of the commercial pressures 'were not really a move to control journalists.' To the commercial managers this must be a highly functional opinion, because whilst they have increasing control, some editorial managers are relatively satisfied. The Deputy Editor of the same paper was as optimistic, 'We have a size relationship with advertising, we always allow late ads if possible, so that later we can get a certain size of paper if the ratio goes against us.' This is somewhat of a fallacy for editorial have no authority to overstep ratios, even if favours are owed, for the process of control is one way. In a similar fashion the Assistant Editor (morning) felt that if advertising encroached any further then the editor would be strong enough to resist.

> 'The war stage has not yet been reached, it was at another centre and the editor had to use strong action to gain a bigger foothold of space. It is as likely to happen here as anywhere else, as Ads are doing very well in their bleak period in the summer.'

This infers that the editor is both capable of, and has the authority to rebuff advertising, a conclusion contrary to the evidence presented here.

At Centre B many editorial managers also falsely perceived the power and positions of the editor within the organisation. Only one editorial manager saw the relationship of the editor to the managing director in managerial matters, whilst the rest saw it in all matters. The Editor of the Evening Observer referred to 'the functional relationship' with the Editorial Director at group level, and the Editor of the Evening Times thought that 'the editor is always above other managers.' He even pointed out that he has 'power, total power, it's my paper and nobody interferes with me - there's nothing like being in the firing line.' Although this has an accent on megalomania, it can be understood if it is placed within certain limits, and those limits have been increasingly defined by the commercial manager.

Their false perception of their ability to control their own work is highlighted (and to a certain extent qualified) over the advertising/editorial ratio. The Deputy Editor (Observer) said,

> 'There is always the problem of fitting advertising. We need a greater understanding by Ads, but they are our natural enemies. Even so more ads gives greater editorial freedom. It means more news, although on overall, less percentage. But we are guaranteed 70 columns.'

By reference back to an earlier section it can be seen that in the period studied the number of editorial columns only once exceeded 70.

Even given this false perception of the editorial managers of their position, there was bound to be some sort of reaction from the others affected, the journalists. The next chapter examines the form of this reaction and the attitude of the managers towards it.

8 Managers and journalists in reaction

8.1 INTRODUCTION

The whole notion of the freedom of the press can be seen both as an attempt by owners to maintain their freedom to publish their own views, and a continued plea from journalists that they should be protected from outside pressures, which may limit or change news collection and presentation. Sometimes the two have been connected, whilst most often they have been opposed because journalists have seen owner influence as an unwarranted outside pressure. The use of the freedom of the press has been used by journalists whenever they have felt under threat, although such notions can only be used where threats are overt, and their effects can be effectively seen or judged. Much of this study has argued that such pressures as do exist are more covert, operating to routinise the work of the journalist. To those upholding the freedom of the press this is not a pressure which affects such freedom and therefore no defence of the journalist is necessary. Where such commercial pressures are overt, in increased concentration, then help is on hand in the form of the monopolies commission.

Thus there is no outside support for the journalists and they then turn to internal remedies to rectify their falling position within the newspaper hierarchy. They turn to militant action, strikes, which at first would seen anathema to them in terms of their profession, their ethics, their flair and artistry which produces a 'living thing', the newspaper. There are, however, catalysts in the process, not least the graduate intake, who perceive that professionalism, reliance on ethics, flair, artistry etc, no longer can exist in the climate of commercialism. They react to preserve pay and conditions, but of greater significance the reaction is against the loss of status.

8.2 THE JOURNALISTIC RELIANCE ON THE SUPPORTERS OF THE FREEDOM OF THE PRESS

One reason for the setting up of the 1947 Royal Commission of the Press was that journalists had complained of the pressure that owners had applied to publish their opinions. These opinions often meant certain names or firms could not be mentioned, and journalists felt they could do little to stop the extension and implementation of such a list.(1). The journalists had a fairly influential lobby group, for instance there have always been several Members of Parliament who had been journalists, and in fact the two N.U.J. members opened a debate in 1946 in the House of Commons to demand an inquiry into the press. When the Commission was finally set up much of the N.U.J. evidence was concerned with the proprietorial influence on the journalist's activities in presenting the news. Although nothing substantial emerged to defend the journalist's interests the mere fact of a public airing was sufficient to preserve some of their freedom of expression, in collection and presentation, and indeed there was a Press Council formed to monitor any improper development in the Press. Its power has been small, and thus it has respectfully kept in the distance, only really speaking when invited to, and then on some uncontroversial topic.(2). But the events were probably sufficient to satisfy the journalists concern over the developments in the press.

If the 1947 Royal Commission was about group ownership and its ability to influence press content, then the 1962 Commission was concerned with group ownership closing unprofitable newspapers and providing a monopoly of news. Journalists were concerned with this, in both the case of redundancies, and that news reporting and presenting was being monopolised. The outcome produced a more powerful, but not powerful enough to be influential, Press Council, and that mergers of newspapers had to be referred to a new, special section of the Monopolies Commission. Again it was the airing of views rather than of substantial results which satisfied the journalists.

The third Royal Commission on the Press was concerned if any newspapers would survive at all. But again it was formed in part by the pressure from journalists, and again the airing of views has been all that the journalists have gained. The Monopolies Commission and the Press Council are in a similar category; they have not stopped mergers, indeed they have found newer and less tangible reasons why they should continue, although these are forums where views can be placed. That they have had little or no influence on the newspaper world as a whole, and on the plight of the journalists in particular, has led the journalists to react in other more direct ways.

8.3 JOURNALISTS ON STRIKE

With the onset of commercialism, directed by the new owners, or the new style of old owners of the regional press, the position of journalists has declined in terms of salary, working conditions and status, which are tangibles easily perceived by journalists and their managers alike. (The processes producing such a situation are rarely or only hazily perceived by the journalists.) As long as they are seen not to be interfered with in the collection and presentation of news then recourse to the supporters of the freedom of the press is useless. In fact they are seen to be relatively free from the influence of advertisers, and owners. The Fleet Street proprietors have been replaced with owners like Thomson, who have publicly guaranteed editorial independence, but that freedom as traditionally defined is being eroded in more covert and undetected ways, and thus journalists, to rectify any of their grievances, have to do it themselves.

In Centre A and Centre B, this they did in a series of strikes, work-to-rules, overtime bans etc, in the period 1972-1974. The reasons for going on strike have been enunciated, and it can be said their grievances were genuine and substantial. The strikes that did take place involved everyone in the editorial department, except the editor, this because of the rules of the National Union of Journalists, which tries to enforce a closed shop in the editorial department and in most offices this is the case, but a few journalists do join the Institute of Journalists. All members are full members, except the editor who takes associate membership, and this means he does not have to abide by any decisions taken at a mandatory chapel meeting, and it is only at such meetings that industrial action can be voted upon.

At Centre B during the research it was possible to attend two mandatory chapel meetings, the agendas of which were mainly concerned with such action. At both meetings the feelings of the journalists was one of frustration with working conditions and resentment of management, local and central, for not rectifying grievances. The first meeting was held on the third day of one of a series of three-day stoppages co-ordinated by the N.U.J. Regional journalists as a whole were in dispute with the employers' association over the interpretation of phase 3 of the government's pay policy (1972-4), and strike action in support of the journalists case was to take place on Tuesday, Wednesday and Thursday of successive weeks until a satisfactory settlement had been reached. The effectiveness of journalists striking is nearly always reduced by the continued publication of the newspaper single-handed by the editor (or, with the deputy editor), which tends, as it did in this case, to increase the frustration and bitterness of the journalists. From a management point of view the economic hardship of a strike is reduced, as the paper, albeit with less editorial, is published with all its advertisements, and thus revenue is maintained whilst some costs are reduced. Readers, in the short term are not dissatisfied, so as a bargaining strategy, strikes by journalists have to be longer rather than shorter.

Of course other ploys can be used, but support from the print unions or the editors is usually neither sought nor given. However, this dispute at Centre B was most unusual because of action by the van drivers, members of the Society of Graphical and Allied Trades (SOGAT), who had refused to cross picket lines physically manned by journalists at the exist normally used by the vans. The newspaper on the Tuesday and Wednesday had been printed but not published.

The meeting took place at the factory gates, and was held primarily to discuss further action in the light of the relative success achieved in the previous two days. There was a high turn-out of the chapel to this meeting, and a lively discussion ensued over the continuation of the stoppage until Friday. Many younger members were in favour of this, and no doubt in colloquial terms would be termed 'militants', although all they were doing was to try to resolve the dispute more quickly by applying further pressure on the management. Some older journalists (the 'moderates') had been against industrial action in the first place and thus were against this proposed extension. Because any new action would be in isolation of the rest of regional journalists the moderates held sway and the motion was rejected narrowly. (A call for support to picket the delivery of local papers, was after this rejection, easily carried.)

The dispute at Centre B worried some senior managers. That the NUJ and SOGAT had colluded was cause for consternation, but most felt that it was a token gesture by the SOGAT men, who had unsettled grievances of their own. After all if the print union supported the journalists, then the print workers would be laid off, thus losing pay, and in the event of a reverse of this situation, the journalists could afford no help to the print unions, technologically being unable to do so. It was this thinking that led management to reject the possibility of bringing in police to clear the right of way. In any case publicity from such a confrontation would be positively harmful, and they felt that the dispute should be channelled through the agreed procedures.

The meeting quickly turned to other issues through which latent frustration could possibly become overt. There was some criticism over the handling of the dispute, especially of management, but also by some, of the mother of the chapel, a rather attractive young lady in her early twenties. Confusion was agreed to be the cause and discussion centred on proposed management action to cancel rest days if, in the normal course of events, they would have been taken during the strike. Nearly all journalists expressed alarm at this and the general attitude was that if management pursued this policy, then a further meeting should be immediately called to discuss strike action. It was becoming clear that a national dispute for these journalists at Centre B, was only a vehicle to voice local grievances. The danger, of course, as many realised, was that the airing and settlement of the national dispute might cloud or even erase local issues. However, it was these local issues which were at the centre of the second meeting some two weeks later.

This was also a mandatory chapel meeting held in the canteen and, being highly formal, permission was sought for and granted to enable my attendance. The national dispute had now ended but the dissatisfaction over the level of settlement served only to make this meeting more militant than it otherwise might be. The four issues on the agenda, some of them relating back to the increasing bureaucratisation of journalists work, were movement of staff, replacement of staff, expenses, and a possible overtime ban. On the first, movement of staff, management (in this case the editors) had proposed that, as one paper was understaffed and the other overstaffed, than one or two journalists could move papers. As a general trade union principle, movement of staff is either strongly resisted, or only done with union approval, and in this case there was the complication of loyalty to newspapers. Traditionally in a newspaper centre where at least two newspapers are published, there exists a loyalty amongst journalists for each newspaper which is often manifested in rivalry, particularly where the two newspapers are evenings. Thus any flexibility in the utilisation of journalists between newspapers is abhorred. If there is a shortage and a surplus, then this is rectified by advertising for new journalists and natural wastage and if a journalist wished to switch newspapers then this would involve a resignation and a reappointment with a fresh contract.

The discussion followed these trade union principles until verification of the facts was sought from the News Editor of the overstaffed newspaper. He was unaware of such a situation referring to the absence on leave (more or less permanently) of a features writer, to the journalist who was on a training course lasting nine months, and to what appeared to be a new practice of counting juniors as full-time equivalents. It was accustomed practice to count them only as one-half, which thus left the newspaper under, not overstaffed, all of which was seen as a management ploy to cut the staffing levels. Flexibility in the utilisation of labour in this case would have allowed a false situation of overstaffing on one paper to legitimise under-staffing on the other. If one newspaper was say, one over-staffed, and the other two understaffed, the movement of one journalist would, at least in the short term, avert the need, from management's point of view to recruit new staff, and the longer such a situation persisted, the more credible it becomes.

This naturally led to the second point, the replacement of staff, particularly on the "officially" understaffed paper, for which journalists had been interviewed but none had been taken on, management saying that they were not of a sufficiently high quality. Opinion at the meeting however, felt this was another management ploy to permanently reduce the editorial budget, and many knew unemployed journalists who, they felt, <u>were</u> of a sufficient standard to be employed on the newspaper. The matter rested with instructions to the mother and chairman of the chapel to pursue the matter further with the editors.

The same conclusion was reached over the issue of expenses. Central management had issued to each centre, a directive over the control of expenses, some of which were to be curtailed, whilst others had to be investigated, and those incurred in "chasing" a lead which results in no story would no longer be bona fide. Such an instruction clearly inhibits and then limits the journalists ability to pursue stories, leaving investigative reporting as a luxury not only to the newspaper but to the journalist as well. (Later, expenses incurred after 5.30 p.m. would, except in the most special of cases, not be allowable, which of course, further restricted the journalists ability to research news stories. The position of editorial managers, particularly the editor is interesting here. They can play 'Caesar's wife' without great difficulty, agreeing with central management, whilst sympathising with their staff, or even promising to make representations they know are doomed to failure. At Centre B where the editors were more managers than journalists, such a position was easy to construct and maintain.

The meeting was fairly hostile, because of management action or inaction, and because the NUJ appeared powerless to successfully intervene and change matters. The outcome was merely that the leaders have discussions with management, although some NUJ members, who wished to give their leaders more bargaining power proposed an overtime ban in the event of no satisfactory settlement of the issues raised.

Unfortunately for the journalists such a move, though appearing fairly militant, and giving the chairman and mother of the chapel more power in negotiation, actually plays into the hands of management, as an overtime ban means no overtime pay, and thus a cut in costs. Certainly it will mean fewer stories, but as expenses after 5.30 p.m. were under scrutiny anyway, the number of stories lost would be minimal and the newspaper would be little different, with perhaps more management of the existing news, although this is exactly what central management requires. After a period the local managers can effectively say that overtime by journalists is inessential for the publication of a successful newspaper, and thus in the end it is the managers who will ban overtime.

Given the structure of the NUJ there is an anomaly, because managers are morally pressured to join the trade union of their workers. At first sight this invokes an interesting paradox because it cuts across the normal "two-sides" of manager and subordinates, an authority relationship which according to Dahrendorf (1959) provides the two-sided structure often referred to in industrial relations. A strike, or any action against management's decision highlights this paradox. It exists for both sides, the managers having to abide by union decisions taken in the main by a majority of their subordinates; and for the subordinates themselves, who, while objecting to a management decision, by the authority of the union, see the managers supporting their objections. Whether the editorial managers perceive the situation as a paradox depends on their allegiance to or perception of management or journalism, something found in their attitudes to the strikes and other industrial action.

8.4 JOURNALISM: PROFESSION OR OCCUPATION?

If it can be argued that journalism is a profession, with a particular professional culture, then managers may find it fairly easy to associate with their subordinates on issues concerning that professionalisation. Such issues might well be status and working conditions as well as salary. Oliver Boyd-Barrett has considered whether, in particular the recruitment and training of journalists can provide a basis for considering journalism as a profession. He uses the outline given initially by Ernest Greenwood who

> 'defines an occupation as a profession according to the possession or otherwise of five major attributes -
>
> i) a systematic body of theory
> ii) professional authority
> iii) community sanction
> iv) ethical codes
> v) a professional culture.' (1970, p.181).

On all counts he suggests that journalism is lacking and he turns to the definition of Millerson who favours a continuum approach to professions, defined as a type of

> 'higher-grade, non-manual occupation, with both subjectively and objectively recognised occupational status, possessing a well-defined area of study or concern and providing a definite service, after advanced training.' (1964, p.10).

Boyd-Barrett found a lack of subjective identification with professionalism, quoting Tunstall's study of one journalistic elite, the Westminster Lobby Correspondents. (1970a). With his own sample he found journalists perceiving their own role in technical rather than professional terms, although there are several signs that professionalisation is occurring. For instance, the regulative role of the Press Council, and the continued existence of a professional association, the Institute of Journalists, although it only has about 2,000 members. Training is also undertaken by the following bodies: The National Council for the Training of Journalists, the Industrial Training Board and various journalist training centres (e.g. at Harlow and Cardiff.) Unfortunately these for Boyd-Barrett are not enough, for to him journalism is not a profession, although the

> 'NCTJ fulfils some of the objective conditions for success in professionalisation, its function in this respect is hindered by a relative lack of independence from employing associations, an alien occupational ideology and non-standardised structure, its own perceptions of its role and the perceptions of those outside the occupation, and certain possible consequences of self-selection amongst its trainee recruits.' (1970, p.201).

Tunstall also using Greenwood's framework concludes,

> 'It is extremely improbable that Journalism could ever acquire these professional attributes to the extent of, for instance, medicine. A more realistic objective, if the occupation wished to pursue it, would be to make journalism into a semi-profession - in the way that teaching, for instance, is a semi-profession.' (1971, p.69).

Carr-Saunders and Wilson (1933) some 40 years earlier had arrived at similar conclusions, which in total now justifies the rejection of the hypothesis that managerial commitment to journalism is based on professionalism. Part professionalism may be allowable, but there must be other reasons for the allegiance, for instance, consciousness of being a separate well defined occupation. However, enquiring into that, other aspects of consideration here are the journalist's perception of their role to the role of others, and the relative status of their occupation. In the Fleet Street model, journalism was very important, indeed central to the publication of a newspaper, as editorial controlled the areas of interchange between themselves and other departments, thus ensuring a news orientated organisation and newspaper. All other functions, advertising, production, circulation etc, existed because of news and were therefore seen as service departments to allow the publication of news. The journalists thought that the gathering, writing and presentation of news was a specialised process, not emenable to normal managerial techniques of control. For instance, productivity per man was an oft-quoted phrase concerning print workers, but never journalists. Thus journalists saw their role as more important than any others, one of high status, a view with which the rest of the enterprise did not disagree. Given this situation some form of editorial consciousness would develop. The accent would be on artistry and flair rather than managerial skills, and senior editorial staffs would not perceive themselves as managers.

The bulk of the research has suggested the opposite, that senior editorial staffs do act as editorial managers, and that the rest of the organisation sees editorial as a necessary input to a commercial operation, although as such it needs to be managed and controlled. The rest of the organisation, particularly the commercial aspects, are now in control of the areas of interchange, and only require a basic editorial content to be able to market their product as a newspaper. Thus the perceived status of editorial is much lower, as their role vis-a-vis other roles is gradually reduced. This diminished role of editorial would affect the level of consciousness of journalists as an occupation. The emphasis for senior editorial staffs is on managerial skills and administrative work, or an ability to organise journalists to collect sufficient news from routine sources to fill the space in the paper allocated to them by the commercial side of the firm, whilst for the journalists there is only this diminished role to be conscious of. Normally this would detract from any strong group cohesion, but, given the threats to their position from commercial pressures, it may, at least initially, reinforce any consciousness that exists, as the journalists attempt to defend their position. Thus the reduced role and status is likely to divide journalists and their managers apart, rather than together, as managers begin to ally more to management than to journalism.

There is however a unifying force which provides more than a degree of group cohesion, and a consciousness of being part of an occupation. This is in terms of their commitment, for most, to newspapers in general, and for some, the present newspaper in particular. Journalists regard newspapers as a living thing, something they have created, and therefore something to protect, rather than treat abjectly or even kill (by means of a strike). During the disputes that occurred this commitment to the paper was evident amongst the editorial managers; the Editor (Times, Centre B) remarked during the dispute, 'the show must go on. Its part of the mystic of journalism, the paper is a living thing.' A Deputy Features Editor (evening, Centre A), 'Journalism, a calling, a profession in the blood, its there.' The News Editor of the same paper, 'I'd rather see the paper on the street than strike with the trade union.' The Deputy Editor (Observer, Centre B), 'But we must have loyalty to newspapers, often at all costs.' The Deputy Editor (Times, Centre B),

> 'We've never stopped in a dispute - this because of our loyalty, our professional ethic, after all it is a living thing .... I've sympathy with the grievances, but I must ensure that the paper comes out.'

These statements declaring commitment to the newspaper were typical of many comments, although, however, such commitment was voiced in reaction to a strike, and it is thus obvious that the commitment to the newspaper does not, in this case, lead to journalistic consciousness. Indeed it is the reverse, for these senior editorial staff were reflecting the managerial position that they were in. There are further reinforcing tendencies towards this managerial ethic. For instance, the career pattern is seen to be primarily out of journalism, whilst Fleet Street is no longer the main attraction, rather it is managerial careers. That the newspapers are part of a group provides easy access for promotion (and indeed to their other interests), and even within the editorial departments there is a proliferation of managerial posts. In the morning at Centre A, there was in the editorial department, Editor, Deputy Editor, Chief Assistant Editor, Assistant Editor, and nine other managerial posts. With so many, (and so few Editor's jobs to accede to), managerial experience can and was being gained. It will be remembered that one Deputy Editor at Centre B had moved to be Assistant Managing Director, at Centre A the Assistant Editor was being groomed for such a move, two other Editorial Managers saw the possibility for themselves, and several saw no reason why editorial staff should not take senior management posts. Finally, and again from the previous chapter, the increased amount of administrative and organisational work suggests that the senior staffs have to become more managerially conscious, even if initially they appear to abhor such trends.

It is now clear that there are influences suggesting a different outlook for the Editorial Managers and the journalists, and if this is applied to the diminished status of journalism perceived by the editorial managers, it refers more to the reporters than to the managers. They after all are now managers and have a different basis for their status. By reference to the last chapter and the section on pay and status it can be seen that it is the status of the journalist that has been reduced, 'their' status, not anyone elses, and the conflict is over the reduction of their status.

8.5 THE EDITORIAL MANAGERS' PERCEPTIONS OF THE INDUSTRIAL CONFLICT

The difference in consciousness of editorial managers and journalists became apparent when they were asked of their attitudes to the various forms of industrial action undertaken. These attitudes need to be seen in relation to the editorial manager's opinion of the grievances, which were low pay, and poor working conditions, although diminished status, as an underlying cause cannot be overlooked. The attitudes expressed in the last chapter suggest a great deal of sympathy with such grievances, as indeed some of them affected the editorial managers (no car, old typewriters, etc.). As a group the managers could say that the journalists 'had been taken advantage of because of their attitudes.' (Deputy Editor, Times, Centre B), and the Chief Assistant Editor (morning, Centre A) said, 'We have been used by management because of the lure of the job, the intrinsic value etc, the journalist always puts the paper first.' The Deputy News Editor, (evening, Centre A), 'Journalism is a profession and management have used us in this way.' The Features Editor (morning, Centre A),

> 'Well, the journalist has never really been organised because of individual professional pride. We've been

'totally dependent on individuals, never worked as a team.'

The Chief Sub-Editor (Centre B, Times) thought that because 'the Journalist has never had the power to stop the paper they've always been treated with contempt.'

The Managers perceived the journalists grievances not only in material terms, but in the general treatment that journalists had had from management, whom they thought had for too long taken advantage of the journalists empathy for a newspaper, that they would not kill what was to them a living thing. The Editorial Manager's sympathetic attitude led to a justification of industrial action in global terms, to rectify the grievances. They referred to the production workers and the way their methods had been successful. One Editor (Centre B, Times) said that the reaction of the production worker had been to 'strike first, ask later', and 'that journalists should use such tactics.' His Features Editor said that 'if the journalists are treated like ordinary workers, they react like ordinary workers.' The Deputy Editor (Centre A, morning) was more adamant, 'the printers just fart and always get their way,' and according to the Deputy News Editor (Centre A, evening), 'it is significant to some people that the production workers get more money.' This led one Deputy Editor to conclude, 'Management have given way to production, why not journalists.'

However, individually, the Editorial Managers found it hard to justify the industrial action, partly for the journalists, and certainly not for themselves. At Centre B, there had been constant overtime bans, and work-to-rule periods, but Editorial Management had found great difficulty in operating them. The Sports Editor of the Evening Observer said he had 'to sneakily not be seen to be not working to rule.' The Chief Sub-Editor remarked he did 'not know what to do when we're striking; I'm not in favour of the strike even though the pay is bad.' At Centre A, several strikes had taken place, but the Editorial Managers did not want to be part of such action. The Deputy Features Editor (morning) said 'I'm a professional, no strike ethics - and in any case overtime pay is not a striking matter.' The Deputy Editor (evening) was 'against striking because it doesn't achieve anything.' Overtime bans which came as a result of reduced expenses would, a Deputy Editor said (Centre B, Times), 'Only damage the editorial material that we have, and eventually damage the status of the journalist.'

Industrial action of several forms had taken place at both Centre A and Centre B, and of the twenty seven editorial managers interviewed in these centres, twenty three had taken part in such action. The four Editors concerned are allowed associate member status in the NUJ and are not required to attend, as all other members are, mandatory chapel meetings, where decisions on strikes are made. The Editorial Managers were concerned to explain why they had taken part in such industrial action, and in all cases they decided it was nothing to do with them. Without exception the Editorial Managers at Centre A said it was the influx of graduates who had 'stirred up trouble', and it must be remembered that these graduates formed the increasingly qualified entrants to what was becoming a more routine and less demanding job. The following comments were made on these intruders at

Centre A, 'The graduates have made the union turn left. They're revolutionaries, Trotskyites.' (Assistant Editor, morning), 'This influx of graduates, they're all politically motivated.' (Deputy Editor, Evening), 'But these graduates, university has given them a political awareness, they've become unsettled.' (Deputy Editor, morning), 'Over the last five or six years these graduates have been introduced. With their background and university environment, it breeds militants. They tend to ask more questions.' (News Editor, evening),

> 'The journalists are on strike because of an influx of left-wing graduates - leftish intellectuals .... maybe symptomatic of society today - got to conform but they don't want to. Well knowing from experience if they had their way they would kill the baby.' (Chief Ass. Editor,morning).

At Centre B where graduate entry had been in operation since the newspapers had started, graduates were not seen as the main problem causing the conflict. It was the proximity to a major city with higher rates and differing standards of journalism which compared very favourably with the position at Centre B.

The graduates were determined, so the Editorial Managers thought, to rectify the low pay and status by militant action, which the Managers thought came easily to this student intake, because of their political awareness and proven ability to act in a decisive manner. From sit-ins, demonstrations (even Paris 1968 was mentioned) it led easily in employment to the 'let's screw the employer' attitude and the strikes, go-slows, overtime bans and work-to-rules, that occurred. One Deputy Editor (evening, Centre A), told of a resignation interview with one of these 'lefties'. He was going to be a reporter for the 'Socialist Worker' and would be back with hob-nail boots on, although unfortunately he did not get the job and had to take part-time employment with the 'Tailor and Cutter'.

When questioned about how strike decisions could be passed at the mandatory chapel meetings, the Editorial Managers referred to the general apathy of the non-militant members who could be swayed by the Marxist demagogues. The Deputy News Editor of the evening at Centre A explained,

> 'There is a great deal of apathy and left-wingers have taken a grasp. Journalists haven't been used to this situation and certain sections have led on others. Important decisions are pushed through. People are swayed at the mandatory chapel meeting when strike action is taken.'

There is an unpleasant irony for the journalists in actually taking industrial action. Fundamentally they were concerned with status, but by striking to complain of lost status, they are further demoted in the opinion of the rest of the newspaper staffs. This further demotion strengthened the editorial managers consciousness of being a manager rather than a journalist, although this did not stop them, and the graduate issue reinforced this, reminiscing on how, once journalism had been a profession, and the NUJ a type of professional body. The Deputy Features Editor (Centre A, morning) said 'the NUJ is now a trade union, but it was then a professional body.' An Editor (Centre A, evening), 'The NUJ is a type of professional association although it is becoming more militant.' His Features Editor agreed, 'The NUJ is now a trade union - but in the past it had tended to be more of a professional association.' A News Editor (Centre B, Evening Observer), 'The NUJ was a professional body'. A Deputy Features Editor (Centre A, evening), 'Now a trade union, then a professional body.' All these comments exhibit the 'Rebecca Myth', which Gouldner uses to describe changes in a factory.

> 'Some years ago, Daphne Du Maurier wrote a book about a young woman who married a widower, only to be plagued by the memory of his first wife, Rebecca, whose virtues were widely extolled. The idealisation of the absent is a well-known phenomenon.' (Gouldner, 1952, p.346)

In this case it was an idealisation of a previous situation which rather than absent was mythical. It has already been decided that journalism has never been a profession, and the NUJ a professional body, however this 'Rebecca Myth' serves a very useful purpose for the editorial managers, for it reinforces, along with other things, their managerial rather than editorial consciousness. They can reject the new trade union type militancy found in the NUJ because they cannot identify with it, which also correlates with the demotion in status of journalism. They, as managers see this affecting them less than the reporters themselves, and therefore the militancy is not concerned to rectify their position but is thus something outside their sphere of consciousness. The NUJ has become more militant, although was always a trade union, but the change is perceived as much greater, of kind rather than degree. The editorial managers can now act as managers and not journalists and be subjectively justified in doing so.

The editorial managers then went on at length to explain these differences, in terms of their early careers, and the attitudes of the new graduates. One Editor at Centre B (Observer) remarked, 'When I was a young journalist I enjoyed the job but this is not the case of the young journalists now.' The Chief Assistant Editor (Centre A, morning)

> 'the older, over 30's were against the strike action - the voting for strikes was very narrow, the bulk of those voting for action were under 30. They have no feeling for the paper, that journalists once used to have. Its much more a job or work now. They only want an 8 hour day, the rest is overtime. I've worked 12-16 hours a day and never claimed overtime.'

A Deputy Editor (morning, Centre A), 'We had grievances years ago, but we had the enthusiasm for the job, and this was enough to overcome them.' The News Editor (evening, Centre A) continued in the same vein, 'It's a combination of status, pay, conditions - we used to have a professional core. When I was Chairman of the local branch, right-wing people ran the show. I suppose intrinsic satisfaction gone, the varnish of the job wears off more quickly now.' The last two comments are indication that the editorial managers were realising that the journalists job is now more routine and less demanding. However, being managers, they saw such routine aspects as necessary and continued to condemn the new graduates in terms of their lack of commitment, to a job which is now somewhat unattractive. The Deputy Editor (evening, Centre B), said 'Journalists now don't want to work the hard news stories.' The Features Editor (Centre A, evening) continued,

> 'They want to be specialists, but they need to learn the basis of journalism. It's a less attractive job for these more sophisticated people, but they have to do the court reports etc.'

The Deputy Editor (Centre A, morning) isolates one reason, 'There's much less investigating reporting, but some journalists want to become columnists, but see that their ambitions are blocked off at an early stage.'

From these attitudes there leads a path to managerialism, and much of that has been documented. However for the editorial managers there now appeared to be a paradox with the membership of the NUJ, in that it contains both workers and managers. A Features Editor (Centre A, evening) said the Chapel, 'was composed of 30% management' and the Editor (Centre B, Observer) talked of being a 'line manager' in industrial relations. He also saw the problem for his closest subordinates, the Assistant Editor and Deputy Editor, both of whom also had to act as 'line managers' for industrial relations problems. 'Its very difficult for my immediate deputies. They cannot come to work in a strike.' This led a Deputy Editor (Centre A, morning) to suggest that

> 'all three editorial executives should be associate rather than full members of the NUJ; it is a difficult position; unionwise I'm a worker; firmwise I'm a manager. I'm too close to the editor to wear a union hat.'

The Features Editor (Centre A, evening) saw that there were 'clear lines of demarcation, we are NCO's rather than officers.' Being tied to chapel decisions was becoming too much for some editorial managers, associate membership being one solution, but a more dramatic one was suggested by the Sports News Editor (Centre A, evening),

> 'there has been talk of a mangement association for people of my level and upwards, as we think more like management. But it has not got any further than that.'

The paradox of managers in a workers trade union is central to the discussion of the closed-shop in newspapers, which journalists see as essential so that their bargaining strength is increased by any threat of a strike. If several editor executives were only associate members of the NUJ then a reasonably-sized paper could be produced every day, and this is no doubt part of the thinking of those opposing any closed shops, the freedom of the press being only a surface issue, improperly defined anyway. This paradox was highlighted in an incident mentioned earlier at Centre B. The NUJ house chapel had called a mandatory chapel meeting between nine o'clock and five o'clock, a pseudonym for a strike. Under NUJ rules the editors need not attend, but in this case both deputy editors worked normally, and together the four of them produced the two evening papers, with less editorial than normal, but sufficient to look like a newspaper. The paper was printed but the drivers refused to cross the picket lines of the journalists. The incident highlighted the paradox for an editorial manager. Had the editor by himself produced the paper, no picket lines would have been justified.

8.6 POSSIBLE SUPPORT FROM COMMERCIAL MANAGERS AND CONSOLIDATION OF COMMERCIALISM

This chapter so far has been concerned with the reactions of editorial staff, managers and journalists, to the increasing control of their work. Nearly all of them resented the process, but given the advantages of more space, and guaranteed continuation of publication, they felt unable to resist. The journalists felt more concerned as the industrial action shows, but with senior staffs acting as editorial managers their chance of success was minimal. One source of encouragement, however, was found during the research. Whilst most non-editorial managers welcomed the control of editorial by increased commercialisation, some expressed concern as to how far such a process could go. It was producing the near complete domination of the organisation by the drive to sell advertising space, to produce a newspaper overfull of advertising, and decisions internally based on the benefit for advertising. This domination, abhorrent to editorial, was questioned by some non-editorial managers. The Assistant to the production manager (Centre A)

> 'Ad sales rather than circulation sales dominate this newspaper. We are therefore revenue orientated. This is somewhat misguided - the size is governed by ad sales, not news. If there are small levels of ads, then no paper .... This had led to there being too much management for instance in display.'

The Deputy Chief Accountant (Centre A)

> 'The revenue side of the business is given too much importance. There is no check on how much is spent by advertising. The priorities are wrong. They spend money fairly liberally - each agent puts in £5-£7 for entertaining a rep .... Editorial is not so important here, because of advertising - it is becoming like an Ad. journal. This is all wrong as the quality of the paper is going downhill - its got a reputation that it is now an advertising medium. I would increase the editorial quota in each newspaper and pay for this by staff savings and making the operation more efficient. But I think this emphasis on advertising is common to many newspapers ..... There are ridiculous anomalies .. .. Some individuals are grossly overpaid - some ad men become administrators and retain the use of their company car.'

Others echoed these sentiments often in a way suggesting that there ought to be some form of balance between editorial and advertising, not only in the newspaper itself, but with the organisation. The Chief Accountant,(Centre A) 'We must maximise profit in a manner which doesn't conflict with long term assets. A realisation that we provide the community with news, entertainment, goods to buy and sell. We must align with the community.' The Advertising Manager (Run of Page, Centre A) 'We need more co-operation at senior level between Editorial and Commercial; we want quality not quantity from editorial.' The Circulation Sales Manager (Centre B)

> 'The paper has too many ads. Its a mistaken understanding by people. When we sit in a Commercial Meeting the emphasis is on paper and advertising input. There's always a reduction of editorial quota. Ads like it then, but I don't. We need adverts but there's too many now. Editorial have less say - editor is always short of staff, and when he's under pressure he readily agrees to a lower quota.'

Finally the Assistant Managing Director at Centre B

> 'a newspaper - a matter of selling ads and selling the paper. A commercially orientated paper - its built in - it can be no other way. Given this its then a question of who tits in with the job. But there has got to be a balance between profit and the paper. We need to make a profit, but we need a good paper - We've probably got too many ads.'

At Centre B the move towards their balance of advertising and editorial was occurring because of the importance of production. The production manager could limit the activities of advertising in the areas of interchange, particularly in deadlines and late advertisements. He would have to keep inside his own budgets, as late copy means extra overtime, which means increased costs. Even the advertising managers were realising a balance was necessary. The General Advertising Manager (Centre A) commented, 'I need to know more about other departments, I need to understand the working of editorial for instance.' The realisation is that a certain amount of editorial is necessary, quality as well as quantity is important. However this conclusion is not to suggest that commercialism is withdrawing its influence, rather it is consolidating its position, for it is the commercial managers who decide what the balance is going to be.

One apparent aspect of this consolidation was the reduction in mobility of managers. It will be remembered that a major spur to bureaucratisation was the movement of managers through a series of various decision-making situations. As a consequence managers became more experienced and their organisations more rule-dominated. Moreover if the overall strategy was to induce commercialism by a succession of managers, then at some point it must be determined that newspapers were sufficiently profitable, and thus the movements would slow down. From a corporate point of view, this point had been reached by the early 1970's. Consolidation was occurring, and in fact many executives in newspapers in this and other groups were moving into the other interests of the group, as diversification became popular. It was also possible that the corporate boards had realised that too much mobility might be detrimental to the interests of the newspaper. At least some managers were raising the question, some even feeling that it was exploitation. The Display Advertising Manager (Centre C) remarked that 'the movement of personnel is a two-edged weapon, but since moves has stopped, display advertising has increased.' The Assistant to the Production Manager (Centre A) said,

> 'There are problems of moving executives around the centres - 2-3 years to prove yourself. For instance here the A.M.D. has the objective of looking at wage levels and reducing production unit costs - but by doing that we get the highest earnings of the group which naturally gives resentment elsewhere, in this building and in other centres.'

The General Advertising Manager (Centre A)

> 'The growth of management, big movements between 1963 and 1969 - well its beginning to slow now. Their growth was done far too quickly. The corporate Board had to do something. Now consolidate and in fact the top personnel in newspapers are beginning to be moved into the other interests of the group.'

One consequence of this consolidation was that less qualified managers were needed to organise the various departments. Commercialism over the last decade and a half had rid the enterprise of its 'indulgency pattern', and a structure now existed into which managers could be slotted. Of course this accepts that newspapers will not develop, well at least not at the pace of the previous period. However if it is accepted then the calibre of management need not be so high, and in accordance with this thinking, salaries were low and working conditions (when compared with other establishments) pretty poor.

The Advertising Manager (Run of Page, Centre A) commented,

> 'It seems that in this organisation, production staff have far more benefits than the managerial staff. Someone like Clive Jenkins will eventually get them. For instance at the moment the compositor has four weeks holiday, we have three weeks. They're poor employers.'

The General Advertising Manager (Centre A), 'They're bad employers - no perks, bad benefits, awful pensions, fewer holidays than in my previous job (outside newspaper), few subsidised facilities .... ' The Marketing Services Manager at Centre B was concerned about 'differentials' and also mentioned Clive Jenkins as a possibility. The Key Accounts Advertising Manager at Centre A though 'that the organisation has its shortcomings, particularly its poor pension scheme.'

There are effects from this, the most obvious being that low salaries did produce managers of a lower calibre, and although this is probably more long-term, in a shorter-term low salaries might lead to low commitment, and greater mobility. Such mobility will be diverted by individual choice rather than by corporate planning, but the effect will be much the same, that of maintaining or increasing the bureaucracy.

NOTES

(1) See George Murray: The Press and the Public, Chap 1-4.
(2) See the annual reports: The Press and the People.

9 Conclusion

Studies concerning newspapers have for the most part ignored the processes which shape organisational structure and thus as a whole their examination of the press in society can at best only be partial. The multitude of studies examining the rise of the press as a historical phenomena have been followed by other developing what has come to be termed the sociology of mass communications. Whilst the former group had some general concern with the role of the press in Western democratic societies, the latter focussed more on the effects of communication on various sectors of their host societies. In doing so, some of these studies have ventured within the enterprise but have generally concentrated on editors and their staff,and their relationship to news contacts, and have virtually ignored the commercial side, by implicitly assuming a static organisational model in which the editorial department determines, without question, the activities of other functions. Although with newspapers it is often inferred that the editor and his staff determine what content shall be, their room for manoeuvre may be influenced or even determined by the non-editorial section of the enterprise. This study has tried to show that in the regional daily press these influences are strong enough to raise questions about the processes of how and what should be reported. The major thesis is that such constraints on editorial activities will affect news content, both qualitatively and quantitatively. This has occurred because the press has passed into the hands of business men interested primarily in a return on capital investment.

Editors and their staffs have always had to work within some kind of financial framework, (Lee, 1976) but it has not been until recently that their work has been defined by such financial objectives. Historically they have perceived their work as central to a newspaper enterprise, and that the editorial content must be of a sufficient quality to ensure survival. This emphasis on editorial content, and concomitantly a large staff to collect the required news was exacerbated by competition from similar newspapers and justified by the ideology of publication which was based on propaganda. This legitimated certain editorial activities, leading to editorial domination of the enterprise as necessary for the fulfilment of the objective of publishing a high circulation newspaper to propagate various political and social causes.

Two major changes occurred which altered the internal structure of regional newspapers, and left editorial perceptions of their position in relation to the rest of the organisation, increasingly false. The first concerned the change in ideology of publication which left editorial with little authority to control, and second, the acceptance by owners that advertising and marketing may be more important for profitable newspapers than the latest and most exclusive news. This follows from the realisation that competition from other newspapers was gradually disappearing (or had disappeared completely) and that success was measured not in circulation but in profit.

The onset of commercialism, particularly in the regions was caused, in part, by a change in the ideology of publication held by the owners of the press. Some owners were new and brought commercial techniques from the business world, whilst those owners who stayed realised the benefits that could be gained by making their regional newspapers profitable. Many of these owners were still interested in propaganda, but for this now solely used their national newspapers, which were increasingly supported by the profit from their regional newspapers. Competition all but disappeared for regional newspapers, and thus the emphasis on editorial content and large editorial staffs could no longer be justified by the need for the latest and most exclusive news. Increasing revenue and cutting costs were objectives stemming from this new ideology of publication, and were met by the emergence of new departments and the growth of the often ignored commercial sectors of the organisation. Increases in advertising, marketing and circulation staff were consequences of these changes in ideology and the work activities of these departments assumed a greater importance than hitherto. They perceived the future of newspapers to be secured only by increasing profit, an objective they felt they had the authority to achieve because of the changed ideology of publication.

The position of editorial staffs in these changes became unsure, for no longer did an ideology of publication exist which legitimated their deomination of the organisation. The new wave of commercial managers saw editorial as one input amongst many, and further, an input that could be controlled and directed by commercial needs. On the other hand editorial staffs basing their perceptions on traditional grounds, continued to believe in their own importance as a basis for the success of the newspaper. However their perceptions did not match the reality of this new commercial era which became characterised more by the commercial drive for profit, than by the diligent search for the truth. Those in authority are now the managers who gain revenue, rather than those who select the correct news.

The nature of the underlying change can be considered in terms of the 'gatekeeper' concept, and indeed several writers (1) have utilised this notion to explain, in particular, the operations in the editorial department. In this particular study such a notion could be used to gain understanding of the power and changes in it, of various departments, or key individuals therein. For instance, given that the ideology of publication centres on propaganda, then the newsman who selects which stories should be included, or investigated, in other words, the 'gatekeeper'appears to be powerful. (The strategic contingencies theory would support this.) However, if the ideology of publication changes, as it has done, to centre on revenue and profit, then it is the commercial staff, who control the revenue and thus the profit, who become the'gatekeepers', and concomitantly it is they who assume positions of authority. It is they who determine where editorial material is placed (by the very fact that they determine where advertisements are placed); and it is they therefore that constrict the editorial department in its activities.

Murphy rejects the idea of the gatekeeper approach,

> 'The idea is that certain positions are nodal, and therefore the person occupying the position has power over the flow of information. But the use of the model involves the assumption that journalists such as wire editors do occupy gatekeepers positions. They do not clarify in what types of organisational flow these positions constitute 'gates'. They do not clarify their criteria of nodality. The fact of nodality and therefore of organisational power is assumed by the analysts.' (1976, p.136).

In replacement Murphy suggests analysis should concentrate on the 'continuous and interlinked chains of influence forming a matrix of individuals attempting to pre-empt at various points the actions of other people whom they see as being amenable in some snese to their influence.' (1976, p.137). This has great similarities with the network analysis developed by Mitchell (2) who by taking the notion from Barnes of a 'total network', (Mitchell, 1969, p.12) refines the concept by anchoring the network on some reference point. At first he suggests 'the use of groups as points of anchorage' but

> 'It seems probable that most of the propositions concerning the relationships among groups could be restated at a somewhat lower level of abstraction in terms of the links among the various individuals concerned. If this is so there is much to be said for the presentation of analyses of network relationships as being anchored on an individual chosen particularly because of the part he plays in the events being analysed.' (1969, p.15).

This appears to return to the nodal concept so disliked by Murphy, although this is not quite the case, as far from describing the role of one particular person (i.e. the gatekeeper), the analysis concentrates on the interaction that person has with others in the network. Further, and of more importance, it is crucial to concentrate on that person's perception of who is or is not relevant to him in his organisational or environmental context. However it may be physically difficult to determine all such interactions, and perhaps more significantly, the analysis could easily be abfuscated by the minutiae of such contacts and exchanges, formal, informal, verbal, or written.

Although both Mitchel and Murphy stress the importance of starting the analysis from the level of the individual, at times greater understanding is achieved by considering groups, or in this case, departments. Lewin and others(3) have shown how groups relate to external influences by means of a 'gatekeeper'.

> 'Gatekeeping means controlling a strategic position of a channel - so as to have the power of decision over whether whatever is flowing through the channel will enter the group or not.' (Katz and Lazarsfield, 1960, p.119).

So a gatekeeper appears powerful within the group, but also represents that group to external or outside influences. The authority of the gatekeeper from one department to influence the activities of other departments rests on the nature of the objectives of the newspaper firm (the ideology of publication). This area of incluence occurs in the area of interchange, and thus the interaction of departments concerns the interaction of certain, perhaps crucial members (the gatekeepers) of that department. In this way the important areas of interchange, and the means to control them can be highlighted.

An area of interchange exists between two individuals in an enterprise when one requires a service from the other. The interaction is normally initially beneficial, which is one reason for its existence. Moreover it will not often be the case that the benefits are equal, rather one party will gain more than the other. From this it could be deduced that the party gaining least may not wish to be part of the interchange, however, that the party does gain something, even if it is less than the other, will ensure its participation, unless of course the gain to the other becomes its loss. Whilst game theory may be able to advance and explain such situations, the main concern here is the reason why the losing party continues to be involved in the interaction. Mitchell, in discussing the content of interactions, (which he refers to as links) outlines three elements, communication, exchange and normative content, and he says of exchange, 'a number of actors are involved in a number of transactions which bind them to one another in a series of expectations and obligations.' (1973, p.25). Indeed the existence of certain individuals, or departments, in an enterprise may only be because of the interaction itself. Mitchell explains the normative content by referring to 'the expectations each may have of the other because of some social characteristic or social attribute the other may possess.' (1973, p.26). (In this case organisational rather than social is more apposite.) Thus, for instance the commercialists expect a certain kind of input from editorial, and through the interaction in which the commercialists have power, they ensure that this input is achieved, no less, nor no more.

The domination of one individual over another, or one department over another, however, is the result of the imbalance of power between them. In this context that power can be envisaged as the authority to influence or control the area of interchange. The level of authority and its legitimation in the case of newspapers, stems from the ideology of publication, that certain activities are of greater importance than others. The full significance of interchange can only be gained by analysing the effects of that interaction. That one party has authority to control the areas of interchange also means it has an influence on the activities of the other party, for that party will have to change its activities to produce what is required by the other in the interchange. As the process develops, and as authority to control becomes more sharply defined, then so does the control of one department over the activities of another. It is not direct, rather it is only through the areas of interchange. By this process, and using this model in the case of regional daily newspapers, explanations can be given for the control of editorial work practices by non-editorial functions, even though those involved vehemently deny the existence of any direct influences.

When the ideology of publication is based on commercial principles then the areas of interchange are likely to be more formal, and inevitably rule-dominated. It is the authority to introduce new working practices (for instance, new rules) which is legitimated by the drive to increase revenue and cut costs. Moreoever the very rationality of the rules themselves provide in the Weberian sense a 'legal authority' for their adherence. The introduction of such rules of interchange by the more powerful party means acquiescence by the other party involved in that interchange. In the case of departments whose members' work has been characterised by flexibility and informality, changes are necessary to meet the demands of the interaction. Their work may have to become more ordered, and in doing may also become more dominated. This movement toward internal bureaucratisation signals the success of the control process, and allows the introduction of further rules from impersonal sources (for instance, head office) to which members have to adhere. The internal bureaucratisation means the development of hierarchies of internal control, and in the Weberian sense an administrative staff whose position, and indeed authority depends on the adherence to the rules.

A process of change in this manner may disrupt the organisation. In a department where work is characterised by the discretion allowed to staff this is often because of the nature of the work involved. Indeed several writers (4) have suggested that such departments gain authority and power because of their strategic importance to the enterprise. The perception of those in the strategically important positions may not match with those who have authority with the organisation, and in this case changes will be accomplished by those in authority controlling the work activities through the areas of interchange of those who perceive themselves to be strategically important. However to take away such discretion by the implementation of a network of rules may destroy the ability of the enterprise to provide or produce the necessary service or product. Homans (1951) and Burns and Stalker (1961) amongst others have shown how such a process may signal the destruction of the enterprise. That is, if such discretion is necessary for such work activities to be accomplished. It could be the case that it is the change in the market structures which allows the redefinition of certain work tasks. In the case of regional daily newspapers the market structures changed because of the rationalisation of the regional press, which in turn could change in response to the changed market structures. Thus competition disappears requiring newspapers merely to publish an ordinary diet of news, rather than the latest and most exclusive. In effect the direction of this market change (in part brought about by the actions of newspaper owners) was to give stability in the organisation's environment.

The process of change is facilitated by the mobility of managers.

They provide the catalyst needed to introduce new working practices which appear at increasingly frequent intervals, as they attempt to achieve personal success in the promotion ladder. Such mobility has occurred mainly in the non-editorial departments and has led to bureaucratisation there, which in turn leads to increasing rule domination of the areas of interchange. The organisational change becomes masked by the personnel changes.

Many studies on the press have assumed a particular organisation format within which newspapers are published. Their analysis has, because of this assumption, also accepted that power and authority resides in certain departments rather than in others. For instance, non-editorial departments only exist because of editorial, and their members work to ensure the best possible newspaper, best being defined by criteria of news and nothing else.

It may be heresy to suggest that newspapers could be organised otherwise, but given the lack of concern in communication studies with everything but editorial and its effects, it should be no surprise to find that such assumptions, as made by those studies, are ill-founded. Over time the market for any particular good will by subject to various effects, and changes will occur as some companies cease to market the product, others expand, some develop the product etc. The internal structure of any organisation will change in reaction to these market changes, and in turn the effects of its own changes will force others to react. Therefore not only have studies of newspapers assumed a particular organisational structure in their model, their analysis has been static as well.

Inherent in the assumption of a particular newspaper organisation is the source of authority which editorial have, to determine which activities they and other functions will perform. As a generalisation editorial have been powerful because they deal with the unexpected, the news itself, and more particularly following Breed, it is the gatekeeper who has power because of his crucial position. If, as has been suggested such an assumption is incorrect, then the question of the source of power and authority remains unanswered. Previous studies have not considered this because they have been restricted by the assumption that editorial are powerful because of the reasons stated. To answer the question the analysis must treat newspapers as though they were a commercial enterprise like any other. Because of the nature of news, newspapers have been put in a special position in Western democracies and from this, notions of profit, efficiency, rationality etc, have supposedly been subsumed by the search for truth. Organisational theorists have ignored most of the press, because it appears little was left to explain as the goal of the search for truth was pre-determined, and indeed universal throughout the enterprise.

However, as newspaper owners and managers feel newspapers are just like any commercial operation, so the analysis of organisational processes must rely on organisational theory, rather than some pre-conceived assumption of editorial power. By developing the model of the areas of interchange, and considering the authority the parties involved may have to direct or influence work activities will not only provide understanding for the process of change, but also explain how and why the editorial function was viewed with such pre-eminence.

A source of legitimation of authority to control areas of interchange can be found in the ideology of publication. Such ideologies are held by those who own the press. Rather than give rise to specific objectives or goals, such ideologies give greater meaning to certain kinds of functions to the detriment of others. Ideologies such as this may be confined to enterprises like the press, given their role in society, and indeed are inherent in the kind of press which many think society ought to have. Many ideologies are concerned with the search for truth in some way, often through the use of propaganda, which the libertarian theorists welcomed as competing ends gave different interpretations of news events. It is only when the market is monopolised, or so structured as to reach similar results, that the search for truth is replaced by the drive for profit. Those concerned with the place of press in society initially hardly object, for such profit means the survival of most of the press. What they misunderstand is that news now does not stand for the truth, but rather is the 'bit between the ads'. Certainly chapter two with its analysis of the intervention of the government and the pronouncements of the Royal Commissions sharply highlighted how they have utilised the organisational model based on editorial power. The ideology of publication has changed and now legitimises the authority of non-editorial functions to control areas of interchange and thus the work of editorial.

Therefore in summary the forms of newspaper organisation (Fleet Street to Regional Commercialism to Regional Technology) hypothesised in chapter one appear to have certain characteristics and the direction and process of change can be expressed in terms of the model developed here, as follows.

It is apparent from the evidence presented that editorial feel themselves to be essential to the publication of newspapers, so essential that they must have full power to make crucial decisions concerning the newspaper. Indeed, not only does the law provide support to this, but so also does the vast majority of those concerned with maintaining the function of the press in Western democracies. In the Fleet Street organisational type, the editorial function is superior to all others, and the perception of editorial staff of their position match the reality of their allotted function in a newspaper enterprise. All other departments largely concur and conflict is minimal. With the onset of commercialism, non-editorial as a whole are given the role of eventually producing a product which will provide a sufficient return on capital invested. The new ownership has given them this role, which in carrying it out, involves amongst other functions, the control of the activities of editorial, by means of controlling the areas of interchange; however on a traditional basis editorial still perceive themselves to be paramount. Thus occurs a situation in which perceptions do not ally with the position as defined by the power balance. Conflict is the natural result of this, as was shown in chapter eight, as editorial react to defend what is perceived rather than what is. Such reactions given the authority of non-editorial are generally futile, and editorial have to gradually accept their diminished importance.

In the Fleet Street organisational type the ideology of publication, determined by the owner was based mostly on propaganda and partially on news. These newspapers were owned by influential figures, displaying something akin to 'charisma'. Indeed following Weberian analysis it is because of this charisma that authority is legitimised. More specifically such owners, interested in the right kind of news (i.e. propaganda) needed large editorial departments to find such news, and therefore to execute the policy of the owner. It was thus they who had authority in the areas of interchange. These editorially controlled areas of interchange were characterised by the discretion allowed in the work activities of editorial staff, other sectors being service departments to editorial, which not so much controlled the activities of them, but rather ensured that they performed only the role asked of them. Production, for instance, printed the newspaper but had no say in the page layout or content. Indeed the timing of the printing of the newspaper, and the deadlines for copy were determined by editorial.

As the latter was more informally organised, so then was the nature of their influence on other departments. Work activities, determined by a strict adherence to rules, were abhorrent to editorial, because news itself is not predictable, and given that the newspapers of the Fleet Street type operated in competitive markets, the latest and most exclusive news was at a premium. The various departments had to be ready at all times to change schedules and routines to allow such news to be printed. And it was editorial who made the decisions.

The Fleet Street type of organisation, of flexibility, informality, of editorial dominance etc, was the one that faced the new commercialists. Again by using the model of the areas of interchange it has been possible to explain the process of change in regional newspapers from the Fleet Street type to the regional commercial type.

Pre-commercialism, it was editorial who had authority to control not only their own activities, but also the areas of interchange. This also allows them to influence the other departments who are party to the interchange. But with the change of ownership, physically as with the Kemsley/Thomson change, or in style as with most of the other major groups, it meant that the direct source of authority for editorial control had disappeared. Only on traditional grounds could the editor and his staff still dictate to the rest of the organisation. The new style of ownership interested in monetary returns, had to control costs and increase revenue. The former was achieved by controlling editorial, and the latter by exploiting the market and realising its potential in advertising and copy sales. Authority to control areas of interchange rested with the non-commercial departments but not until they had developed their internal work activities through a bureaucratic framework designed to meet the demands of the new ownership. In pre-commercial days the functions in newspapers were editorial, production, accounting, advertising and circulation. In Centre A the latter two departments were insignificant, advertising having only approximately one per cent of the work force and circulation being nearly totally sub-contracted. One of the first moves therefore to exploit the available market was to establish suitable departments. Advertising quickly split into disply and classified, and was greatly expanded respectively by the effect of television(5) and through the use of American marketing and selling techniques. Concomitant with this was the development of the accounting department capable not only of monitoring, but of controlling costs. These departments, and in addition marketing, were organised on bureaucratic principles through the development of a system of rules, which when followed could deal with almost all cases at work.

Regional newspapers were short of qualified personnel in these areas and recruited managers from outside, who brought commercial techniques into use in an area where creativity and flair had ruled. Certainty replaced instability and rule adherence replaced flexibility. These departments grew as more revenue through advertising increased, for instance, circulation became specialised in terms of selling to those areas where advertisers wanted to advertise. This growth meant the generation of more managerial posts, as hierarchies developed around these bureaucracies, and managers were given great experience in varied decision-making situations. In Gouldneresque fashion this meant an exacerbation of the bureaucracy, as new managers introduced new rules, ones that were enforced, for managers soon realised that the promotion roundabout was based on such short cycles. There was thus only a short time to be successful to ensure an upward and not sideways movement. It was in this way that these new rules were enforced and thus strictly adhered to. However problems arose in the areas of interchange, for here the traditional authority of editorial to maintain flexibility, clashed with the authority of the commercial department to introduce stability and certainty through rules. The problem was solved when the activities of editorial were controlled, and the newspaper became a commercial operation much like any other. This was achieved by control of the areas of interchange.

Working practices in any one department which are dictated by a strict adherence to rules will have effects on other departments through the areas of interchange. For instance, the Accounts department in accordance with the new philosophy began to introduce budgeting. After all if costs are to be monitored and controlled, budgets not only need to be introduced but adhered to. This creates problems for editorial for traditionally the 'flair and artistry' they provide cannot be accounted for by a budget. Costs to them are necessarily incurred in order to report and write news stories. News stories are unpredictable, so therefore are the costs incurred to report them, and an impersonal budget cannot take cognisance of this. A battle, if that it can be called, takes place in the area of interchange. Accounts believe in the authority of the strict adherence to rules, and editorial see their traditional authority allowing them to demonstrate the necessary 'flair and artistry'. Other battles ensue, mostly between editorial and all other commercial departments. Production for the reasons stated in earlier chapters are excluded in these early stages of change, but they too become party to the bureaucratisation, once the new technology is introduced in full. The battles are won by commercialists because of the source of authority, but in addition the working practices of editorial are constrained by other manoeuvres leaving them very much as merely one department dependent on others for existence rather than as the focal point for the publication of a newspaper.

Before mentioning these other manoevres it will be useful to re-introduce the perceptions of editorial staff into the analysis.

It will be remembered that in the Fleet Street organisational type perceptions of the position of editorial were much the same from both the editorial and non-editorial points of view. However, in the regional commercialism type these perceptions begin to differ widely. Whilst editorial staff still see themselves as central and thus of greatest importance to the paper, the commercial side perceive their role to be more subservient. In a rational way non-editorial do not see the need for the latest and most exclusive news if time is the only constraint. For some time competition had ceased to be a constraint, regional newspapers were operating in a monopoly position. All therefore that was required was a diet of local news interspersed with features, and national news 'as it happens' from the wire. Editorial, according to the commercialists, need to process rather than collect news, and that which has to be collected can be done in an orderly and regular way from institutional sources. From the commercial point of view the problem is one of ensuring editorial perceptions are changed, but given the nature of editorial this is highly unlikely, although other methods can be utilised. Control of areas of interchange and their concomitant effect on editorial work practices have been mentioned, and the argument will return to them later, but non-editorial begin to, perhaps unconsciously, play on these perceptions to control editorial.

Hickson et al have shown how departments become more influential if they deal with unexpected cases, in that they gain importance because they are strategically contingent. However, with the nature of news, cases can be unexpected or expected, depending on both your point of view and the required need for certain types of news. To continue the analysis editorial gain influence because news is an exceptional event and it is they who report it. From the commercial point of view if it can be shown that news is unexceptional then according to the Hickson et al argument editorial will lose some of their influence. The onset of commercialism produces more advertising, and given advertising/editorial ratios, more editorial is also required. The editorial perceptions of their own importance are increased because of this extra space. They thus openly welcome commercialism. However, although editorial space in the newspaper nearly doubles, the number of journalists does not increase. As many managers implied, journalistic productivity had to rise, however, to be sure of enough news the work of journalists had to be organised on a stricter basis. Fewer journalists could be deployed for investigatory reporting, and even fewer were allowed to follow-up stories, except if they were very important. To be certain of news, reporters were increasingly directed to institutional sources, and thus news became regular and expected. 'Hold the front page' was a cry of the past, as news was expected from a court session, a council meeting, etc, each providing a story of near predictable length. The editorial department had to bureaucratise itself to ensure all the space was filled.

Another reason why editorial welcomed the onset of commercialism was because it made newspapers profitable, and guaranteed their survival. Further, at least to their thinking, more profit means more resources available to report the latest and exclusive news. Unfortunately, the non-editorial sectors see profit as an end in itself rather than as a means to improve editorial quality. As already mentioned, why improve editorial beyond a certain level, for there is no competition by which comparisons can be made?

Thus although the consequences are dire for editorial they initially welcome the onset of commercialisation. Because of this and of the need for internal bureaucratisation to achieve organisation or reporters, the 'battles' in the areas of interchange are smoother than they otherwise might be. As Accounts, Advertising and Marketing begin to issue rules of interchange, based on their own working practices, then editorial by and large accepts. When the flow of rules increases, editorial begin to react, but still perceiving itself to be central to newspapers, they regard the intrusion of commercialism as a necessary evil. Further control of editorial work practices is achieved by the use of impersonal rules on cars, expenses etc. These ensure that reporting work can only be done at certain times and in certain areas. Not only are costs reduced but the work of reporters is more easily planned, and thus the flow of news more easily organised. To complete the subjugation of editorial to commercial demands, senior journalists such as chief sub-editors, deputy editors etc, appear and act more like editorial managers. Job descriptions involve the organisation of news collection from routine sources, the administration of various sections, and the control of expenses in accordance with the budget, which of course has to be drafted. As the management and organisation of news is more important than its collection these posts proliferate, with senior journalists viewing careers as progressing through such hierarchies. Indeed some see future developments in the non-editorial side; they become managers rather than journalists.

The widespread introduction (6) of new technological printing processes in regional newspapers has increased the bureaucratic tendencies apparent with regional commercialism. The time-served craftsman is no longer the archetype production manager. It is now the engineer, often a graduate, trained in the use of computers, and at the very least an equal to other senior managers. No longer is the production department the plaything of editorial and advertising, for strict deadlines are introduced, and copy of both sorts is planned for several days ahead. Areas of interchange with production become bureaucratised, and this has an affect on the departments providing copy and on those using the computer facilities. Again editorial welcome this development, for the new technologyis more versatile, as colour can be used, and pictures and print are much clearer. However, the end result is further control of their work practices.

Given this concentrated attack on editorial a reaction was almost inevitable. However, such reaction in the form of industrial action has highlighted the manager/worker relationship of senior staff to journalists. The managers went to great lengths to explain away the conflict that had occurred in the early 1970's. It was always the left-wing graduate intake, or a minority of trouble-makers rather than the control of work practices, pay and conditions. The industrial action made overt the latent division of managers and workers in the same trade union, the NUJ. However, the end result is that regional newspapers have become more profitable, and have utilised the latest technological innovations, but at the price of the subjugation of the journalist. Todays newspapers reflect these changes - they are larger, they can produce better pictures, sometimes colour - but the news that is reported is from institutional sources, or from the wire -

its all reactive reporting, a pre-programmed space-filler, as investigatory reporting becomes a thing of the past.

At the design stage of this research it was hypothesised that there were basically three models of newspaper organisation, entitled Fleet Street, Regional Commercialism and Regional Technology. The first was described from investigation and memoirs of editors and the like who worked in the Fleet Street and regional newspapers up to about 1960. As the Fleet Street model was not confined to national newspapers (indeed it could be said to have originated in the region and only developed in Fleet Street) so Regional Commercialism is not solely confined to regional newspapers. However, it was wholly developed there, and the Fleet Street papers by the mid 1970's had only begun to introduce some of its characterisations. The bulk of the empirical work was concerned with describing the regional commercial newspapers and analysing how they arrived at such a situation from the traditionally derived Fleet Street model.

Regional daily newspapers are highly commercial operations which make large profits (except mornings), and support part of the national press. Their main aim is to make a sufficient return on capital, rather than to provide a community with information of local and national events. They do still report local and national news but this is merely a means to an end. Editorial departments are constrained in attempting to search for the 'truth' and have to report that news which is easiest to collect. This is probably the most fundamental result of the resolution of the paradox of commercial ownership of institutions, traditionally thought of as diligently pursuing the truth.

The tensions evolving from the resolution of the paradox have been affected by various constraints. For instance, the market shape and size for newspaper sales has been simplified by the monopoly position, thus allowing newspapers to survive with a lower input of editorial. The demand for advertising has in part been created by the supply of vehicles in which to advertise. The potential of the market has been realised, and in doing so editorial has been more closely geared to the demands of advertising. The process of commercialisation of the regional press was quickened by the hiring of outside businessmen, with few favourable feelings towards the creative aspect of journalism. The news they required could be found in more routine and rational ways. No longer do newspapers sell themselves by scoops and exclusives, but rather they are now marketed much like any other manufactured goods. Finally the onset of the new technology has ended the slavery of the production department to the whims of the editorial. The last-minute rushes to get a news story on the front page, is replaced with the orderly flow of news copy, allowing a planning of work in the production department. In this way the costs of the two largest departments in newspaper enterprises are reduced and controlled. It is commercial criteria which dictate the activities of the editorial departments, and anything which is seen to contradict the demands of commercialism is eradicated.

It could be envisaged that this process of commercial domination will continue until any quality of new editorial, will suffice, as long as it fulfils its role as the 'bit between the ads'. However, it is suggested here that one phase of change in regional newspapers may have been accomplished. Regional newspapers are profitable, and are now going through a process of consolidation. The realisation that an advertising-dominated newspaper may strangle itself as editorial becomes too insignificant appears to be one of the main elements of that consolidation.

NOTES

(1) See W. Breed: Social Control in the News Room, Social Forces No. 33, 1955; R. E. Carter (Jr) : Newspaper Gatekeepers and the Sources of News, Public Opinion Quarterly 22(2) 1958; L. Donohew : Newspaper Gatekeepers and Forces in the News Channel, Public Opinion Quarterly 31(1) 1967; D. Manning White : The Gatekeeper, A Case Study in the Selection of News, Journalism Quarterly 33, 1956.

(2) See J. C. Mitchell : Networks, norms and institutions in J. Boisseran and J. C. Mitchell (eds) : Network Analysis, Studies in Human Interaction, and J. C. Mitchell : The Concept and Use of Social Networks in J. C. Mitchell (ed) : Social Networks in Urban Situations.

(3) The notion of the gatekeeper was first used by K. Lewin : Frontiers in Group Dynamics II. Channels of Group Life : Social Planning and Action Research, Human Relations, Vol. No.2, 1947. See also K. Lewin : Group Decision and Social Change in E. E. Macoby, T. M. Newcomb and E. L. Hartley : Readings in Social Psychology. See also note 1 and E. Katz and P. F. Lazarsfeld : Personal Influence, who have utilised this approach in respect of the media.

(4) See G. Homans : The Human Group; D. J. Hickson et al, op.cit; C. Perrow : A Framework for the Comparative Analysis of Organisations; American Sociological Review 1967.

(5) See Table 5. Appendix on Statistics, Royal Commission on the Press 1977.

(6) See Financial Times, August 17th 1978.

Methodological appendix

Most of the empirical work presented here is based on a series of interviews in which was used a semi-structured open-ended questionnaire with the interviewer asking the questions. Generally the first part of any interview was centred around personal demographic factors, about which the interviewee could respond fairly easily, and without fear of contradiction or of being controversial. To a large extent in this early part it was necessary for the interviewer to establish his 'credentials' in such a way that the interviewee felt the disruption to work caused by the interview was not without reason, and that the research being conducted was worthwhile. At the same time a relationship of confidence could be established between the interviewee and the interviewer, a rapport between them so essential for the interviewer to be more successful later in obtaining lengthy and in-depth answers to what may appear to be more controversial issues. As the median time of interviews was 1 hour, 40 minutes, such an introduction was vital to the success (1) of the interview.

Generally the second part of the interview was dictated by what the interviewee wanted to say, for given that the first part was successful in establishing a relationship of trust, when the interviewee wanted to speak at length on issues which he/she felt were important not only to his/herself but in relation to their role vis-a-vis others in the enterprise, and the success of the newspaper organisation, he/she were encouraged. Indeed it was made clear at the start of the interview that the questionnaire was designed to secure the manager's view of the organisational requirements of a newspaper and his particular role in that organisation.

Where interviewees did diverge and make tangential comments this was not generally discouraged, except where such a diversion went outside of the rather wide scope of newspapers and the people who work in newspaper organisations. The semi-structured aspect of this part of the interview contained prepared questions concerning certain areas of newspaper organisation. Many of these questions however remained unasked in this form, because interviewees either 'volunteered' the information, or by their very answers they suggested alternative questions which were related to the prepared ones. The prepared questions did not attempt to secure specific information, rather they directed the interviewee to talk about specific matters, or areas of operation. There were a few questions to which short answers were required which were generally given, and some of these appear in the text.

The interviews were prefaced with an introduction by the interviewer, outlining the general aims of the research. Contact was made by letter through the supervisor of this research, Professor G.F.Thomason, and interviews arranged, by phone, at mutually convenient times. Overall, permission to interview managers at or above a certain level was obtained from the Personnel Manager at Centre A, and the Managing Directors at Centres B and C, who remarked that it was up to each individual manager to agree or not, except in the case of editorial managers, where the relevant editor's permission was needed. This was achieved by interviewing the editors first, and which because of relatively successful interviews, gave some sort of 'bona fide' status to the interviewer.

The design of the questionnaire was helped in the initial stages by informal talks with the Personnel Manager and Executive Assistant to the Managing Director at Centre A. I had become acquainted with both of these, and other managers at Centres A and C during the summer of 1972 when many of them had lectured on a management training course for newspaper managers, on which I was course tutor. Not only did that course, in the series of lectures given by managers, help to focus my mind on relevant areas of study, but gave me a much needed introduction to many of the managers who were later interviewed.

The interviews normally took place in working hours and in the office of the interviewee. For some editorial managers, where their 'office' was the general work room for journalists, unoccupied or interview offices were used. (In one case the canteen was used, and in another for the night editor, the bar of a local hotel). This was generally less satisfactory than where a personal office could be used, because managers were taken out of their own environment, but as it concerned few of the interviews its effects were minimal. During the interviews copious notes were taken, and immediately afterwards these were more formally constructed into a report on the interviews, containing not only what the interviewee said but implications of it for the final work and for other interviews. This technique has been used successfully elsewhere, (2) and in this case the reports on interviews exceeded well over 100,000 words. It was thought that the use of a tape-recorder would inhibit discussion particularly of sensitive organisational problems, and indeed without it, many managers were relatively forthright on controversial issues.

NOTES

1. The definition of success is not here a subjective one in that the interviewee responds in such a way that it gives the interviewer the information required. Rather it centres on the notion of interviewees responding positively to questions and giving their viewpoints on a variety of questions.
2. see J. Tunstall: The Advertising Man: Chapman & Hall, 1964

QUESTIONNAIRE

SECTION I : Individual

I. Present appointment
2. Age
3. Past experience/occupational history
4. Education
5. How many years have you worked with your present paper?
6. Why did you join your present paper?

SECTION 2 : Organisation (see blank chart at end of questionnaire)

I. Who is the man to whom your immediate supervisor reports?
2. Who is your immediate supervisor?
   (The man who controls your work and to whom you report)
3. Who are the men at the same level as yourself who report to the same supervisor as you do?
4. Who are the men who work under your control and who report directly to you?
5. Are you given any organisational chart to follow?
   If so, does it conflict with the one you have drawn?
6a. Could you give me a job description?
6b. Do you have a set job objective?
7a. With reference to newspaper, how effective is the organisation, in your opinion?
7b. Could you suggest any improvement in management structure?
8. Are there any ways in which you could improve the effectiveness or efficiency of your department?
9. Do you think it advantageous that your paper is part of a newspaper group?

SECTION 3

I. Which other members of management and supervision do you contact during a week? (Please note frequency of contact)
2. How would you say these contacts are primarily conducted?
   a) by telephone
   b) by written message
   c) verbally
   d) a third party
3. If you had a problem, with whom would you discuss it?
4a. Do you have any difficulties as regards communications?
4b. Can you suggest any improvements?

SECTION 4 : Attitudes

I. How well informed do you feel you are with regard to what is happening in the firm?
   a) I am completely informed
   b) I know most of what goes on
   c) I am moderately well informed
   d) I am left in the dark about many things
   e) I am left completely in the dark

SECTION 4 (Cont'd)

2. How easy do you find it to get the information you need to do your job properly?
3. If you had an idea which would make the job more efficient how easy would it be to get people above you to listen to you?
4. How often do the instructions you get from different sources conflict with each other?
5. How do you like your job?
6. Is there any way you feel you could improve your job?
7. How satisfied are you with the firm as an employer?

N.B. At first most of these questions had a series of pre-set answers, but as these inhibited discussion, they were fairly quickly dropped, and only offered as an answer if the interviewee found difficulty in expression.

SECTION 5 : Miscellaneous

I. Do you have any problems concerning industrial relations? Is there any policy laid down concerning industrial relations?
2. What effect, if any, does unionisation and closed shops have on the running of your department, and the firm?
3. Does the personnel manager deal with any problems relating to members of your department?
4. How do you see the role of the personnel manager in this firm?
5. Do you think newspapers need a different kind of organisation/ management structure because of the nature of the produce?
6. Do you think the policy of moving executives from centre to centre has many advantages?
7. Do you meet any of your fellow employees outside the firm?
8. Do you consider editorial staff suitable for higher managerial positions?

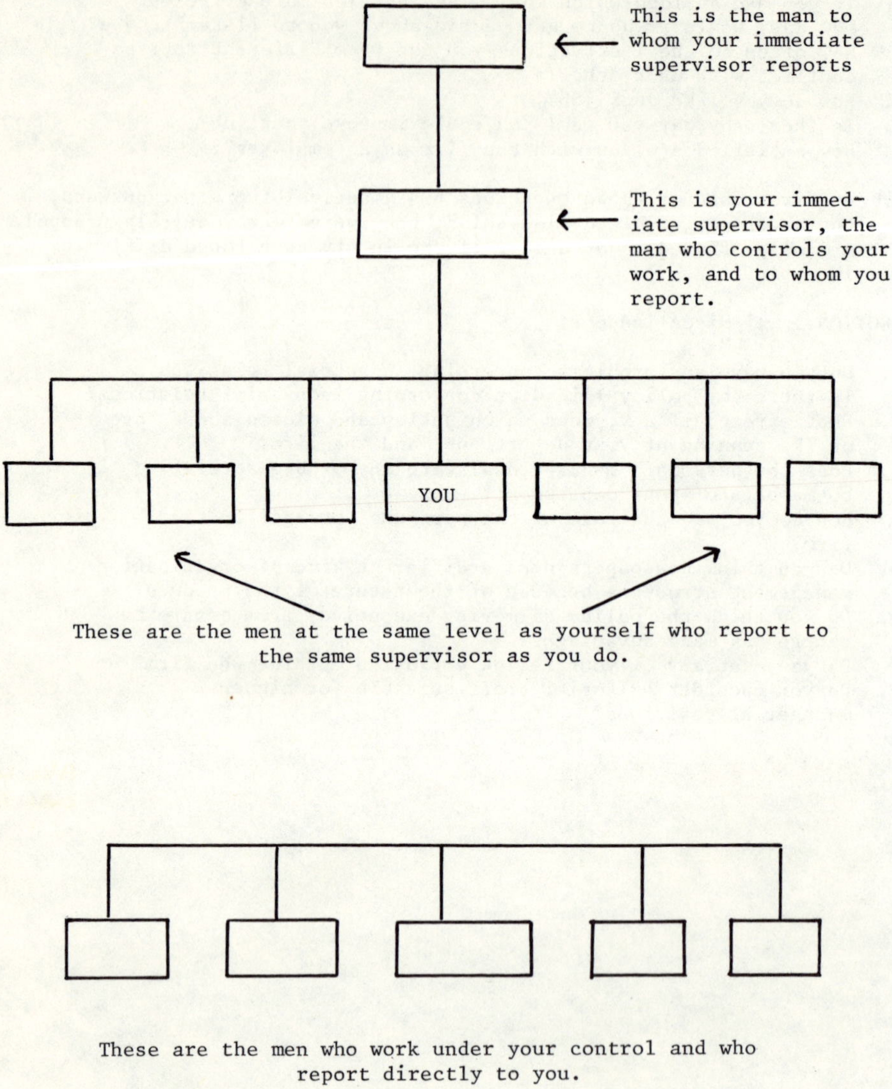
This is the man to whom your immediate supervisor reports
This is your immediate supervisor, the man who controls your work, and to whom you report.
YOU
These are the men at the same level as yourself who report to the same supervisor as you do.
These are the men who work under your control and who report directly to you.

Bibliography

Albrow, M., Bureaucracy, Macmillan, London 1970.

Andrews, Sir Linton, Autobiography of a Journalist, Ernest Benn, London 1964.

Andrews, Sir Linton, Problems of an Editor: A Study in Newspaper Trends, Oxford University Press, London 1962.

Arensburg, C.M. and McGregor, D., 'Determination of Morale in an Industrial Company', Applied Anthropology, 1942.

Ayerst, D., Guardian, Biography of a Newspaper, Collins, London 1971.

Bairstow, T., 'Anatomy of a Crisis' in Boston, R. (ed.), The Press we Deserve, Routledge & Kegan Paul, London 1970.

Barnard, C., The Functions of an Executive, Harvard University Press, Cambridge, Massachusetts 1962.

Beavan, J., 'The Press and the Public', Fabian Tract 338, 1962.

Benn, The Newspaper Press Directory, Benn, Annual.

Bennis, W.G., Changing Organisations, McGraw Hill, New York 1966.

Bernard, C.I., 'Functions and Pathology of Status Systems in Formal Organisations' in Whyte, W.F. (ed.), Industry and Society, McGraw Hill, New York 1946.

Blau, P.M., The Dynamics of Bureaucracy, University of Chicago Press, 1963.

Blau, P.M. and Meyer, M.W., Bureaucracy in Modern Society, Random House, New York 1956.

Blau, P.M. and Scott, W.R., Formal Organisations: A Comparative Approach, Routledge & Kegan Paul, London 1963.

Boissevain, J. and Mitchell, J.C. (eds.), Network Analysis, Studies in Human Interaction, Monton, The Hague 1973.

Boston, R. (ed.), The Press we Deserve, Routledge & Kegan Paul, London 1970.

Boyd-Barrett, O., 'Journalism, Recruitment and Training' in Tunstall, J. (ed.), Media Sociology, Constable, London 1970.

Braddon, R.D., Roy Thomson of Fleet Street, Collins, London 1965.

Brech, E.F.C., Principles and Practice of Management, Longmans, London 1953.

Breed, W., 'Social Control in the Newsroom: A functional analysis', Social Forces 33, 1955.

Brown, R.L., 'Some Aspects of Mass Media Ideologies' in Halmos, P. 'The Sociology of Mass Media Communications', Sociological Review Monograph, No.13, January 1969.

Bundock, C.J., The National Union of Journalists, A Jubilee History 1907-57, Oxford University Press, Oxford 1957.

Burns, T. and Stalker, G.M., The Management of Innovation, Tavistock Publications, London 1961.

Camrose, Viscount, British Newspapers and their Controllers, Cassell & Co.Ltd., London 1948.

Carr-Saunders, A.M. and Wilson, P., The Professionals, Clarendon Press, Oxford.

Carter, R.E. (Jr.), 'Newspaper Gatekeepers and the Source of News', Public Opinion Quarterly 22(2), 1958.

Child, J. and Mansfield, R., 'Technology, Size and Organisation Structure', Sociology, Vol.6, No.3, September 1972.

Child, J., Industrial Relations in the British Printing Industry, George Allen & Unwin Ltd., London 1967.

Christiansen, A., Headlines All My Life, Heinemann, London 1961.

Clarke, T., Northcliffe in History, Hutchinson, London 1950.

Clarke, T., My Northcliffe Diary, Gollanz, London 1931.

Clegg, S., Power, Rule and Domination, Routledge & Kegan Paul, London 1975.

Cleverly, G., The Fleet Street Disaster: British National Newspapers as a case study in mismanagement, Constable, London 1976.

Cohen, S. and Young, J., The Manufacture of News, Constable, London 1973.

Collett, D. Collett, History of the Taxes on Knowledge, Watts Thinker's Library Edition, April 1933.

Coote, C.R. Editorial, Eyre & Spottiswood, London 1965.

Cranfield, G.A., The Development of the Provincial Newspaper 1700-60, Clarendon Press, Oxford 1962.

Crozier, M., The Bureaucratic Phenomenon, Tavistock Publications, London 1964.

Cudlipp, H, Publish and Be Damned; The astonishing Story of the Daily Mirror, Andrew Dakes Ltd., London 1953.

Cudlipp, H., At Your Peril, Weidenfeld & Nicholson, London 1962.

Cudlipp, H., Walking on the Water, Bodley Head, London 1976.

Dahrendorf, R., Class and Class Conflict in an Industrial Society, Routledge & Kegan Paul, London 1959.

Dalton, G. and Lawrence, P., Motivation and Control in Organisations, Irwin Dorsey Press, Howeward, Illinois 1970.

De Fleur, M.L., Theories of Mass Communication, McKay, New York 1970.

Dexter, L.A. and White, D.M., People, Society and Mass Communications, The Free Press of Glencoe, 1964.

Donohew, L., 'Newspaper Gatekeepers and Forces in the News Channel', Public Opinion Quarterly 31(1), 1967.

Driberg, T., Beaverbrook, A Study in Power and Frustration, Wdidenfeld & Nicholson, London 1956.

Drucker, P.F., The Practice of Management, Heinemann, London 1955.

Economist Intelligence Unit, The National Newspaper Industry 1966, prepared for the Joint Board for the National Newspaper Industry by E.I.U. Ltd., 1966.

Edelman, M., The Mirror, A Political History, Hamish Hamilton, London 1966.

Emery, F.E., Systems Thinking, Penguin, Harmonsworth 1969.

Fenby, C., 'A deserving share for the regional papers', Financial Times, 26 June 1967.

Gabriel, H.W., Techniques of Creative Thinking for Management, Prentice-Hall, Englewood Cliffs, New Jersey 1961.

Golding, P., The Mass Media, Longmans, London 1974.

Gollin, A.M., The Observer and J.L. Garvin 1908-1914, Oxford University Press, 1960.

Goulden, J. Newspaper Management (under National Council for the training of Journalists.) Heinemann, London I967

Gouldner, A.W. 'On Weber's Analysis of Bureaucratic Rules', in Merton, R.K. et al (eds.): Reader in Bureaucracy, The Free Press, New York I952.

Gouldner, A.W. 'The Problem of Succession', in Merton, R.K. et al (eds.) Reader in Bureaucracy, The Free Press, New York I952.

Gouldner, A.W. 'Patterns of Industrial Bureaucracy', The Free Press, Glencoe I954.

Gouldner, A.W. Wildcat Strike: A study of unofficial strike, Routledge and Kegan Paul, London I955.

Greenwood, E. 'Attributes of a Profession', Social Work, July I957

Gross, G. (ed), The Responsibility of the Press, Fleet Publishing Corporation, New York I966.

Hadley, W.W. 'The Editor, in Viscount Kemsley (ed)': The Kemsley Manual of Journalism, Cassell, London I950

Halloran, J.D. Control or Consent, Sheed & Ward, London I963.

Halmos, P. (ed), 'The Sociology of Mass Media Communications'. The Sociological Review Monograph, No.I3, University of Keele I969.

Hamilton, D. 'The Making of a Newspaper in Viscount Kemsley': The Kemsley Manual of Journalism, Cassell, London I950

Hansard, June I967

Hearn, R. A Study of the Production of Accounting Information and Statistics for Management in the Newspaper Industry. M.Sc. unpublished thesis, Cardiff I97I

HMSO, Court of Inquiry Report into problems caused by the introduction of web-offset machines into printing industry. Cmnd.3I84 HMSO I967

HMSO, White Paper on Productivity, Prices and Income Policy after I969. Cmnd 4237, HMSO I969.

HMSO, Economic Development Committee for Printing and Publishing NEDC, Printing in a Competitive World, HMSO, London I970.

Hickson, D.J. 'A Convergence in Organisation Theory.' Administrative Science Quarterly, Vol.II, Sept. I966

Hickson, D.J. Hinings, C.R. Lee, C.R. Schneck, R.E. Pennings, J.M. 'A Strategic Contingencies Theory of Intra-Organisational Power' Administrative Science Quarterly, Vol. I6, No.2, I970

Hirsch, F. and Gordon, D. Newspaper Money, Hutchinson, London I975

Hobson, H. Knightley, P. Russell, L. The Pearl of Days: Memoirs of the Sunday Times I822-I972, London I972

Hoch, P. The Newspaper Game Calder and Boyars, London I974.

Homans, G.C. The Human Group, Routledge and Kegan Paul, London I95I (I975 edition)

Hood, S. The Mass Media, MacMillan, London I972.

Hunter, L.C. Reid, G.L. Boddy, D. Labour Problems of Technological Change, No.I8: University of Glasgow Social and Economic Studies, George Allen and Unwin, London I969.

International Press Institute, The Editor and the Publisher, I.P.I., Zurich I957

Jackson, I. The Provincial Press and the Community, Manchester University Press, I97I

Janowitz, M. The Community Press in an Urban Setting, University of Chicago Press, Chicago I967.

Katz, E. and Lazarsfeld, P.F. Personal Influence, The Free Press, Glencoe, Illinois I960

Kemsley, Lord (ed), The Kemsley Manual of Journalism, Cassell, London 1950
King, C. The Future of the Press, MacGibbon and Kee, London 1967
King, C. Strictly Personal, Weidenfeld and Nicholson, London 1969
King, C. The Cecil King Diaries 1965-1970, Jonathan Cape, London 1971
King, C. The Cecil King Diaries 1970-1974, Jonathan Cape, London 1975
Lee, A.J. The Origins of the Popular Press 1855-1914, Croom Helm, London 1976.
Lee, A.J. 'The Management of a Victorian Local Newspaper', Business History, 1973.
Levy, H.P. The Press Council, MacMillan, London 1967
Lewin, K. 'Frontiers in Group Dynamics II; Channels of Group Life; Social Planning and Action Research.' Human Relations Vol.I, No.2, 1947
Lewin, K. 'Group Decision and Social Change', in E.E.Macoby, T.M.Newcomb and E.L.Hartley, Readings in Social Psychology, 3rd edition, Henry Holt, New York 1958
Likert, R. The Nature of Highly Effective Groups in New Patterns in Management, McGraw-Hill, New York 1961
Mabane, W.'Management Problems', in Viscount Kemsley (ed.): The Kemsley Manual of Journalism, Cassell, London 1950.
Macoby, E.E. Newcombe, T.M. Hartley, E.L. Readings in Social Psychology, 3rd edition, Henry Holt, New York 1958
Madden, L. How to find about the Victorian Period, Pergamon Press, Oxford 1970.
Maier, N.R.F. and Hayes, J.J. Creative Management, John Wiley & Sons, New York 1962.
March, J. (ed), The Handbook of Organisation, Rand McNally, Chicago 1965
March, J.G. and Simon, H.A. Organisations, John Wiley & Sons, New York, 1963
Martin, K. The Press the Public Wants, Hogarth Press, London 1947
Matejko, A.'Newspaper Staff as a Social System' in J. Tunstall (ed): Media Sociology, Constable, London 1970
McQuail, D. (ed). Sociology of Mass Communications, Penguin London 1972
Merton, R.K.'The Unanticipated Consequences of Purposive Social Action', American Sociological Review I, 1936
Merton, R.K. 'Bureaucratic Structure and Personality', Social Forces 1940, reprinted in Reader in Bureaucracy, Merton et al, (eds.)
Merton, R.K. Gray, A.P. Hockey, B. and Selvin, H.C. Reader in Bureaucracy, The Free Press, New York 1952
Miller, E. and Rice, A.K. System of Organisation, Tavistock Publications Ltd. London, 1967
Millerson, G. The Qualifying Association: A Study in Professionalisation, Routledge and Kegan Paul, London 1964
Mitchell, J.C. (ed.) Social Networks in Urban Situations, Manchester University Press 1969
Mitchell, J.C.'Networks, Norms and Institutions' in J.Boissvain and J.C.Mitchell (eds), Network Analysis, Studies in Human Interaction
Mitchell, J.C. 'The Concept and Use of Social Networks', in J.C.Mitchell (ed). Social Networks in Urban Situations.
Monopolies Commission, Report on the Times Newspaper and the Sunday Times Newspaper, HMSO, 1966.
Monopolies Commission, Thomson Newspapers Ltd and Crusha & Son Ltd. HMSO, 17th January, 1968
Monopolies Commission, The Berrow's Organisation Ltd. and the County Express Group, HMSO, 24 April, 1972

Monopolies Commission, Westminster Press Ltd. and Kentish Times Ltd. and F.S.Parsons Ltd. HMSO, 25 October 1973a

Monopolies Commission, Report into transfer of Courier Printing and Publishing Co.Ltd. to Associated Newspapers. HMSO, 1973b

Moonman, E. (ed), The Press: A Case for Commitment, Fabian Tract 391, March 1969

Morriss, C. I Bought a Newspaper, Arthur Baker, London 1963

Muller, H.D. Press Power; A Study of Axel Springer, Macdonald, London 1969

Murphy, D. The Silent Watchdog: The Press in Local Politics, Constable, London 1976

Murray, G. The Press and the Public,(The Story of the British Press Council), Southern Illinois University Press, 1972

National Board for Prices and Incomes, Report No.2, Wages Costs and Prices in the Printing Industry, Cmnd. 2750, HMSO 1965.

National Board for Prices and Incomes, Report No.19, General Report, April 1965 to July 1966, Cmnd. 3087, HMSO August 1966

National Board for Prices and Incomes, Report No.26, Prices of Standard Newsprint, Cmnd. 3210, HMSO February 1967a

National Board for Prices and Incomes, Report No.40, Second General Report, July 1966 to August 1967, Cmnd. 3394, HMSO August 1967b

National Board for Prices and Incomes, Report No.43, Costs and Revenues of National Daily Newspapers, Cmnd. 3435, HMSO, 1967c

National Board for Prices and Incomes, Report No.77, Third General Report, August 1967 to July 1968, Cmnd. 3715, HMSO July 1968d

National Board for Prices and Incomes, Report No.115, Journalist's Pay, Cmnd. 4077, HMSO June 1969e

National Board for Prices and Incomes, Report No.122, Fourth General Report, July 1968 to July 1969, Cmnd. 4130, HMSO July 1969f.

National Board for Prices and Incomes, Report No.141, Costs and Revenues of National Newspapers, Cmnd. 4277, HMSO February 1970g.

New Statesman, Series on the Press Proprietors.
In Charge of the Clattering Train - Sir Max Aitken. No.1, 20. 9.74a
Lord Hartwell, No.2, 27.9.74b
Male Heir - Vere Harmsworth, No.3, 4.10.74c
By Rags to Riches - Rupert Murdoch, No.4, 11.4.74d
The Emperor Unclothed - Lord Thomson, No.5, 18.10.74e
The Silver Spoon - D. Astor, No.6, 25.10.74f
The Master of the Enterprise - Sir Don Ryder, No.7, 1.11.74g
K.G. and PRO - Earl of Drogheda, No.8, 8.11.74h

Parsons, T. The Structure of Social Action, The Free Press, Glencoe, 1968

Parker, S.R. Brown, R.K. Child, J. Smith, M.A. The Sociology of Industry, George Allen and Unwin, London 1967

Perrow, C. Organisational Analysis (A Sociological View), Wadsworth, Los Angeles, 1970.

Perrow, C. A Framework for the Comparative Analysis of Organisation, American Sociological Review, 1967

Peterson, T. 'The Social Responsibility Theory of the Press,' in F.S.Siebart et al, Four Theories of the Press, University of Illinois Press, 1963.

Political and Economic Planning (P.E.P). Performance of the Press, P.E.P. London 1956

Pound, R. Harmsworth, G. Northcliffe, Cassell, London 1959

Press and the People, The. Annual Reports of the Press Council,1954-79. The Press Council, London
Price, W.C. The Literature of Journalism: An Annotated Bibliography, University of Minnesota Press, 1960.
Price, W.C. and Pickett, C.M. An Annotated Journalism Bibliography, 1958-1968, University of Minnesota Press, 1970.
Pugh, D.S. (ed.) Organisation Theory: A book of readings, Penguin, Harmondsworth, 1971.
Pugh, D.S. Hickson, D.J. Hinings, C.R. Writers on Organisation, Penguin, Harmondsworth, 1971, 2nd edition
Read, D. Press and People, Edward Arnold, London 1961
Richardson, J. Hall, From the City to Fleet Street, Stanley Paul and Company, London 1927.
Robinson, I. The Survival of English, Cambridge University Press, 1973
Roethlisberger, F.J. and Dickson, W.J. 'Formal and Informal Status', in R.K.Merton, et al, (eds), Reader in Bureaucracy, Free Press, New York 1952.
Royal Commission on the Press 1949, Report, HMSO, 1949a
Royal Commission on the Press 1949, Memoranda of Evidence, HMSO, 1949b
Royal Commission on the Press 1961-2, Report, Cmnd.1811, 1962a, HMSO, London.
Royal Commission on the Press 1961-2, 6 Vols. of Documentary Evidence and 3 Vols. of Oral Evidence, Cmnd. 1812, HMSO, 1962b.
Royal Commission on the Press 1974-77, New Technology and the Press, A Study of Experience in the United States by R. Winsbury, Working Paper No.1, HMSO, London 1975.
Royal Commission on the Press 1974-77, Interim Report, The National Newspaper Industry, London, Cmnd. 6433, HMSO, 1976a.
Royal Commission on the Press 1974-77, Review of Sociological Writing on the Press by Denis McQuail, Working Paper No.2, HMSO, London 1976b
Royal Commission on the Press 1974-77, Final Report, London, Cmnd.6810, HMSO, 1977a.
Royal Commission on the Press 1974-77, Working Paper No.3, by O.Boyd-Barrett, Dr. C. Seymore-Ure, and Prof.J.Tunstall, HMSO, London 1977b.
Royal Commission on the Press 1974-77, Industrial Relations in the Provincial Newspaper and Periodical Industries, A Report by the Advisory, Conciliation and Arbitration Service, Research Series 2, Cmnd. 6810-2, HMSO, London 1977c.
Royal Commission on the Press 1974-77, Concentration of Ownership in the Provincial Press, Research Series 5, Cmnd. 6810-5, HMSO, London 1977d.
Rucker, F.W. Newspaper Circulation, Iowa State College Press, 1958
X Rucker, F.W. and Williams, H.L. Newspaper Organisation and Management, Iowa State University Press 1965, 2nd edition.
Sadler, P. and Barry, B. Organisational Development; Case Studies in the Printing Industry, Longmans, London 1966.
Schramm, B.W. (ed.) The Process and Effects of Mass Communications, Harper and Brothers, New York 1949
Seymore-Ure, C. The Press, Politics and the Public, Methuen, London 1970
Seymore-Ure, C. The Political Impact of Mass Media, Constable, London 1974.
Siebart, F.S. Peterson, T. and Schramm, W. Four Theories of the Press, University of Illinois, 1963.

Silverman, D. The Theory of Organisations, Heinemann, London 1970

Simpson, D.H. The Pattern of Constraint on Management Decisions in the Newspaper Industry, Ph.D., Wales, 1979

Sisson, K. Industrial Relations in Fleet Street, Basil Blackwell, Oxford, 1975

Smith, A. (ed). The British Press Since the War, David and Charles, London 1974

Southern, M. 'The Adman Cometh', in R. Boston, The Press we Deserve, 1970

Spector, C. Management in the Printing Industry, Longmans, London, 1967

Starbuck, W.H. Organisational Growth and Development, Penguin, Harmondsworth, 1971

Taylor, A.J.P. Beaverbrook, History Book Club, Hamish Hamilton, London 1972

Taylor, H.A. The British Press; A Critical Survey, Arthur Baker, London 1971

Thomas, H. Newspaper Crisis in Britain, The International Press Institute, Zurich, Switzerland, 1968

Thomason, G.F. The Management of Research and Development, Batsford, London 1970

Thomson, Lord. After I was Sixty, Purnell Book Club Edition, Oxford, 1975

The Times, The History of, Vol. iv 1912-1948: The 150th Anniversary and Beyond, The Times, London 1952.

Trist, E. et al, Organisational Choice, Tavistock Publications Ltd. London 1963.

Trist, E. and Emery, F. 'The Causal Texture of Organisational Environments', Human Relations 18, No.1, 1965

Tunstall, J. Journalists at Work, Constable, London 1971.

Tunstall, J. The Westminster Lobby Correspondents, Routledge and Kegan Paul, London 1970a

Tunstall, J. Media Sociology, Constable, London 1970b

Tunstall, J. 'News Organisation Goals and Specialist Newsgathering' in D. McQuail (ed) Sociology of Mass Communication, Penguin, London 1972

Tunstall, J. The Advertising Man, Chapman and Hall, London 1964.

Unwin, G. Industrial Development in the Sixteenth and Seventeenth Centuries in England, Clarendon Press, Oxford, 1904.

Vines, C.M. A Little Nut-Brown Man, Readers Union, London 1969.

Vroom, V.H. Methods of Organisational Research, University of Pittsburgh Press, 1967

Walpole, K. and Hudson, R. Community Press, New Society, 24th Sept. 1970

Watkins, A. My Days with Beaverbrook, New Statesman, 1st September, 1972.

Waugh, E. Scoop, 1938, Penguin, Harmondsworth, 1967 edition

Weber, M. The Theory of Social and Economic Organisation, translated by A.M.Henderson and Talcott Parsons, The Free Press, Glencoe, Illinois, 1947.

White, D.M. The Gatekeeper; A Cast Study in the Selection of News, Journalism Quarterly 33, 1956

Williams, F. Nothing so Strange, Cassell, London 1970

Williams, F. Dangerous Estate; The Anatomy of Newspapers, Longmans, London 1957.

Williams, F. The Right to Know; The Rise of the World Press, Longmans, London, 1969.

Williams, R. Communications, Penguin, Harmondsworth, I962.
Williams, R. The Long Revolution, Chatto and Windus, London I96I
Winsbury, R. Government and the Press, Fabian Tract 379, Feb. I968
X Wintour, C. Pressures on the Press, Deutsche, London I972
Wood, A. The True History of Lord Beaverbrook,
Woodward, J. Industrial Organisation; Theory and Practice, Oxford University Press, London, I965.